Gender and Society:
Feminist Perspectives on the Past and Present

Series Editor: June Purvis
School of Social and Historical Studies,
University of Portsmouth, Milldam,
Portsmouth PO1 3AS, UK

This major new series will consist of scholarly texts written in an accessible style which promote and advance feminist research, thinking and debate. The series will range across disciplines such as sociology, history, social policy and cultural studies. Before submitting proposals, a copy of the guidelines for contributors to *Gender & Society* should be obtained from June Purvis at the address above.

Out of the Margins: Women's Studies in the Nineties
Edited by Jane Aaron, *University College of Wales*, and Sylvia Walby, *London School of Economics*.

Working Out: New Directions for Women's Studies
Edited by Hilary Hinds, *Fircroft College, Birmingham*; Ann Phoenix, *University of London*; and Jackie Stacey, *Lancaster University*.

Making Connections: Women's Studies, Women's Movement, Women's Lives
Edited by Mary Kennedy, *Birkbeck College, London*; Cathy Lubelska, *University of Central Lancashire*; and Val Walsh, *Edge Hill College, Lancashire*.

Mature Women Students: Separating or Connecting Family and Education
Rosalind Edwards, *South Bank University*

Gendered by Design?: Information Technology and Office Systems
Edited by Eileen Green, Den Pain, *Sheffield Hallam University*; and Jenny Owen, *UMIST, Manchester*

Forthcoming

Women and Careers
Millicent Poole, *Queensland University of Technology*, and Janice Langan-Fox, *University of Melbourne*

Feminist Politics and Education Reform
Madeleine Arnot, *University of Cambridge*

Women and Modernism
Gabrielle Griffin, *Nene College, Northampton*

Feminism, Sexuality and Struggle
Margaret Jackson

Subjects and Objects: Gender and Schooling
Jenny Shaw, *University of Sussex*

Friendly Relations: Mothers and their Daughters-in-Law
Pamela Cotterill, *Staffordshire University (Stoke-on-Trent)*

Aids: Gender and Society
Tamsin Wilton, *University of the West of England, Bristol*

Women in Britain 1914–1945
Edited by Sybil Oldfield, *University of Sussex*

Mature Women Students:
Separating or Connecting Family and Education

Rosalind Edwards

Taylor & Francis
London • Washington, DC

UK   Taylor & Francis Ltd, 4 John St., London WC1N 2ET
USA Taylor & Francis Inc., 1900 Frost Road, Suite 101, Bristol, PA 19007

First published 1993

A Catalogue Record for this book is available from the British Library

ISBN 0 7484 0086 9
ISBN 0 7484 0087 7 pbk

Library of Congress Cataloging-in-Publication Data are available on request

Typeset in 9.5/11pt Bembo
by Graphicraft Typesetters Ltd., Hong Kong

Printed in Great Britain by Burgess Science Press, Basingstoke on paper which has a specified pH value on final paper manufacture of not less than 7.5 and is therefore 'acid free'.

Contents

List of Tables and Figures

Feminist Perspectives on The Past and Present
Advisory Editorial Board

Acknowledgments

The responsibility for this book lies with me alone. There are, however, several people without whom completing it would have been a difficult, and less enjoyable, task. My thanks to Miriam David and Jane Lewis; I am grateful to them for their time and attention. Miriam's support, especially, has been invaluable. Jane Ribben's willingness to discuss every aspect of the work at great length, day and night, went beyond the bounds of friendship. Thanks also to Jo Campling. My family displayed endless patience. Particular thanks to Alice for hours of checking transcripts and references, and to Clive for support and interest, and for not minding.

Chapter 1

The Political and the Personal

It is a common-place wisdom that gaining an education affects women's positions in the 'public' world (particularly in the area of paid work) and within the 'private' family sphere (especially in their personal relationships with men they may live with). This assumption is not only so for many academics; it is also held in the public mind generally, especially with regard to the latter sphere. The headline to an article in a popular daily newspaper reporting on aspects of the research that formed the basis for this book, conjured up the obviously instantly accessible imagery of the film *Educating Rita*: 'Educating real life Ritas "can lead to marriage break-ups".' What is it about gaining a higher education that means it is viewed as so potentially disruptive to relationships between women and the men with whom they live? Annette Lawson points us towards an explanation when she argues:

> Education has the power to change people in fundamental ways . . . *power* is the clue. People with traditional backgrounds feel it unnatural that wives should be more independent, more capable, more educated than their husbands. It reverses long-accepted understandings of the proper place for each to occupy. This reversal becomes confusing and threatening (1990, pp. 187–88; her emphasis).

However, popular assumption and lived reality do not always bear each other out. Moreover, not all those writing on education view it as undermining social power relationships, but rather as reinforcing them.

Educating Women for Equality or Subordination?

In the sense that it has been seen as an instrument for and of power, education may be deemed political. Education has been viewed as offering a way out of inequality and oppression both by and for groups who are powerless. For women in particular, education has been looked to by some as an escape route from do-mestic life and second-class citizenship into the public sphere. Many nineteenth-century feminists, both white and black, focused on education, and entry to higher education in particular, as fulfilling a right to intellectual development and the need for better employment opportunities (Banks, 1981; Hooks, 1982). The fight for admission to universities was based for at least some on the premise that education would give (middle-class) women the opportunity of access to the public world of the professions and to economic independence (Purvis, 1991). Similarly, in the 1960s, Betty Friedan, at the beginning of the second wave of feminism, saw 'serious' higher education for women as the 'key to the problem that has no name' (Friedan, 1965, p. 362) which she had identified; the isolation and dissatisfaction of suburban housewives completely immersed in the private sphere and their wifing and mothering roles:

> The feminine mystique has made higher education for women seem suspect, unnecessary and even dangerous. But I think that education, and only education, has saved, and can continue to save, American women from the greater dangers of the feminine mystique (Friedan, 1965, p. 357).

Juliet Mitchell (1971) and Janet Chafetz (1989) have pointed to the role that the expansion of higher education in the 1960s played in the growth of feminism.[1] Black feminists (Bryan, Dadzie and Scafe, 1985) have shown black people's, particularly black women's, belief in education as both a way out of poverty and exploitation and as necessary for them to achieve anything in the face of racial discrimination.

Feminists have also voiced concern over women's continuing relatively poor access to the higher levels of educational institutions and their poor representation in the prestige subjects, with the underlying assumption still being that women can use education as a bridge to a more secure place in public life. Eileen Byrne has charted the inequalities for women in higher education, and education generally, and believes that 'only the fullest educational opportunity' (Byrne, 1978, p. 12) — that is, access to the same education as men — is the key to women's freedom of status, career and personal fulfilment. She calls for the redirection of resources in education towards this end. Tessa Blackstone has argued that women will remain a disadvantaged group so long as their education is restricted, and that 'better educated women are more likely to be politically active, to be employed, to believe in sex equality' (Blackstone, 1976, p. 200). Margaret Stacey and Marion Price state that:

> Education has been one of the few resources that women have been able to use to free themselves from the constraints of the traditional role. Providing both sexes with routes for upward mobility in a changing society, education has made it possible for women to stand alongside and against men in the public political arena (1981, p. 173).

They see women seeking positions of power in the public world of politics and work as the way forward for women who want changes in society.

Moreover, education has also been seen not just as a way of combating inequalities in the public world of paid work and politics for all groups, but also as affecting the 'private' but 'political' personal relationships between men and women. Olive Banks (1981) maintains that many of the nineteenth-century feminists who advocated higher education for women as a means of improving and diversifying their position in the public world of paid work also felt it would enhance and elevate relationships between middle-class women and husbands in the home. Allowing women to become intellectual equals with their husbands would undermine the pettiness of domestic life and prepare them more effectively for the role as wife and mother. Banks states that few nineteenth-century feminists actually wanted to challenge the fundamentals of the marital relationship itself. Carol Dyhouse has taken issue with this view, to argue that:

> Almost all feminists wanted to see change in certain areas, and their criticism of existing patterns of family life was particularly likely to focus around issues of economic and domestic organisation, and in the area of marital and sexual relationships (1989, p. 185).

She goes on to say, however, that there was not always unity in this critique, with divisions of social class and political allegiance.

Later, in the 1960s, though, a strand of thought that regarded higher education as enhancing women's roles as intelligent companions for men and for their future role as mothers responsible for their children's development was still apparent. In advocating women's entry to the public world via education, for example, Friedan had not envisaged any changes in the private sphere. Nevertheless, higher education for women is usually now regarded by many feminists and others as an important factor leading to greater equality in the personal relationships between men and women in the private sphere. Lee Comer (1982) has argued that wives gain power in marital relationships by having more education than their husbands and by being equally or more involved in organizations outside the home. Stacey and Price cite studies (such as the one by Pleck, 1985) which show that highly educated women have a greater influence in the public sphere and that this increases their power within the family. The shift in the balance of power between men and women is regarded as coming about because gaining an education changes women's opportunities, expectations and self-conceptions. Rose Coser (1974) suggests education, in allowing the chance of a career, will lead women to reassess their position when they realize there are realistic chances of achieving a more equal status with their husbands. David Morgan feels that education, and especially higher education, may cause 'some women to pause and examine, quizzically, their own marriages or relationships' (Morgan, 1985, p. 94). He goes on to say that, collectively, the: '. . . changes in roles and statuses of women in education and work can be seen as having some kind of cumulative effect on relationships within the family' (1985, p. 96).

Nevertheless, Morgan does caution that the processes by which this change takes place are not straightforward. The vast majority of those who have advocated education as an important step forward in changing both women's public and private relations have acknowledged that education is not sufficient in itself and that other changes are necessary too. Rosemary Deem (1978), for example, maintains that 'the connections between knowledge and action are rarely as close as either reformers or revolutionaries sometimes think they are' (p. 138), and that it is possible for women who have received higher education to enter into traditionally feminine paid work or to treat their jobs as less important than a man would.

However, over the last twenty years, some feminists have produced critiques of education, including higher education, which argue that the educational system and the knowledge that is promulgated within it, far from leading to potential equality between men and women, merely maintain notions of women's 'proper' place and women's work. Therefore, as it stands, education cannot bring about change. They have looked back at the energy that women put into gaining entry to higher education — to the source of gaining power it was thought to embody — and questioned why, for example, women are no closer to being full members of the educational élite that sets agendas and priorities than they were 150 years ago:

> . . . women have never participated fully in the decision-making pro-
> cesses of the educational world. As in all other spheres of public life,
> where the power is women are absent (Dale and Foster, 1986, p. 66).

Dale Spender believes that education is still 'a political weapon' used against women (Spender, 1985, p. 180). Spender and others have propounded a view of education as flawed and biased, rather than the benign, neutral, value-free system it claims to be, because, they say, most of what we know has been constructed by white men (Bryan, Dadzie and Scafe, 1985; Spender, 1982; Belenky *et al.*, 1986). Jane Thompson (1983) states that while it has been assumed that access to higher education for women is the issue, if the only education is 'men's education', equal access will not alter the basic relationship between men and women. She and other feminists contend that the knowledge taught in higher education and the education system itself explains and legitimates, reflects and reinforces patri-archal, middle-class and white norms and values. Certainly, in Britain, the Department of Education includes among the 'aims and purposes of higher education' the 'transmission of a common culture' (DES, 1987, p. 1). For many feminists and others this common culture is one that is particularly slanted in the way described above.

Higher education, according to such critiques, will teach women only more about subordination, unless there are profound changes both within the insti-tutions and within society. Miriam David (1986) argues that while governments may at some time have been committed to equality of educational opportunity between the sexes as a means of improving paid work opportunities, none has been committed to transforming their responsibilities within the private family sphere, either through education or by any other means. Education and the family, she says, jointly act to reproduce gendered identities, materially and ideologically (David, 1980). This is further compounded by changes in the view of the nature of education as a vehicle for social change. Notions of education as creating forms of social equality and social cohesion are coming to be replaced by those of individualism and competitiveness in the educational and other marketplaces (David, 1989).

For some, all of this leads to a disenchantment with education as a way out of inequality and oppression for women from different classes and races. Spender quotes Adrienne Rich on the matter: 'a woman's integrity is likely to be under-mined by the process of university education' (Spender, 1985, p. 186). However, Janet Finch (1984), Gillian Pascall (1986) and others see education as contradictory and contested ground, with both opportunity for liberation and reproduction of subordination existing side by side. Pascall warns against drawing simplistic conclusions with regard to education's role in the expunging or reinforcement of inequalities. While education is an important means of transmitting dominant ideologies it also constitutes an important resource for social movement. Thompson (1983), despite her criticisms of higher education, feels that it does at least improve the chances for women competing in the male world of work. Sandra Acker, too, hopes that, in spite of higher education's integral part in reproducing an unequal and hierarchical society, 'a little learning will deepen discontent — and ultimately be a dangerous thing' (1984, p. 30), while Sylvia Walby feels that 'during the twentieth century, education has been the least patriarchal institution' (1990, p. 108).

Others also have faith that if a feminist perspective is incorporated into higher education, particularly via Women's Studies, then education will play an important part in the transformation of human relationships and of society. Gloria Bowles writes of how she and other feminists in academe have: '. . . a basic belief in the potential power of the university, in the value of education for enriching individual lives and for improving society' (1983, p. 38), and Madeleine Arnot is optimistic that 'wherever women are found, the messages of the women's movement seem to take root and grow, whatever the political top soil' (1985, p. 123). Deem (1983), too, has postulated that where women's own experiences, problems and social position have some influence on the educational context it does meet a real need among women and can offer them a positive experience. Indeed, women academics have been successful, at least to some extent, in introducing feminist perspectives into teaching in many countries, especially in the area of social sciences (Maynard, 1990; Lie, 1990). Moreover, the profile of students studying within higher education is changing. Non-traditional students, particularly mature and/or black and working-class women, are being encouraged into higher education.

Wanted: Women — Mature, Working-class, and/or from Minority Ethnic Groups

Demographic trends mean there is, and will be for some time, a shortage of conventionally qualified 18-year-old students to enter full-time higher education in many Western countries. Both governments and education institutions are looking to other than traditional sources of students to fill places on degree courses. In Britain and the United States, for example, widening access to higher education for mature students, women, the working-class and those from minority ethnic groups has been laid down as a major aim (Department of Education and Science, 1987; HM Inspectorate, 1991, Appendix V). The development of specific routes into higher education for mature students has occurred in many countries. Colleges and universities in the US have developed 'gateway' or 'bridging' courses (HM Inspectorate, 1991). In Britain and several other European countries there are 'Access' courses that direct their mature participants towards higher education, and/or institutions of higher education themselves have special entrance examinations (Commission of European Communities, 1991).

Although Arlene McLaren (1985) found that as women increased their investment in education in the 1970s the economic situation worsened — a situation that is repeating itself — mature women seem to be responding to the call for their increased participation in higher education. There has been a rise in the number of full-time mature students entering higher education in many countries, with the number of female mature students at all levels and all modes of study often increasing at a faster rate than that of men. In Britain, for example, the figures show that between 1979 and 1988 there was a 37 per cent increase in full-time mature students (part-time numbers increasing more sharply), with the proportion of women rising steadily from 41 per cent in 1979 to 48 per cent in 1988 (Department of Education and Science, 1991). In the US, women and older students now comprise 53 per cent and 39 per cent of enrolments respectively (US Department of Education, 1988), with the mature student trend increasing sharply.

Despite governments' stated desire to expand the numbers in higher education many have, at the same time, introduced student loans and/or imposed severe restrictions upon the sector's public funding. Pressures on finance have, however, led to cuts in 'non-essential' areas of provision which affect women, such as day nurseries in institutions, and in areas of study that also particularly affect women. Those disciplines and courses, such as the physical sciences, which readily admit quantification and produce 'hard' facts are attracting resources while more philosophically-based subjects, such as social sciences and humanities, are becoming marginalized (David, 1989). Education and social science subjects are the 'choice' of the majority of all mature students, but especially of mature women (for example, Department of Education and Science, 1991).

David predicts that all these factors will mean 'a return to a more uniform system of relatively privileged access to higher education' (1989, p. 175). At present, though, the main aim of the push to widen access on the part of governments and/or institutions seems to be to boost the numbers from under-represented groups in higher education.[2] They are, however, most often concerned with 'how many' as an indicator of equal opportunities in access to higher education and not with the power aspects of inequalities in the qualitative experiences of women in general and women from different races and classes, once admitted as students to the institutions. Little attention has been paid to aspects such as discrimination and harassment, curriculum review and the overall institutional ethos. Governments and institutions have largely abrogated responsibility for the experiences of under-represented groups once they have succeeded in gaining access. In Britain, the Commission for Racial Equality has noted that:

> It is necessary to ask what inequalities there are in the experiences of groups, once admitted as students. If the qualitative experience of different groups are the subject of policy proposals, then very different forms of monitoring are necessary . . . this would require the collection of a range of data on course satisfaction, academic progression and success, perceptions of treatment by staff and peers, key curricular foci, incidents and trauma etc. (Williams *et al.*, 1989, p. 21).

The American Council on Education's Office of Minorities in Education has also made similar points. Clare Ungerson has remarked with regard to women students particularly:

> For women of all social classes to be further liberated, *both* access to . . . institutions *and* the content of what is taught there should be increasingly

woman-centred in order to gain the ground that until now has been very largely occupied by men (1986, p. 123; her emphasis).

The subject areas that women are 'choosing' to study, however, are those which are very much channelling women towards traditional roles in the public world as teachers, social workers and so on, and are, like other areas of knowledge, ones that feminists have criticized as having a male bias. On the other hand, these are areas in which a feminist perspective on women's positions might well be expected to form at least part of the curriculum, even within a context of cutbacks. Despite the drive to reduce inequalities in numerical access to higher education and the rationale of higher education policies generally being accompanied by an absence of any commitment to reduce inequalities within the private sphere, gaining a higher education may have such implications for relationships between men and women.

Exploring Experience

The experiences of thirty-one mature women students, from different races and classes, form a basis for the explorations in this book. Each was interviewed two or three times during the years 1988 and 1989.[3] (See Appendix for brief details of each woman). The interviews I conducted with them were loosely structured and were concerned with collecting 'family-education' biographies from childhood to the present (see Edwards, 1990b and 1993a, for a more detailed account of the methodology and issues arising from it). The women were all at various stages of a social science degree level education, and were drawn from two universities and three polytechnics[4] in the southeast of England.

Table 1.1: *Numbers and sources of women interviewed*

	Polytechnics			Universities		Total
	A	B	C	A	B	
First year students	6	1	3	1	—	11
Third year students	3	2	2	3	2	12
Graduates	3	—	3	1	1	8
Total	12	3	8	5	3	31

I interviewed the women who were in their first year of degree study once (occasionally twice) at the beginning and once (again, occasionally twice) at the end of the academic year. They thus provided me with a picture of their feelings about being a mature student as they were currently experiencing them. The women in their third year of study were interviewed twice at the beginning of the academic year and then once just after they had graduated. They were thus able to give me both retrospective and current accounts. Those who had graduated recently were interviewed two or three times, and so provided me with a retrospective account of their years of studying. All the women, of course, provided retrospective accounts of their childhoods.

The women were what can be called an 'opportunistic case study sample' — they were volunteers defining themselves as fitting certain criteria. These criteria were that they should have at least one child who was either below school age or in full-time education and for whom they were still responsible. Additionally, they should have, or had, at the start of their degree course, a man whom they considered to be a long-term partner.[5] A year-long relationship with their partner seemed to be the minimal definition of 'long-term' for the women, but many of them had been with their partners for at least five years, and just under half (fourteen women) had been with their partners for ten years or more. Most of the women were married or in cohabiting relationships that were akin to marriage upon commencing their studies, but several were in long-term relationships where their partners did not live with them permanently (see Chapter 3). For the most part, the women's partners came from the same race or a similar class background to themselves. Both the women of 'mixed' race, however, had white men as partners, perhaps reflected in their not defining themselves as black, while one of the white women had an Asian partner.

All the women defined their own status in terms of whether they considered themselves working-class, middle-class, black or white and so on. In their own terms, they came from a diversity of races and classes. Of the white women, ten referred to themselves as middle-class, and twelve as working-class. Seven of the women (one originally from Africa, and the others from the Caribbean) described themselves as black, while two others were of Asian and white ('mixed') parentage and did not feel 'black'. Only one of the black women referred to herself as working-class as well as black, and the 'mixed' race women did not 'class' themselves either. Thus, all but one of the black women, and the women of 'mixed' race, rejected social class as part of their identity and felt reality; for them the class system appertained to white British society. It is also a view shared by many of the black people whom Nancy Foner (1979) interviewed in her study of Jamaican migrants in London. On the other hand, for the white women class was a part of their identity, although not necessarily in an uncomplicated way.

Over the past fifteen years or so, women's relationship to class and their social mobility have been topics of constant debate. There has been much literature on the subject, with feminists and others criticizing conventional stratification and mobility theories' stances towards women because they ignore married and cohabiting women's relation to the labour market, the role of their educational qualifications, as well as their domestic and cultural work within the home. Such models are also argued to ignore patterns of resource distribution inside households (also taken as representing unequal power relationships). Many have offered alternative systems, but there has been no general consensus about this even within feminism. The complexity of the debates themselves have been summarized cogently elsewhere (for good accounts see Abbott and Sapsford, 1987; Charles, 1990; Payne and Abbott, 1990). In assigning the women to a status, I took their own definitions of their position. The women's own perceptions of their position, as they live it, served as a better guide to many of their understandings of the effects of their gaining an education upon their social relationships. For example, in a later chapter I will discuss black and white working-class women's worries that education could somehow move them apart from their peers in an élitist way. These worries were related to their own race or class sense of identity rather than their partners', or their own previous, occupation. Also, elsewhere (Edwards, 1990a, b), I have shown how race was fundamental to the black women's understanding of their place in, and their views of, the education system, and detailed the ways in which race determined the women's reactions to the research and to me. While economic and political structures may 'do' things to defined groups of people, these groups of people, individually or collectively, not only respond to these forces but may also reshape them. As Anne Phillips (1987) points out, material and structural definitions may be useful in identifying an important basis of economic power, but in the end they evade people's sense of themselves and the world in which they live.

So, what does gaining an education mean for the lives of women as students, workers, users of services, partners, mothers, daughters, friends and so on? Questions concerning the relationships of power within women's lives, as they see them, both outside and inside 'the family', and whether these perspectives shift and change over the course of a three-year period of degree study, will be addressed within this book. They are pertinent questions at a time when more women are being encouraged to enter higher education as mature students in order to facilitate the expansion within the sector required by governments and higher education institutions. Many of the women drawn into higher education through Access courses and so on, have families. Concern among educationalists, however, has not just centred around a pondering of the effects of gaining an education upon these women's family lives. Their family responsibilities are often regarded as 'interfering' with their ability to study. Moreover, any problems the women may experience in combining family and education are conceptualized in particular ways which place the onus for dealing with them upon the women themselves.

The 'Bag and Baggage' of Mature Women Students

As governments' and higher education institutions' interest in mature students heightened, research studies on this topic also proliferated. One overview of the literature of the late 1970s and early 1980s from several countries (Osborn et al., 1984) cites over 120 studies of mature students in all areas of education. Many of these studies note that, for women with a family, returning to study means a radical change in their way of life, and may entail particular stresses that men do not experience. There can be no doubt that a substantial number of mature women students have partners and are responsible for children. An OPCS survey (1989a) concerned with British mature students' finances revealed that almost half the women surveyed aged 26–35 were married or cohabiting, and 37 per cent of them had children (my calculations from their figures).

Acker has asked, 'Should we be more concerned about the dilemmas women present for higher education, or the difficulties higher education presents for women?' (1984, p. 25). These studies tend to display the former rather than the latter concern. Nearly all them approach the subject from the perspective of 'education' rather than that of mature women students. That is to say, they are concerned with the interests of the education institutions — reaching and retaining more students — and with what is often termed the 'external pressures and problems' (Woodley et al., 1987, p. 119) of other aspects of students' lives (such as family, friends and so on) on their ability to study successfully and pass exams.

Because of this orientation, the difficulties faced by those who are combining domestic responsibilities with education are written about in certain ways:

> . . . all the bag and baggage of their lives, with their families, with their jobs, with their attitudes and with their experiences. I'm talking about it coming from a background of sociology, emphasising *the impact of their lives on their studies* . . . and the tensions and pressures this creates (McIntosh, 1981, p. 5; my emphasis).

> In particular, financial needs and *family responsibilities impeded women's educational activities* to a considerable extent (Osborn *et al.*, 1984, p. 93; my emphasis).

Mature students, however, do not just bring their experience with them, they *are* their experience. To talk of their lives in terms of being 'bag and baggage' and 'externalities' reveals whose interests are paramount in shaping these studies. Moreover, the bag and baggage of higher education is rendered invisible.

While research about mature students rarely investigates the effects of their educational activities on the students' home lives from their perspective, many of the studies make observations on the subject, and in particular on relationships with partners, because of their concern with the effects of these relationships upon mature students' ability to study. Some address the issue of education itself as leading to a re-evaluation of relationships with partners, arguing that where study had an effect on the mature students' marriages it was due to intellectual growth not being shared with their partners (for example, Hopper and Osborn, 1975; Johnston and Bailey, 1984; Smithers and Griffin, 1986). Thompson (1983), from a perspective more grounded in women's than in institutions' interests, also remarks that for many of the students she has taught, using feminist perspectives, studying was accompanied by a stocktaking of personal relationships; this 'stocktaking' was not always negative because, for some, seeing the structural side to the relationship helped. For other women, however, it did not have this accommodating effect and their relationships came to an end. Alice Lovell, also taking a feminist perspective, found that while many of the married women in her study said they received support from their husbands their replies to other questions she asked proved contradictory. She argues that some of the women 'were blocked from achieving their objectives by domestic psychological pressure which amounted to "sabotage"' (Lovell, 1980, p. 94). This would indicate that something more than mismatched intellectual growth was taking place. Another of the problems with the studies of mature students, as Rita Johnston and Roy Bailey (1984) note in their own large-scale snapshot, is that longitudinal research is thin on the ground. The majority of studies are based on large samples, re-searched through self-administered structured questionnaires, with sometimes a few in-depth back-up interviews. Thus the processes by which varying scenarios of support or strain may occur in family relationships and any movements over time remain unexamined. Moreover, quite what is being supported or strained is not really satisfactorily addressed.

By far the majority of the studies that discuss the effects of study on domestic life seem to be, implicitly or explicitly, organized around the idea of roles, role strain and role conflict. Many of the studies of mature students that address the issue state that few of the women appeared to have help in their 'dual roles' of wife/mother and student from within the family (see Osborn *et al.*'s, 1984 overview). Jenny Martin and colleagues, for example, state that the women in their study were determined to 'fulfil their roles as wives/mothers as well as to remain industrious students' (Martin *et al.*, 1981, p. 119), organizing their days so that all the different demands were met with a high degree of motivation and determination. They note, however, that the women did have difficulty in making a shift from one role to the other — although they do not say why this might be. Quite a few of the studies note how much more intense role conflict is for women students than for men (among others, Gilbert and Holahan, 1982; Johnston and Bailey, 1984; Woodley *et al.*, 1987). This conflict is because, it is argued, their student role requires attitudes and behaviours that are inconsistent with traditional female spouse and parental roles. Once again, what those inconsistencies might involve are not really made explicit. One study (Gilbert and Holahan, 1982) argues that women who recognized the societal influences and ideologies which keep women in their place were more successful in reducing stress and conflict by changing or restructuring the role demands made upon them — although quite how the women managed this shifting we are not told.

In centring what attention they do pay to the domestic side of students' lives on role strain and conflict these studies are subject to the criticisms that have been made of role theory generally. They make little attempt to consider the material of structural circumstances of students' lives, and so levels of role stress related to women's structural positions are not really addressed. Women's roles are treated as ahistorical 'givens', ignoring the social and ideological context in which they are defined. The use of the term 'role' loses connotations of socially-defined expectations and provides a static social picture. Shifts in substance and emphasis are not accounted for, thus using a role framework makes it hard to think about power and resistance (Ross, in Rapp, Ross and Bridenthal, 1979). The term depoliticizes relations between men and women, and between races and classes. Tension and conflict are only explained as a product of multiple roles that are only explained as a product of multiple roles that are failing to mesh. The implication is that if the multiplicity of roles disappeared or a bit more skilful juggling took place, conflict would cease. This blames the victim, making the conflict the personal possession of each individual woman who merely has to arrange for the restructuring of her roles. The reality of struggle and resistance as a permanent part of social life is left untackled (Anyon, 1983) because the idea of roles is not complex enough to take account of the emotional (and sometimes physical) working out of sexual politics.

Taking account of these ties, Jean Elshtain has questioned whether 'wifing' and 'mothering' can be termed roles in the same way as, in this case 'student' may be:

> Mothering is *not* a 'role' on a par with being a file clerk, a scientist, or a member of the Air Force. Mothering is a complicated, rich, ambivalent, vexing, joyous activity which is biological, natural, social, symbolic, and emotional. It carries profoundly resonant emotional and sexual imperatives. A tendancy to downplay the differences that pertain between, say, mothering and holding down a job, not only drains our private relations of most of their significance, but also oversimplifies

what can or should be done to alter things for women, who are frequently urged to change roles in order to solve their problems (Elshtain,
1981, p. 243; her emphasis).

Being a wife and mother are more than merely roles for Elshtain, they are core
identities invested with blood, sweat, tears and toil. They are therefore not things
that women can easily split off from the rest of themselves but are integrated
aspects of their whole personas.

Because the concept of sex roles, even when used by feminists, shovels the
complexities of actual behaviours and characters of men and women into two
vast heaps, it can lead to an oversimplified description of social life. The complexity of attitudes, and both the normative and individual ambivalence and
contradictions around roles, are not addressed; differences between women are
glossed over (Eichler, 1980). The concept of roles thus suggests some sort of
determinate, stereotypical reality in which absolute order exists, with the actual
content of roles taken as generally agreed upon. Role theory fails as an explanation because it does not allow for variations, complexity, or for a notion of
'self' other than a cluster of roles (Stanley and Wise, 1983). It is a generalized
abstraction that tells us little about lived experience and feeling, and that mirrors
assumptions rather than explicates them. Yet, as Ellen Ross has reluctantly
concluded, 'all of us will continue to use these terms because it is hard to find
substitutes' (Rapp, Ross and Bridenthal, 1979, p. 188) — although she urges their
careful use.

When it comes to the situation of mature women students with families,
then, certain questions are left unanswered by previous studies. What do the
'roles' of student and partner/mother mean to the women and what do they
require of them? How do being a student and being a partner/mother relate to
each other under the different or similar social circumstances of the women's
lives? Are studentship and partner/mothership themselves incompatible or contradictory, and if so in what way?

The Academic as the Personal

It has not only been on 'objective' intellectual grounds that I have found the
literature on mature women students wanting. Indeed, my interest in the whole
topic has not been motivated by an academic concern alone. As Acker has
commented, 'Many of us study aspects of our autobiographies partially disguised
as a "detached" choice of an interesting problem' (Acker, 1981, p. 96). My own
experiences as a mature women student with a family led me to feel detached
from many of the studies of mature students. While to some extent they statisti-
cally noted the stresses that I, along with others, had undergone, they told me
nothing satisfactory about what had been going on in my life. Role strain seemed
a curiously hollow sounding thing that did not touch upon my feelings and
experience.

I went to do a full-time degree course at the age of 30, having left school at
16, with a few qualifications, to be channelled into secretarial work, marriage(s)
and motherhood. Studying for a degree had been a long-held ambition and
education itself held a certain status in my eyes. I was thus very proud to have

obtained a place at the local polytechnic, and was determined to study success-fully and also to be a 'good' wife and mother. Over the course of my first year at the polytechnic, however, my life seemed to become split into two: doing the course, and being a wife and mother. The two did not seem to meet in any way, whereas I desperately wanted them to. This was not merely a matter of having two different roles in my life. I had previously done this without any problems when in paid work. Family and education both seemed to require me to play not a role, but to be wholeheartedly involved in each to the exclusion of the other.

I did try to mesh the two in various ways for a while, one of which was an attempt to draw my education into my family life. My husband, however, was not interested in coming up to the polytechnic with me, reading essays I had written or in discussing what I was learning at all. While my academic books entered the home, the ideas they generated in my head were not welcomed. Indeed, the children got a little fed-up with long lectures on the subjects of sexism, racism and so on. My husband attempted to push education outside our family life while I attempted to draw it in. We began to have tremendous rows, ostensibly about such things as whose turn it was to do the washing up. In fact, by the beginning of my second year of study we were sleeping in separate rooms.

Despite all the domestic stress, I was doing well at the polytechnic. Indeed, I was determined that it should not affect my studies, and to prove that I was just as capable as any 18-year-old straight from school. I felt that if only I could devote all my time to study I could do more than well. I was enjoying the content of my course, but I did not find it as exciting as the Open University courses I had previously studied. There did not seem to be so much room for my own thinking; the main idea seemed to be to get through the exams, and the way you did this was to regurgitate what everyone else had said on a subject. I quickly learnt to do this, and to regard my own life experiences as no basis for challeng-ing 'received wisdoms'. What the course did given me, however, was confidence in my opinions. I no longer just had opinions, I had informed opinions that could be supported. They were therefore validated in a way they had not been pre-viously. I began wondering what my life would have been like if I had never married and had any children, and dreamed of unending time to study in a flat of my own. I felt isolated and lonely at home in a way I did not when I was in seminars and lectures. At the polytechnic, with my family life hidden from view, I was successful; at home, I was a failure.

Halfway through the second year of the course my husband, with my grudg-ing acceptance, arranged for us to see a counsellor. While the problems of combining family and education did not go away, they slowly came to appear less threatening to both of us. I managed to create mental space for myself to work in bursts when I needed to, gave the family the attention they seemed to need when I did not, and stopped trying to involve them all in my education. My husband became more overtly supportive of my studies, and we ceased arguing about the washing up. Overall, by the final, and obviously crucial, year of my degree I felt that I was doing what I wanted to without it being disastrous for my family relationships. However, the basic tension between family and education remained (and remains). My family and I had just managed to accommodate, rather than resolve, it — a process requiring constant negotiation. I will argue that this basic tension is due to the socially-constructed value base of each institution.

Frameworks and Concerns

These were the experiences that led me to want to look at the interactions of family and education in the lives of mature women students. At the time I had no means to explain or control what was going on in my life. I felt buffeted around by emotions. Marge Piercy has said:

> If you do not have a vocabulary, you cannot handle your own experience. One of the things feminism does for women is that it names things. Once you name something, it exists for you, you can handle it in your mind, you can turn it around, you can decide what to do about it (Quoted in Forster and Sutton, 1989, p. 14).

One of the objectives of this book is to name rather than to quantify the experiences of mature women students for them. I hope to lay out how their experiences are shaped by factors that extend beyond their individual lives and which are political rather than merely personal. In doing so, I also move beyond each women's experience in an attempt to contribute to accounts and explanations of women's lives generally. A flexible framework and concepts for analyzing women's everyday experiences in both public and private worlds is generated, one which is applicable across race and class and which can take account of different accounts, from each other and to my own. And yet there are some common dilemmas and themes that run throughout both their and my accounts. The experience of being a mature woman student creates some shared ground, but there are also other factors that can lead to differences in the perceptions and experiences of this shared situation of combining education and family life. The dilemmas and themes explored in this book concern separations and connections between family and education; they concern the bases of educational and family knowledge and their relationship to one another; and they concern many kinds of 'differences': differences of status, differences between men and women, differences between women, and differences between students.

The interactions between family and education for mature women students, and the effects of pursuing an education on women's family relationships, may be pertinent areas to examine at a time when more mature women students are entering higher education — and concomitantly at a time when concern is being expressed over the fate of 'the family' in many Western countries today. Nevertheless, the spotlight should not just be turned upon women themselves and their individual situations and personal relationships. To do so would be to ignore the fact that women who have families and who enter full-time higher education become students in certain social, political and ideological contexts. These contexts include 'the family', with its particular ethos, values and construction of women's role within it, and women's position in the public world generally, but they also include the ethos and values of higher education itself and what being a student means within it.

Having rejected role theory because it does not fully address social and political issues, Chapter 2 discusses other explanations of women's lives, and of tensions that may occur within them, which provide a more comprehensive base for understanding. With some modifications, concepts are used that are derived from the ideological notions of public and private spheres, and of male and female psyches as developed within these differentiated contexts. These explanatory concepts are held up against the women's accounts of their lives throughout the following chapters.

Public and private worlds generally, and specifically here in the form of education and family, are not separate entities. They interact and impinge upon each other, with particular implications for the position of women within each. The interactions between the two, and the implications for women with families who become mature students are a major concern of this book. The meanings of education and of family life for the women taking part in the research, from childhood through to the present, are examined in Chapter 3. Within their retrospective accounts emerge images of differences between home and education, particularly in the form of schooling, overlaid by race, class and gender. These images are also contained within the women's accounts of their lives at the time the interviews with them were carried out. These are also other images contained within these accounts, to do with the nature of higher education and being a student within it, and the nature of being a mother and a female partner. Some of the interactions between family and education and their effects upon the women's lives in childhood are discussed in Chapter 3, while the following chapters look at the effects for them as mature women students. Chapter 4 examines the social and institutional contexts within which the women are partners/mothers and full-time degree students, and which result in the women having certain expectations of themselves. It considers what this means for the ways the women organize their time and their responsibilities, and for how they feel about this organization. In the next two chapters the separations and connections between education and family are discussed, focusing upon the ramifications of each for the other in terms of the women's relationships in both public and private worlds. Chapter 5 concentrates on the ways in which the family lives and responsibilities of women shape their experiences as students and their interactions with other students and with lecturers. The women's understandings of the ways in which they are perceived by these and other people in the public sphere are also examined. Chapter 6 is concerned with the ramifications of being a full-time student for the women's family lives. It particularly examines the power issues raised for the women in their relationships with their partners, but also with their children and parents. Chapter 7 sets out the various and varying patterns created by the coexistence of family and education in the women's lives and what this means for the ways that women's lives are conceptualized. It then examines these patterns in the context of an intermediate public/private sphere: the women's friendships. In conclusion, Chapter 8 draws out and assesses some of the implications arising from the analysis of the experiences and perceptions of the women taking part in this study, for higher education itself and for women's position in public and private worlds.

Notes

1 Mitchell, however, sees this expansion as a contradictory outcome, in that she believes that the overall female experience of education is one of devaluation.
2 Usually, as in Britain, this push is fuelled by a preoccupation with improving the performance of the economy (McIlroy, 1989).

3 Pseudonyms have been used for the women and their partners and children. In some cases they chose these names themselves, in others they left it up to me.

4 At the time of the research, Britain still retained a binary divide in higher education. Along with some other countries (for example, Australia) steps have been taken to replace it with a unified system.

5 The men with whom the women had relationships will be referred to as 'partners' in any general use, in order to cover the variety of husband and live-in/live-out boyfriend relationships that there were (see Chapter 3). In specific cases the actual type of relationship is referred to.

Chapter 2

Separating and Connecting Public and Private Worlds

Actually, one of the other girls in my group got your letter [requesting respondents]. And we were talking about it and somebody else came in and said, 'Well, I wouldn't want to give personal details to a stranger'. And I thought well, you know. I said to her, 'Well, what about you, if you was in that situation, you know, doing that, you know, you'd want help' (Wendy, a white working-class woman).

This quotation from one of the mature women students I interviewed illustrates some of the themes pursued within this chapter. The sentiments Wendy expressed are not unusual in comparison with the other women, she just conveniently expressed them together. Wendy's words show that there is a boundary in the other student's mind, which she also accepts, about what should remain personal. The details of her family life I had indicated I wished to talk about with her and make public in the form of research are something that should remain private. Her words also show that, while Wendy accepted the boundary, her own decision to participate was based on a projected affiliation between us. She made a connection between how she would feel in the same situation and how I would feel.

This chapter examines the concepts of public and private spheres that set up boundaries between the worlds, and of a feminine psyche (difference theory) that sets up women's need to feel affiliated. It draws out from them the ideas of separation and connection that I will be using to look at the ways in which women have family and education in their lives. The use of the concepts of public and private worlds and of difference theory is not without problems. I will argue, however, that, despite criticisms of them as ahistoric and asocial dichotomies, the dismissal of the concepts that some feminists have advocated risks 'throwing the baby out with the bathwater'. Taken as ideological distinctions rather than as empirical categories, it can be seen that the concepts operating as norms within society throw up irresolvable tensions with which women have to deal. Separations and connections between worlds are crucial for an understanding of what women have to say about having both family and education in their lives, and how they report the reactions of other people to this. As notions, they pervade Wendy's words and structure meanings for her and many of the other mature women students.

Juxtapositions of the public sphere with the private sphere and related notions of a female identity also pervade and structure other accounts of women's lives. They have been frequently used in feminist research and discussion. Sometimes the public/private division is made explicit in analysis, sometimes it is left as implicit. Sometimes there are conflations between or slippages from the broad public/private dichotomy to the narrower production/reproduction, family/work dichotomies. Sometimes the public and private is treated as subsumed within a broader concept such as patriarchy, sometimes it is seen as synonymous with it. Sometimes there are even distinctions made between what is seen and what is unseen, between actions and beliefs, or between the known and the unknown, and these are labelled public and private.[1] Between usages there is a confusing diversity in what exactly is meant by the concepts. However, an overview of the assumptions underlying use of the public/private spheres concept is as follows.

In general the public sphere is regarded as associated with the male world. It is the world of paid work, politics, formal education, culture and the general exercise of power and authority. The private sphere is also associated with men, because they move between the two spheres, but the private sphere is particularly women's place. It is the domestic domain, the world of family, home, children, domestic labour. As such it is of lower status and less authority than the public sphere. Women are said to have a special relationship with the private sphere of 'the family' because it is the primary site of both their work (domestic and reproductive) and of their social and personal identity. Housework and looking after people are not just another species of work, or even just women's work, they are women's identity and are part of their psyche, it is argued (for instance, Graham, 1983; Pascall, 1986). In their daily actions within the private, domestic sphere women do have power, especially with regard to the rearing of their children, but it is an informal, fragile and constrained power (Elshtain, 1981; New and David, 1985).

Women's position in the private world of the family is said to relate to their position in the public world; they are trapped between subordination in the private sphere and subordination in the public sphere (Pascall, 1986). The private world of the home, of childcare and of care of people as women's work and identity is therefore often regarded as crucial to an understanding of women's place in the public world (New and David, 1985; Pascall, 1986) although some, such as Sylvia Walby (1990), argue that it works the other way around, with women's place in the public world structuring their position in the private sphere. Even when women do go outside the home to do a paid job they have been said to do so almost as 'migrant labour' (Porter, 1983, p. 124), and are crossing a boundary into a world that is not their own. They carry the aura of the private sphere with them when they venture into the public sphere. Men, however, are felt to have an unquestioned place in both worlds, and to carry the authoritative and powerful aura of the public world even while in the private sphere. This sort of analysis obviously has implications for women who are combining the public world of paid work or formal education and the private world of their family lives. How far do these women feel that there are boundaries and differences between the worlds, and what does this mean for their identities? Before discussing this, the public/private dichotomy and its relation to the production of gendered psyches needs further examination.

Theories of the Public and the Private

Notions of a split between public and private/domestic spheres, with the former being the world that men can move in and the latter being the world that women naturally remain in, are often traced back to nineteenth-century urbanization and industrialization, whereby production became radically separated from the household, and to bourgeois liberal thought (Pateman, 1983; Davidoff and Hall, 1987). The period saw the emergence of the idea of the domestic sphere as a private space. What is often called the cult of domesticity embodied the split whereby women's 'natural' sphere was seen as the home, within which they could carry out the domestic and caring tasks for which they were suited, while men were predominant in the public world of paid work, politics, formal education and so on, for which they were 'naturally' suited.

The public/private dichotomy thereby also casts the characteristics of the domestic sphere in opposition to the presumed characteristics of the public sphere: affective, altruistic and non-goal oriented as opposed to unemotional, competitive and mercenary. This characteristic opposition of the two spheres matched the separate characteristics and roles of men who operated in the public world, and of women contained within the private sphere. Additionally, one was thought necessary to the other. The private sphere acted as a refuge from the public world, a private haven for men to retreat to from the heartless public world. In nineteenth-century liberal bourgeois proseletyzing (Davidoff, 1979), and in twentieth-century British conservative philosophy, political rhetoric and prescriptive agenda (David, 1986), the antithesis between the two spheres was, is, and should be, definite. Indeed, part of the construct is the privacy of the private sphere. It is a domain into which the public world and its concerns and institutions should not penetrate (provided things are as they ought to be). The private sphere of the family is 'paradigmatically private' (Pateman, 1983, p. 286), an area of relationships to which access, scrutiny and control from the 'outside' should be restricted. It is 'under culture constraints to appear as autonomous and private' (Rapp, Ross and Bridenthal, 1979, p. 288).

Others, however, see the division between public and private spheres at the base of a wider patriarchial rather than just a bourgeois ordering of social life. The use of the public/private model by feminists as an explanation for women's oppression was originally conceptualized in the writings of American feminist cultural anthropologists in the early 1970s, most notably in Michelle Rosaldo and Louise Lamphere's (1974) book of collected writings, *Women, Culture and Society*. In this volume Rosaldo and others argued that all societies and cultures have and do distinguish between men and women. No matter what form the sexual division of labour within them took or takes, they argue that the assignment of men to the public sphere (everywhere regarded as more significant and important) and of women to the private sphere (everywhere regarded as less significant and less important) is a universal asymmetrical characteristic, operating across time and place: 'everywhere men have some authority over women . . . a culturally legitimated right to [women's] subordination and compliance' (Rosaldo, 1974, p. 21). This universal differentiation, and opposition, between the public and the private/domestic spheres was, for Rosaldo, based on women's childbearing and rearing activities and responsibilities. These led women to participate less than men in public life and thus to a differentiation between the spheres:

[Private] refers to those minimal institutions and modes of activity that are organized immediately around one or more mothers and their children; 'public' refers to activities, institutions, and forms of association that link, rank, organize or subsume particular mother-child groups (Rosaldo, 1974, p. 23).

The opposition underlay rather than determined sexual asymmetry.

While Rosaldo did not argue that women were completely devoid of power within either the private or public spheres, she saw any power they exerted as exercised through informal rather than formal authority. Rosaldo contended that men, because of their association with the public sphere and its institutions and because of their ability to distance themselves from the private/domestic sphere, held both legitimate and formal power and authority. In fact, Rosaldo proposed a relationship between the amount of separation between the public and private spheres in a culture or society and the degree of subordination of women's position: 'Women's status will be lowest in those societies where there is a firm differentiation between domestic and public spheres of activity' (Rosaldo, 1974, p. 36). In societies where men were more involved in domestic life, allowing women to participate in public life and making distinctions between the two spheres less clear-cut, men's degree of authority and power over women was less than in societies where men held themselves apart from the private sphere. Rosaldo's solution to women's oppression was thus dual, or shared, parenting — a solution other feminists have put forward too.[2]

Rosaldo saw men's dominant power and authority as legitimated by the cultural value assigned to their tasks and activities because these tasks and activities took place in the public sphere. In the same volume, Sherry Ortner (1974) builds on this point (although she focuses on division of labour) to argue that women are universally subordinate to men because women, due to their reproductive function, are universally associated with nature. Men, on the other hand, are associated with culture, and culture is universally seen as separate from and superior to nature. Ortner then goes on to state that because of this socially constructed public/culture and private/nature split, men and women inhabit separate worlds, and women develop a different psychic structure to men. This postulated feminine psyche also has universal characteristics in that it is concerned with the interpersonal, the subjective and the particular (as opposed to the objective, abstract male psyche developing out of men's social conditions in the public world).

A Feminine Psyche: Difference Theory

Ortner's ideas on the creation of a feminine personality, which has its base in the universal assignment of women to the private sphere because of their association with childrearing and nature, are closely allied to those put forward by some feminist social psychologists (notably Chodorow, 1978; Gilligan, 1982). They have also argued that women's primary existence within the private sphere of nurturance and self-sacrifice results in the development of a distinctive psychological personality that is inherently relational. For boys and men, they say, separation and individuation are critically tied to gender identity, since separation from their mothers is essential for the development of masculinity, whereas for girls and women issues of femininity or feminine identity do not depend on the achievement of separation from their mothers or on the progress of individuation:

> The sexual and familial divisions of labour in which women mother and are more involved in interpersonal, affective relationships than men produces in daughters and sons a division of psychological capacities which leads them to reproduce this sexual and familiar division of labour (Chodorow, 1978, p. 7).

Girls thus develop a different personality structure, rather than merely learning roles.

Carol Gilligan's ideas have been particularly influential among many feminists and have gained wide scholarly attention. She argues that women have a greater orientation towards empathetic and compassionate relationships and towards interdependence. It is necessary to recognize the importance of attachment, affiliation and connection for them, compared with the male celebration of separation, autonomy and individuation. Women 'define their identity through relationships of intimacy and care' (p. 164) and stress 'continuity and change in configuration, rather than replacement and separation' (Gilligan, 1982, p. 48). They judge themselves on their ability to care for others and to maintain ongoing social ties. Women stay with, build on, and develop in, the context of affiliation and attachment. According to Gilligan, women's sense of self becomes organized around being able to make and maintain affiliations: 'to see themselves as women is to see themselves in a relationship of connection' (Gilligan, 1982, p. 171). Women's sense of identity is thus never a separate one, in the way that men's is, but is defined in relation to others. Indeed, Gilligan maintains that separation and individuation can leave women feeling anxious and unconnected, whereas men can feel uneasy about interdependency and connection.

A consequence of this type of difference theory is that men are seen as incapable of operating fully in the nurturing, caring private sphere and women are similarly seen as incapable of operating fully in the public sphere. Nancy Chodorow (1978) has stressed that gender differentiation and sex oppression will continue to exist as long as women continue to be totally responsible for mothering.

How Useful Are the Concepts?

The public/private dichotomy and difference theory have been criticized as a tool of analysis by other feminists. Three strands can be discerned within these critiques. Although the strands are not easily distinct, I have split them for ease of discussion. The first criticism does not dismiss the dichotomies but says that as formulated they are acultural, ahistorical and asocial. The second also does not entirely dismiss the dichotomies, but is concerned to show how the two spheres and gendered personalities are integrally connected and related to each other rather than separate. The third argues that the whole notion of the dichotomies cannot be sustained and therefore should not be used.

Acultural, Ahistoric, Asocial

The universalities of the public/private distinctions as originally conceived by Rosaldo and others, and of the notion of a feminine psyche put forward by Chodorow, Gilligan and others, are said to ignore, or at best obscure, the workings of social processes. They leave the two spheres presented as timeless, distinct and unchanging. If there is no awareness of the varieties of women's experiences over historical time and in different cultures, it is only too easy to accept some features of a society as essential parts of the human condition rather than as cultural constructs. Christine Gailey states that while the public/private split certainly characterizes all class societies, the existence of such a division in other societies (such as uncolonized kin societies) is questionable. As she says: 'We can find similarities of form everywhere if we ignore the meaning and dynamics of the relationship for the particular society or type of society' (Gailey, 1987, p. 48). She gives examples of societies where women's work was not given a lesser status. Similarly, it has been argued that ideas of nature and culture, as used by Ortner and others, are relativized concepts which can be entirely different in non-Western societies (Pateman, 1983), while Leonore Davidoff and Catherine Hall (1987) state that constructs of masculinity and femininity are specific to, and must be understood within, historical time and place. They are categories that are continually being forged, contested, reworked and reaffirmed. Thus, it is argued, universalistic notions of public/private and masculine/feminine dichotomies are projecting the social constructs of one time and place onto other times and places, producing unilinear evaluations that cannot be upheld. They leave us unable to analyze or explain shifts in activities or characteristics. The terms may remain constant but what is contained within their definitions may change over time.

Davidoff and Hall, and others, have also pointed out that a conflation of the private sphere and female roles with women's nature also ignores social differences between women (and between men) within the same society; specificities of class and of race are overlooked. Evelyn Glenn (1987), for instance, draws attention to the way that the specific cultural ideology of children being brought up by their mothers does not fit some ethnic groups where nurturance may be shared among female kin, thus throwing one of the difference theorists' basic assumptions into question (albeit not entirely; the main carers are still women). It is argued, often by black feminists, that many feminist analyses have, from a narrow base of white middle-class experience, purported to speak for all women whatever their race, and led to the myth that being socially designated a woman was a comparable source of oppression for all women. Boundaries between the public and the private do not just shift between cultures and over historical time, they are different for the different social groupings within that one culture or society.

Diane Lewis (1983) and Carol Stack (1986) maintain that the relationship between blacks and whites in society and the relationship between black women and black men casts doubt on the full validity of Rosaldo's and others' theories of female inequality, and Gilligan's and others' theories of personality structure:

> The systematic exclusion of black men from the public sphere suggests
> that black sex-role relationships cannot be adequately explained by the
> notion of a structural opposition between the domestic and public

spheres or the differential participation of men and women in the public sphere (Lewis, 1983, p. 172).

Black women and men have a very similar experience of class, that is, a similar relationship to production, employment, and material circumstances . . . there is a convergence between women and men in their construction of themselves in relationship to others (Stack, 1986, p. 323).

Lewis and Stack do not, however, appear to dismiss the dichotomy for white women. According to them, because of black men's exclusion from status jobs in the public sphere, black women have had to enter the public sphere of work in order to make an economic contribution to their families' upkeep. For Lewis this gives black women some power in terms of access to resources. Furthermore, she argues, both black men and women are excluded from political power.

Neither Lewis nor Stack answers the question of precisely how this, on its own, makes black women's situation different from that of white working-class women, who are, arguably, in the same position. White working-class men could also be said to be excluded from status jobs and formal power in public life. Nevertheless, Lewis does state that we need to look at hierarchical arrangements in a society in terms of access to power and resources.[3] She goes on to suggest that the gender inequalities black women suffer in their private lives are different from those of white women. In contrast to Rosaldo's hypothesis that egalitarian relationships will be based on equal access to both spheres on the part of men and women, Lewis argues there is evidence of a stronger egalitarianism in black sex-role relationships generated by black men and women's shared unequal access to public power and resources. Similarly, Stack argues that because black men and women share a subordinate position in the public world, and because of racism, they have a similar relationship to the private world. She says this produces a cultural alternative to Gilligan's model, with both black men's and women's identity vested in the private sphere, and stressing relationship, continuity and social ties. Again it would seem that white working-class women and men could well be said to be in a similar position here (although not with regard to racism). Other black feminists, too, have argued that while the private sphere may be a source of oppression for white women, for black women it is a source of support and resistance against the controlling, racist demands of the public sphere (Hooks, 1982; Bryan, Dadzie and Scafe, 1985) — in fact, another version of the haven in a heartless (racist) world.[4] Anne Phillips, however, disagrees with this idea. She locates differences between women in terms of class and race as predicated upon their position in the public rather than the private sphere, with divisions running along full-time/part-time (race) and professional/non-professional (class) lines. For Phillips, 'in the privacies of the household we may face the same problems; in the publicity of our jobs we are not all as one' (Phillips, 1987, p. 149). Either way, the public/private dichotomy still operates in both analyses.

Hester Eisenstein (1984) argues that US interpretations of the public/private divide, with their concern with its biological and psychological aspects, have perpetuated the ignoring of historically and culturally specific moments (feeling that British feminists, with their concentration on the sexual division of labour in the workplace as well as the home, have to some extent avoided this blind spot).

To reduce sexual asymmetry down to biology, as she says Rosaldo, Chodorow and others implicitly do when they link women's association with the private sphere to their association with childbearing, ignores the social relations of each time and place that produce different types of social divisions. No explanation of the variety of social and cultural constructions of sexual asymmetry is provided. In fact, Rosaldo herself, in a reconsideration of the public/private split, admitted oversimplification in her original concept. While she still maintained that when any power women wielded was held up against that of men's, 'the vast majority of opportunities for public influence and prestige . . . are all recognized as men's privilege and right' (Rosaldo, 1980, p. 400), she amended her ideas to take account of the understanding that sexual asymmetry was not everywhere determined by the same concerns but was shaped by complex social forces and the meaning women's activities acquired in a society. Chodorow (1989), too, has developed her arguments and stressed her rejection of pre-given biological differences as either necessary or universal.

Integral Connections

Janet Sharistanian feels that, while the public/private model remains useful, its greatest drawback was:

> . . . not any particular premise that it encompassed but its tendency to stress the separation of, or opposition between the domestic and public domains rather than their complex, multilevelled, highly variable, and frequently shifting interdependence (Sharistanian, 1987b, p. 179).

If not properly explicated the public/private model and the male/female psyche model leads to a tendency to focus attention on the two constituent parts as separate rather than as interpenetrating. They miss the fact that women's lives do, and have, straddled the two spheres, both in terms of their work inside and outside the home, and in that women are the ones who usually mediate between the spheres on behalf of their children (New and David, 1985). They also ignore the economic and social structures that push women into particular familial, caring roles (Graham, 1983).

Christine Bose (1987) stresses that even in the nineteenth century the cult of domesticity obscured the fact that women outside the white middle-classes have always had the double day of productive work and domestic work in the home. Natalie Sokoloff, too, has shown that women's roles were never as separate from the male-dominated productive sphere as the public/private ideology implied. She argues that there is a reciprocally reinforcing relationship between the two spheres that is shaped by the separate but interacting forces of the needs of capitalist production and patriarchal ideologies of male authority and power:

> Instead of seeing the home as women's sphere and the market as men's sphere it becomes necessary to understand that both the home and market are mutually interpenetrating and are organized by the dialectical relationship between patriarchy and capitalism (Sokoloff, 1980, p. 222).

Similarly studies of wives' incorporation into the work of their husbands (see Finch, 1983a) show the way the public world of organizations is able to use the idea of a private sphere as separate in such a way as to cross the boundaries in fact, but to maintain them in fiction. Other feminists have also exposed the fiction that the domestic sphere operates autonomously, untouched by the state, and exposed the ways in which state policies have, and do, work to strengthen, if not to create, the ideal of the privacy of the private sphere while in fact regulating it. In particular, Miriam David (1985, 1986) has pointed to the role state policies play in controlling and shaping motherhood and 'the family' for women, and women for motherhood and 'the family', and the ways in which this controlling is shot through with class differences. Rayna Rapp (Rapp, Ross and Bridenthal, 1979) also warns that we must not ignore the class and race aspects of any interactions between spheres.

With regard to notions of a feminine psyche, Eisenstein has argued these reduce the subordination of women to a private struggle in the minds of individual women and men, ignoring the underlying public political, social and economic factors. She says this attitude gives women the impression that in order to transform their situation it suffices only to change the way they think about the world:

> It needs to be stressed that the psychological interacts with the economic,
> the social and the political. A feminist analysis that locates power only in
> individual psychology is both naive and damaging (Eisenstein, 1984,
> p. 132).

Similarly, Hilary Graham (1983), while she accepts the need for a psychological understanding of women's caring, stresses the need to see how it results from the particular way in which economic and social reproduction is organized. Ketayun Gould (1988), however, argues that not only does the notion of a feminine psyche, as used by Gilligan in particular, fall into the trap of individualizing, but also that it dangerously reifies and reinforces the 'natural' stereotypical qualities attributed to women. It leads to the conclusion that women really are more nurturant than men. The association of women with feelings of connection, caring and responsibility for others is just a new version of a traditional view of women that appeals to feminists, she says, because it affirms the feminine characteristics that society devalues. The danger, for Gould, in difference theory is that it ignores the fact that women have these traits assigned to them because women are subordinate. Linda Kerber, in a comparable critical analysis, wonders how Gilligan's conception of women's personality can deal with the 'self-indulgent, selfishness, and meanness of spirit which women display as much as do men' (Kerber, 1986, p. 309). David Morgan has also stressed that adhering to rigidly dichotomous constructions of gender differences, with male and female being taken as discrete, non-overlapping categories, runs the risk of reproducing stereotypical assumptions: 'In contemporary society there is not one version of gender differentiation but a range of versions available for use by different persons in different situations' (Morgan, 1986, p. 35). Others too have claimed that men and women are more alike than they are different (Greeno and Maccoby, 1986), particularly when class and education are controlled for — at the upper levels sex personality differences are said to evaporate (Luria, 1986).

Morgan does, however, accept notions such as the sexual division of labour, the distinction between home and work, and associated divisions such as public and private, as a crucial factor in our society.

Throwing Out Dichotomies

Some feminists maintain that the whole nature of working with dichotomies, and with these dichotomies in particular, is suspect. Indeed, as Carole Pateman has pointed out (although she does not appear to totally reject the dichotomy herself), the very slogan associated with feminism, 'the personal is the political', implies 'that no distinction can or should be drawn between the two spheres' (Pateman, 1983, p. 295). The model of a public/private split is said to so distort important features of society that it is not only a misleading tool of analysis, but also a dangerous one.

Stephanie Coontz (1988) argues that it does not make sense to define 'the family' as a private institution because it is a culture's way of coordinating personal reproduction with social reproduction. This coordination is so whatever the social ideology, the 'socially necessary illusion', about its apartness. Additionally, any separation obscures the extent to which household activities, particularly women's domestic labour, are economic activities (Finch, 1983a). We need, says Coontz, to reconceptualize the public and the private as an organic, changing whole. Sandra Harding, too, regards the idea of a split as an ideological construction emanating from the perspective of the dominant group: 'They are not only false and "interested" beliefs but also ones that are used to structure social relations for the rest of us' (Harding, 1986, p. 657).

So, within this strand of thought, rather than public/private and difference theory explaining women's subordination, they are a major component of gender ideology. In effect, using the dichotomies means judging women from the perspective of men. Bose (1987) illustrates the ways in which she feels the public/private ideology has served the interests of both capitalism and patriarchy (middle-class men). By using these dominant ideological constructs feminists are upholding and legitimating the imposition of them on subjugated groups, and in effect are supporting their usefulness for those who presently hold power. The public/private split and notions of male/female psyches are, therefore, inappropriate tools for a feminist analysis. Anna Yeatman (1987) states that what feminists should be doing is 'forswearing' dichotomies such as those of the public/private, even those that privilege women's female psyche, in the interests of exposing how 'factitious' they are.

Rescuing the Baby from the Bathwater

While accepting that the public/private split and notions of a female (and male) psyche are oversimplified and do not represent conditions of living for all women, I would not go along with writers, such as Jane Atkinson, who have concluded that 'the long-questioned domestic/public dichotomy has for many outgrown its usefulness' (quoted in Lewis, undated, p. 2). We cannot, in fact, forswear the dichotomies if we seek to understand women's perspectives on their lives. One of the important points with regard to the dichotomies is the very one the critics castigate: that they operate as ideological distinctions, as particular world views. The public/private and male/female oppositions are of interest precisely as ideological world views, not as absolute categories of analysis (although they do have some 'real' basis as well). Indeed, within her reply to her critics, Gilligan (1986) notes that they often say that her analysis seems intuitively right to many women, but then go on to say it is not sustainable. The use of the distinctions as descriptions of society, and men and women within it, in themselves necessarily presuppose the existence of social norms and assumptions. While these norms are not necessarily universal or necessary concepts, they are profoundly significant ones in Western society, patterning key features of the framework for daily life in terms of both physical settings and social relationships. The fact that the two domains and the psyches that inhabit them are ideological constructs rather than factual descriptions does not make them any less important for our perceptions of social reality. As Anne Phoenix (1987) has pointed out, black people are subject to the same dominant ideological forces as white people. Due to the pervasiveness of such ideologies, many black people subjectively accept aspects of them because they espouse the attitudes of those who are perceived to be more powerful and do not wish to be subject to stigmatization. To this idea I would add that black people, and indeed the white working-classes, may espouse certain aspects of dominant ideas but impute a different meaning to them (see below with regard to privacy). Ideologies do not exert pressure on individuals from a distance — people can redefine them in various ways.

The idea of a sphere that is private and is women's special responsibility is both deeply ingrained and emotionally loaded, to the extent that acute discomfort or guilt can be felt if the norms are violated. Women with children who do not take on this special responsibility are regarded as deviant by the state, and can be 'punished', for instance by having their children taken into state care or their mothering supervised. Moreover, as social norms, even as idealizations of reality, such notions could not have endured for so long unless they linked into assumptions that were, and are, held by people, and unless they touched upon people's experiences in some way:

> In our personal myths home is the place where we are fully accepted. It is linked with the idea of a woman, mother . . . Appeals to defend 'the privacy of the family' evoke powerful memories and dreams, and are thus able to strike chords in many hearts (New and David, 1985, p. 54; see also Ribbens, 1993, forthcoming).

The public/private split and difference theory can be used in a particular way as an important key to women's lives. They are ideas that shape, and are shaped by, women's experiences, and are reflected in women's everyday attempts to straddle the social divisions between the spheres. Even some of the critics who have attempted to show that the dichotomous models do not exist in practice accept that they do penetrate this society's cultural beliefs. Janet Finch, for instance, while destroying the model of public/private boundaries in her review of studies of wives' incorporation into their husbands' paid work, accepts that the boundary still exists 'because the domestic sphere is treated as private, the notion that it *ought* to be private penetrates cultural practices' (Finch, 1983a, p. 112; her emphasis).

The privacy of the private sphere as a concealed area to which access is restricted is something that retains a particularly strong currency in conventional wisdom. This privacy covers both physical access and knowledge of detail (Allan and Crow, 1990). A domestic space in the form of a home is regarded as essential for family life, and there is a general acceptance that domestic problems, conflicts and tensions occurring in it should be kept within 'the family'. As Christopher Gonin puts it, writing in the British National Marriage Guidance Council's (now named 'Relate') journal, 'Many of us would fight for the personal life of individuals or couples to remain private' (Gonin, 1984, p. 2). The ideology of the bounded private sphere is effective. David Clark and Mike Samphier, in their study of public attitudes towards problems between husbands and wives, note the 'highly privatised nature of the contemporary marital relationship' (Clark and Samphier, 1983, p. 6). Their study shows how most people believe problems should remain a private affair, to be sorted out by the couples themselves (including the option of splitting up) rather than calling in outside help. In the main, outside intervention is seen as only validly taking place for the sake of the children. Researchers often mention the strength of the norms of privacy as an obstacle in investigating family life and relationships. The idea of the domestic family sphere as a fundamentally private place, into which outside intervention is unacceptable, means that information about what goes on in it is regarded as private — not only by respondents, but also by researchers. Julia Brannen, in writing of the difficulty of researching sensitive subjects, such as marital difficulties, indicates how she was acutely aware of this privacy, even if her respondents showed more abandon:

> Once the interview was underway it was as if the floodgates had opened and she appeared to no longer care what she said. I was afraid that people might overhear and that she might later regret this. I suggested we move to another room for greater privacy (Brannen, 1988, p. 560).

Yet, the notion of a bounded private sphere that is *private* may not always mean the same thing to all sections of society. For instance, those espousing traditional 'family' values may feel privacy and a lack of outside intervention from the apparatus of the state is necessary for the family to exist as the stable unit that they regard as the basis of society (Mount, 1982; Anderson and Dawson, 1986). For those who are working-class, privacy may be bound up with notions of respectability (Finch, 1983b; Allan, 1990), while black people, regarding their families as a haven from racism, may wish to keep their family lives especially private where white people and those in authority are concerned (Edwards, 1990b). Nevertheless, whatever the links into the belief in a bounded private sphere, the norm exists. As such it is a form of social closure that people desire and work towards, although their actual abilities to achieve it will depend upon the material resources available to them. The public/private split can be used in a revealing way and can offer an open and flexible perspective, provided it is recognized that the divisions and boundaries between the two are not only not constant, but are to some extent different for each person according to structural and other factors operating on or in their lives. It must also be recognized that the factors operating on/in a person's life may, to some extent, change over time, not just at a generalized overall level, but also at an individual level.

Not only is the privacy of the domestic sphere regarded as an important ideal, but the sphere is still regarded as, and overwhelmingly is, women's responsibility and special place.[5] What this attitude means for women attempting to combine such responsibilities with gaining an education will be examined in the following chapters. For now it is relevant to note that boundaries between the public and the private may well be seen as shifting, or as applying in a different way to women of different races and classes, if one looks at women entering the public sphere of paid work and the changes or differences in assumptions about what work women should undertake. Or again, the boundaries may be seen as disappearing if one looks at the incorporation of the domestic sphere into the public sphere. And yet little seems to change with respect to women's responsibility for home and family. A fundamental difference in the nature and balance of the public and private exists between men and women despite any social changes or differences that might logically result in their blurring. No matter what women's activities in the public sphere, no matter what their race or class, and no matter what interactions there are shown to be between public and private spheres, women have retained a special relationship with, and responsibility for, the latter sphere that is rooted in their childbearing and childrearing responsibilities. Moreover, these responsibilities are for a large part carried out in private. This fact is of key importance in understanding and describing women's lives. Brannen (1990) has found that even when women are in dual earner relationships they construct the rewards of motherhood according to features of the dominant paradigm of 'normal' (full-time) motherhood.

The particular identification of women with the private, domestic sphere as leading to a different way of thinking and being to men is also a strong social assumption. The notion of a feminine psyche stresses that women have a need to feel interconnections, and indeed this could be said to be part of a common-sense view of women's personalities. An article in *The Guardian* newspaper (3.1.89) about a woman running workplace nurseries for private companies quoted her reflections on 'women's more holistic outlook'. She felt that 'men tend to divide their life into fairly rigidly defined sections', while women 'have always had to juggle with different roles'. Obviously it is implied that for men being a parent and a member of the workforce is not a question of juggling roles but of simply moving between them in an unproblematic way. Maggie Humm's analysis of the autobiographies that mature men and women students were encouraged to write as part of statements used as a means of assessing their suitability for entrance to a course of study, came to the conclusion that men and women run their lives around totally different bases:

> Those written by women (which are often cultural products) . . . locate their multiplicity in the sites of childhood, family and relationships rather than in the practical and career skills privileged by male students (Humm, 1987, p. 16).

A Way Forward

In positing a difference between races and classes of women in relation to the spheres, it has usually been differences in women's position in the public sphere that have been concentrated upon. Conversely, the social psychological analyses have largely concentrated on feminine characteristics as manifested in the private, domestic, personal sphere, rather than looking at the feminine psyche in operation in the public, male world. While sociological studies may show the non-existence of boundaries, or the existence of them only for women of a certain race and/or class, concentration on public activity and externally observed actuality rather than women's feelings and understandings can lead to the position where a model is destroyed but still exists. In observed academically-analyzed reality, a bounded private sphere may not exist, but the domain may well do in feelings and in people's understandings and explanations of their lives. Whether or not public/private boundaries are empirically real is less important than the fact that they are real in their ideological consequences (Porter, 1983); that in an expressive sense there may be 'boundaries to which people actually make reference and which are meaningful to them in their everyday lives' (Morgan, 1985, p. 153).

How women themselves feel about and work with, or do not work with, boundaries or connections in their everyday lives when moving between home and the outside world has not had so much analytical attention paid to it. Nevertheless, as shown below, it is increasingly becoming of popular concern. Women may work towards maintaining boundaries, or may wish to demolish them, and such processes need to be looked at in their own terms. Unless understanding is rooted in women's feelings and understandings as well as their externally observed experiences, it can only be partial.

Sharistanian believes that the public/private model:

> ... is more, not less, useful precisely because the apparent inter-penetration of public and domestic life makes tracing the real ways in which conflicts between these spheres still exists for women an even more subtle and complicated analytical task than before (Sharistanian, 1987b, p. 180).

One particular subtlety that is not usually considered by critics or proponents of the constructs is the interaction between the ideas of public and private spheres and difference theory. As has been explained, the two are conceptually linked — female psyche difference theory arising out of the special relationship to, and place of women in, the private sphere. Placing the two ideological models together is particularly interesting because within what are seemingly unified notions and common-sense wisdoms there appears to be an internal underlying tension. The public/private division, with its notion of boundaries that are to be maintained to keep the private, domestic, sphere an unaffected haven, is in contradiction to, and in tension with, the need for connectedness within the postulated feminine psyche. While the public/private ideology enjoins women to keep the two spheres separate, thereby protecting the private sphere from destructive incursion from the public sphere, the notion of an affiliative feminine psyche calls for women who straddle the spheres to take a more holistic stance and to build connections between them.

How do women, crossing the boundaries between the spheres as they have always done, deal with such ideological tensions between the two? Do they build connections and interdependencies between, in the case of the concerns here, the worlds of education and family in such a way as these are not separate — as their feminine psyches would seem to lead them to do? Or do they keep a strict boundary between the two, as the public/private ideology would have it, not letting public world demands affect their family life? Do race and class affect the ways that women do, or do not, separate the public and the private? Other studies of women combining family and, in the main, paid work, may throw some light on this problem.

Connection or Separation?

Some women would appear to take the private world of family, upon which their status, identity and psyche is so dependent, with them into the public sphere (in addition to being defined in that way within the public sphere by others). A recurring theme in several studies of women in paid work is the way in which women bring family into their jobs. Anna Pollert (1981) stresses that home was something the women brought into the factory; it was always with them. She argues that while men, too, centred on their families and discussed them at work, they related to them differently. Their family was part of their concern as fathers and breadwinners. For the women, family was of immediate, ultimate and daily concern. The actual process of family care penetrated and altered their consciousness of work. Sallie Westwood (1984), in another study of factory workers, describes the way the women decorated their machines with family photographs. She argues they were attempting to insert their lives as wives and mothers into the production process. Margaret Attwood and Frances Hatton (1983) show that the women hairdressers in their study saw their salons as places where domestic experiences could be carried over into the paid work context.[6] More immediately relevant to this study, Sue Scott (1985) found, in her interviews with PhD students, that in general male students did not see domestic aspects of their lives as legitimate topics. The men talked about their lives in linear, unproblematic ways, perceiving their academic lives as separate from their personal lives. Women students, however, wanted to, and were quick to, make connections between the different areas of their lives, and to discuss the problems and tensions with regard to childrearing, housework and so on.

Whether the women in the literature cited above inserted paid work or study into their home lives in the same way is not mentioned. Nevertheless, these particular studies, if arguments about a feminine psyche are accepted, would appear to point to women needing a recognition of, and interaction between, their identity from the private sphere in the public sphere — an integration and blurring of boundaries between the material public world and their private consciousnesses. Angie Pegg, who had been a mature student with children, and whose marriage had ended during her studying, said in the course of an interview about the effect of Simone de Beauvoir's writings upon her:

> My own experience at home was really what informed my studying and it taught me more about the world than my three years at university. I am a teacher now and I'm always trying to make connections between these things. I feel that if any student came to see me at home they wouldn't find an essentially different person (quoted in Forster and Sutton, 1989, p. 58).

This sense of connection on the part of women would be as opposed to the male psyche that would want to believe they are separate. For example, Glenn (1987) states that men (both working-class and middle-class) have been found to typically report little carry-over from job to home even when connections are obvious to an outsider, and Katherine Gerson (1985) states that men are better able to keep paid work and family as separate spheres in their lives.

On the other hand, other studies present a different picture wherein women appreciate keeping parts of their lives separate and displaying different personae. Marilyn Porter (1983) found that while women carry their private identities and concerns with them into the public world of paid work, both they and the men she interviewed saw a gulf between the two worlds, feeling that they were not only of a different order, but that they should be kept that way. Public world identities and concerns were not brought into the home, as far as possible. While both men and women felt the home should be kept as a private haven, however, Porter does say it was particularly part of the men's survival tactics to keep the two worlds separate. Yet Kate Crehan's (1986) study of women working on the shop-floor in the retail trade found one of the reasons the women gave for work-ing in the industry was that it was not a demanding job and there was no problem about 'switching off' when they went home. Julia Brannen and Peter Moss's study of new mothers returning to full-time paid work after the birth of their child shows that one of the ways the women coped with the return was by adopting a mental attitude which compartmentalized the two worlds of employ-ment and home: 'Because of the interdependence of the two spheres of work and home women feel a compelling need to separate them in their *heads*' (Brannen and Moss, 1988, p. 134; their emphasis). In a later paper, Brannen (1990) suggests that they might also do this to cover the discrepancies between their acceptance of the dominant ideologies of motherhood and family life and their actual situations. Jane Lewis and Barbara Meredith's (1988) research concerning daughters who had cared for their elderly mothers at home mentions that one factor determining whether the daughters saw themselves as retaining mutually-supportive relation-ships with their mothers in this situation was the extent to which they (the daughters) felt that they had been able to maintain a separate, compartmental-ized, identity for themselves outside the home, other than that of their mother's carer. Sue Sharpe (1984) also writes about how the working wives and mothers she interviewed perceived themselves as having a separate sense of identity quite apart from their family roles and responsibilities. Additionally, many of these women felt that having a double identity had improved their relationships with their husbands and children. The women in these studies, then, appear to draw boundaries for themselves that permit little integration or blurring of their identities in the two spheres in a way that does not concur with the full notion of a feminine psyche, but which would accord with ideas about a separate private sphere.

On the evidence drawn from the literature above, therefore, mature women students may either try to connect or separate the private world of their families and the public world of education. For women who are partners and mothers, though, doing anything outside the private sphere is viewed as inherently prob-lematic to varying degrees. David Clark and Douglas Haldane report that men frequently see and experience marriage as something that supports them in the world of paid work. Women, by contrast:

... are likely to experience ... tensions between the demands of paid work outside, and those of their unpaid labours within the home. These will not only be pressures of time and physical energy, housework and cooking are also 'moral' categories which 'say something' about a woman's feelings for her husband and their marriage and which communicate to significant others such as parents, siblings and friends (Clark and Haldane, 1990, p. 27).

Inasmuch as Clark and Haldane note how frequently cohabiting relationships are to all intents and purposes often indistinguishable from institutional marriage, the same could be said of them. Much of the intellectually dominant 'two roles' sociological literature of the early 1970s (e.g. Rapoport and Rapoport, 1971; Young and Willmott, 1975) tended to assume that 'things are getting better'. Due to the postulated symmetrification of male and female roles within 'the family', women would no longer experience these types of conflicts. Much feminist research has, however, shown this optimism to be misplaced, and indeed based on a false analysis of the situation. Certainly, even the mature women student literature operating within this two roles paradigm, as criticized in the first chapter, bears this out. On the other hand, black women have had their womanhood constructed in different ways to white women and have always been seen as workers (Hooks, 1982; Phoenix, 1987) — although still retaining responsibility for the private sphere. Any activities within the public sphere may not create such tensions for them (a point returned to again below). Indeed, most of the studies referred to in this section of the chapter are concerned with white women.

Nevertheless, some form of tension between home and paid work is widely assumed. Certainly courses run in order to encourage women returners often include a component on 'balancing home and job', something that it is difficult to imagine included in a similar course for men who, say, have been long-term unemployed. Women's magazines run features on how to be a 'successful' working mother, and books and articles are published that all assume a basic tension between paid work/career and home life, particularly motherhood, for women. Both popular and academic texts tend to evoke the metaphors of balancing or juggling in order to describe the difficulties for women, and the skills involved, in combining roles in two different worlds. For example, Katherine Gieve's edited collection, entitled *Balancing Acts: On Being a Mother*, addresses 'the contradictions between being a mother and maintaining some independence and a place in the outside world' (Gieve, 1989, p. vii); Crehan's (1986) study is entitled 'Women, work and the balancing act'; Suzanne Lie (1990) examines women's participation in academia in a study entitled 'The juggling act: Work and family in Norway'; and Valerie Grove (1987) subtitles her book *Marriage, Motherhood, Career: Can She Have It All?*.

This conflict is often argued to be a structural tension, whereby the institutions of both private and public spheres (family, the labour market, the welfare state and so on), as organized around traditional models of women as the backbone of domestic labour and men as the full-time breadwinners, create the tensions for women (for example, Sassoon, 1987) — the public/private model. It is also conceptualized (sometimes combined with a structural analysis) as a matter of tensions in women's identity — the female psyche. The quotation above from Gieve's book exemplifies this tension, with its idea of a contradiction between motherhood and maintaining independence. There is some evidence to suggest that women wanting separate identities or having a sense of 'wholeness' may be related to social class and race. Mary Boulton found that:

> A sense of being monopolised by children and losing individuality in motherhood was described much more frequently by middle-class women that by working-class women (Boulton, 1983, p. 100).

Boulton argues that this is because middle-class women's material resources appear to allow them time and freedom for other interests apart from domestic life which, when they try to pursue them, are blocked by the inherent restrictions of motherhood as institutionalized in our society. Working-class women, with fewer resources, were less likely to confront these fundamental limits and to articulate a loss of identity. Boulton thus concludes that, given better material resources and hence expectations, working-class women would also feel constrained. Yet, as was noted earlier, black women's identity has been said to be constructed in a different way to that of white women. Yasmin Alibhal feels that, as a black woman, the notion of blocked freedom is anathema to her:

> The internal imagery of childbearing and childrearing in this country seems to me quite different from what it symbolises for me. The strong sense of a child being a burden you unload at some stage of your life, or the process of childbirth and nurturing as something that draws from a woman her selfhood making her socially and politically powerless, are alien images (Alibhal, 1989, p. 30).

Berry Mayall, however, remarks upon the common priorities, concerns and perspectives of the mothers in her study with regard to mothering, regardless of country of origin, socio-economic status and household composition: 'Perhaps the experience of being mothers and carers creates this common ground: they learn from the life, the work and from the children themselves' (Mayall, 1990, p. 197). There are, therefore, not only questions to be pursued here about whether women separate or connect their educational and family lives and identities,[7] but also questions as to the whether and in what ways a woman's class and race affect such separations and connections.

Notes

1 Feminist researchers sometimes make a distinction between what goes on behind the scenes in book production or research and the final product in terms of private and public (for examples see Sharistanian, 1987a; Gordon, 1989). Jean Anyon (1983) distinguishes between public actions and private beliefs, while Jalna Hamner and Sheila Saunders (1983) have argued for an association of the private domestic world with known others and the public outer world with strangers.
2 The idea of shared parenting, a more equitable change in the household division of labour, has been the subject of much discussion and debate (see for example, Ehrensaft, 1981; Elshtain, 1981; Riley, 1983; Eisenstein, 1984; New and David, 1985). Whatever its merits, without other changes white middle-class shared parenting could come to be regarded as ideal and best for childrearing. Black

and/or working-class forms of shared parenting practices could come to be viewed as deviant and unsatisfactory. Valerie Walkerdine and Helen Lucey's (1989) discussion of pedagogy and class in present mothering norms and practices provides an example of an area around which this could coalesce. Moreover, the growing numbers of lone mothers make it a limited vehicle for social change on its own.

3   Phillips has called this approach 'a victimology of those who are the most oppressed' (Phillips, 1987, p. 141). A hierarchy of privilege and suffering (a hierarchical ordering that is surely an anathema to feminism) is erected which, in effect, leaves white middle-class women barely oppressed at all.

4   As Walby (1990) has pointed out, however, by itself, the private sphere as a haven from racism does not mean it is not also the site in which black men oppress black women.

5   Coontz (1988) suggests that different sub-groups within a society will have different relationships to the mode of production of that society, producing different relations within the private sphere (different family forms). Only one ideal type is the sanctioned one, however. Nevertheless, in Western society, whatever the family form, women retain responsibility for it and for associated activities. There may be different patterns in different families with regard to who cooks, shops, vacuums, cares for the children and so on, but responsibility for ensuring these things are done most often rests with the woman (Doyal, 1990).

6   The domestication of the paid work environment seems to many of these authors to be collusive in its acceptance of women's domestic role. They do not consider whether it may be psychologically important for women to integrate different areas of their lives.

7   To some extent, although I do not draw upon Alison Jaggar's (1983) work here, the concept of separations and connections operating in women's lives has some similarities with her ideas about alienation. Looking at the conflicting demands made upon women as wives, mothers, workers, etc., Jaggar uses the concept of alienation to explain how, under capitalism, everything (work, sex, play) and everyone (family, friends) that could be a source of a woman's integration and connection as a person instead becomes the source of her disintegration into separate parts.

Chapter 3

Family and Education: Meanings in Childhood and Adulthood

The story of the educational and family lives of the women on whose experiences this book is based is a familiar one for those who are aware of feminist literature on the subject (for example, David, 1980, 1984; Deem, 1978, 1980; Wolpe, 1976, 1978). It is an almost inevitable pattern given the subject matter. In the main, the women left school with no great career ambitions or direction, and went into traditional female occupations with little status or prospects. After a short time they fulfilled their own and their parents' expectations by finding a man and having children. It is, however, worth looking a little closer at their lives. Children learn what it means to be a male or a female of a particular race or class in the context of family life and at school, as well as within the larger community and stratified society in which they live, and from the place of family and school within that larger society. Any ideas of boundaries between the public and private worlds, and of women's place and responsibilities within them will be, to a large part, formed in this way. Moreover, the women's family and educational histories together help to construct for them the meaning of gaining a higher education, which in turn has implications for the coexistence of family and education in their lives in adulthood.

The first part of this chapter looks at the dominant ideological family and educational context in which the women grew up. It examines the fit between this and their own situations, and the meanings the women attached to family and education in their childhoods. The women's perceptions are, of course, retrospective, and filtered through understandings gained by studying. Nevertheless, retrospective interpretations of the past provide important pointers to the present. Certain themes emerge within the women's accounts of their childhoods that feed into their present understandings of family and education. These themes concern the mental and physical privacy, or otherwise, of family life and what goes on within it; the subjective, piecemeal nature of family life itself; education as conferring status in the public world and as being something for others; the individualized and abstracted nature of education; and that of being different from others. The extent to which the women's perspectives fit with the ideological and common sense beliefs outlined in the previous chapter is examined as part of this exploration. The congruences or disjunctures between the two provide pointers to issues the women had to deal with both as mothers/partners and as students,

Table 3.1:   Age cohorts

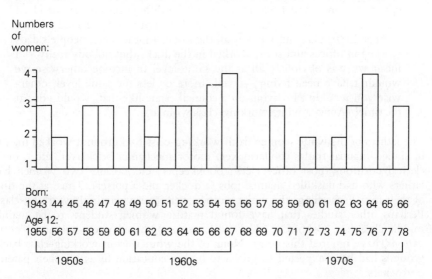

and to the ways in which they went about dealing with these — the topic of the rest of the book.

The Women's Childhoods

Age Cohorts, Class and Race

The mature women students can be divided into three main cohorts in terms of their ages as shown in table 3.1. There is a small group of older women, born between 1943 and 1947, who entered secondary schooling (aged about 12) in the mid to late 1950s, and who were in their early to mid 40s when I interviewed them. Their adolescent years, when they were becoming increasingly aware of the opposite sex and what their future was in relationships with them, were accordingly experienced during the 1950s. The largest group (half the women) were born between 1949 and 1955, and were in their mid to late 30s when interviewed. They experienced adolescence and secondary schooling during the 1960s. The third group, a slightly more disparate one, is formed from the women in their mid 20s to early 30s, born between 1958 and 1966. Their entry to second-ary school and their adolescent years took place in the 1970s.

Far more of the white women identified themselves as having had working-class childhoods. Six of the ten women who had described themselves as middle-class in adulthood felt they had come from working-class backgroungs, making eighteen white women from working-class backgrounds in all. No-one referred to themselves as currently working-class and from a middle-class background. The women's identification of their class backgrounds appeared to be based on their fathers' occupations and the communities in which they lived. Sometimes they also made comparisons with the living conditions of other people outside this sphere of reference:

> It was a big estate and everybody, you know, was all Londoners. We all talked the same, and I wasn't aware of the differences on the outside. I was only a lot older when I realized that. Everybody around us was another Eastender, and we was all the same. I mean some people's dads worked in offices and some worked in the docks, but nobody really — I mean we was obviously all at the same level of income otherwise we wouldn't have been living — well, more or less the same level, otherwise you wouldn't be living on a council estate like that, would you, at the time? (Anne, a white working-class woman).

The fathers of the white women from working-class backgrounds worked mainly in skilled manual trades (boilermaker, motor mechanic, bricklayer, etc.), or in clerical positions (post office clerk, bookkeeper, etc.). Only two women had fathers who had unskilled manual jobs (a docker and a porter). Thus, at the time of their initial schooling, the white women were overwhelmingly working-class. Perhaps other studies that have found mature women students to be mainly middle-class (see Osborn *et al.*'s, 1984, review), based upon husbands' occupations, have ignored this point. None of the women from working-class backgrounds had been expected to go on to higher education by either their parents or teachers.

The remaining four white middle-class women spoke of coming from middle-class backgrounds. Their fathers were in professional or managerial positions. Interestingly, three of these women fall into the third cohort of women, who entered secondary schooling in the 1970s. The fourth was within the middle cohort and was atypical in other ways. She was the only woman who came from an upper middle-class background, attending a private girls' school that specialized in producing 'young ladies' rather than women with academic qualifications. Additionally, apart from her, the other women from middle-class backgrounds had continued their secondary schooling beyond the minimum school-leaving age. Two of them had been expected by both their parents and teachers to go on to higher education (pregnancy delayed this path for one, while the other 'rebelled' against these expectations). The older cohort of women all came from working-class backgrounds and their educational achievements, along with those of the other women from working-class backgrounds and the black women, are discussed below. It may well be that women from middle-class backgrounds are likely to make a decision to return to education as mature students far sooner than women from working-class backgrounds.

The black women overwhelmingly did not speak of themselves in terms of class. In the main their childhoods were lived outside Britain and, for reasons which will become clear, their fathers' occupations did not define their sense of the status of their backgrounds in the same way as it did for the white women — although they too referred to the rest of the community around them. Like the white middle-class women, the black women fall into the latter two cohorts, with the majority in the middle cohort (five of the seven). The timing of their decision to return to higher education is thus probably more to do with establishing themselves as immigrants to this country. The one black woman whose father was in a middle-class occupation (teaching) in this country did fall into the younger cohort, which supports the conclusion drawn above for the white women from middle-class backgrounds.

Family Life Ideologies and Educational Policies

Complementary Roles and Education

The ideal and 'normal' family of the immediate post-war years consisted of a husband playing an instrumental breadwinner role, which dovetailed with his wife's contribution as a full-time husband-and-child-centred carer and nurturer. This unit, effectively, is the separate spheres model, a notion of benignly differing but complementary tasks based upon the implicit naturalness of sexual divisions. The welfare reforms of the 1940s and early 1950s entrenched the view of the wife, as mother, in her dependency on a male wage-earner (Lewis, 1984). The 1950s was a time when the nuclear family came to be especially seen as a private haven, with an additional stress on intimacy between husband and wife. Women were expected to devote their prime years and best energies to home and family in an 'orgy' of ultra-domesticity. As Sylvia Ann Hewlett puts it: 'To be a nurturing and empathetic mother and to be a loving and supportive wife [were] the overriding goals of women who grew to maturity in the 1950s' (Hewlett, 1988, p. 150).

The women in the first cohort, who grew up in the 1950s, (all of whom said they had working-class childhoods) came from two-parent nuclear families. They spoke, however, of having a large extended family network that played a part in their upbringing. Four of these women recalled their fathers as doing little domestically and as not very involved in their upbringing. Yet the other woman remembered her father as 'helping' quite a lot with the housework and with looking after her and her brother. Superficially these women's parents fitted the dependent wife-mother and breadwinner husband mould, with only one woman's mother having a paid job outside the home during her childhood. Nevertheless, two of the women remembered their mothers doing paid work inside the home, such as dressmaking or typing envelopes. The haven containing a woman with sole, and only, nurturing responsibility was thus not quite the complete reality of these women's childhoods.

Yet education policies of the time (as they do now) contained particular ideological views of girls from different classes, and of families. Throughout the 1950s and 1960s, British policy-makers supported the notion that education for girls should be different from that provided for boys (David, 1980, 1984; Deem, 1981). The concept of 'relevance' in schooling for boys' and girls' different adult roles held sway. Boys should have a technical, industrial, job-slanted education, while working-class girls' education concentrated on domestic skills. Middle-class grammar school girls, though, also learned arts, languages and so on, in order to fit them for suitable paid work as well as their future marital life. The main benefits of girls' education was seen as accruing to the private world of their homes and families. During the 1960s there was a gradual shift from selective towards comprehensive secondary schooling, and the removal of the eleven-plus exam,[1] in an effort to reduce class-based inequalities, but sex-based inequalities were left unacknowledged. What this shift meant for the women educationally is discussed below.

Symmetrical Roles and Education

The late 1960s and 1970s saw a general move towards recognition that women, whatever their class and marital status, were part of the workforce (Arnot, 1983). The image of the ideal family was also shifting. The emphasis changed from one stressing 'complementarity' towards a more 'symmetrical' partnership. Studies at the time (Goldthorpe *et al.*, 1969; Young and Wilmott, 1975; Rapoport and Rapoport, 1976) appeared to show that men were becoming more home and family-centred. One postulated outcome of what was viewed as the increasing proportion of married women in paid employment was that this was making marriage a more egalitarian relationship. The 'symmetrical family' has been criticized and exposed as superficial by many feminists. For example, at the time Ann Oakley (1974) showed that, while attitudes might be becoming more egalitarian, changes in behaviour were much less marked. The idea of symmetricality, however, enjoyed a general pervasive influence and popularity, with its comfortable picture of harmony and adaptability, which continues (see Chapter 6).

The white women (seventeen) and the two 'mixed' race women in the second and third cohorts, however, do not remember these facets of their family lives so very differently from the older cohort. Most came from two-parent families. Two women experienced their parents divorcing in their mid-teens, and two had parents who divorced in their early childhoods. Of the latter, one was then brought up by her mother alone and the other's mother remarried after a few years. Extended families, however, did not figure quite so much in this cohort's accounts of their upbringing, regardless of class. This was particularly so in the case of the younger cohort of women. Again, fathers were mainly not recalled as being greatly involved in the women's upbringing or helping out domestically. Nevertheless, some fathers did play a domestic role, taking on shopping, childcare and so on — always described by the women as 'helping' their mothers. Half the women's mothers had paid work in, at least, part-time jobs during their childhoods. Here, however, combined age and class seem to make a difference in terms of the fit between norms and the women's childhood reality. While the women from working-class backgrounds in the middle cohort were evenly divided between those whose mothers had paid jobs and those whose mothers never worked outside the home, the women growing up in the 1970s were divided between the white working-class girls whose mothers did not work outside the home and the middle-class girls whose mothers did. The ideal of complementary roles and sex-based relevant schooling for working-class girls, current during their mothers' teenage years, may be seen in operation.

During the 1970s, however, the assumption that girls needed a different sort of education from boys came, to some extent, to be questioned, accompanying the shift in conceptions of family life towards egalitarianism. Sex-based inequalities of provision were acknowledged in the mid-1970s in Britain, when the education sections of the 1975 Sex Discrimination Act made it illegal to deny a girl access to any particular subject (except sports) on the grounds of her sex, or to operate quota systems. Any commitment to equality between the sexes was very limited however (David, 1983).

Table 3.2: Working-class girls' schools and qualifications

Numbers
of
women:

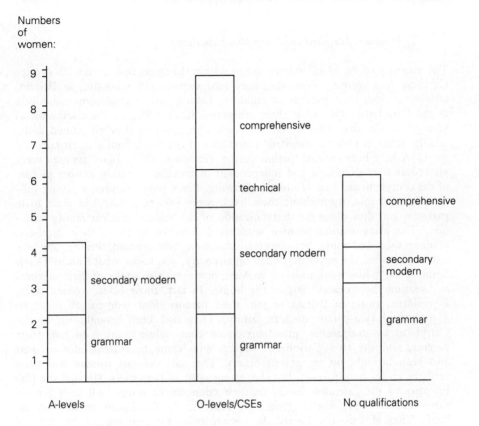

Educational Outcomes

Whatever the twists and turns of education policies, and whatever age cohort the women fell into, the result in terms of paid work for the white working-class women, along with the white middle-class women, was the same, no matter what their educational route. The vast majority ended up in clerical or secretarial jobs, while a few went into nursing, and some worked in shops. Half the working-class girls (nine women) passed their eleven-plus and went to grammar schools or into the top streams of comprehensives. Despite this, just under half of them (four women) left school with no qualifications whatsoever. All but one of them came from the older cohort of women. On the other hand, those failing their eleven-plus and attending secondary modern schools (six women) all, bar one, came away with some qualifications at O or CSE levels, and a couple gained A-levels.[2] Overall, the white women's qualifications as 'working-class girls', by type of school attended, are shown in table 3.2.

In itself, this situation provides some comment on the education system, but the women's perceptions of the reasons for these outcomes are discussed later.

The women had their own views on the relationship between family and education and the way it had shaped their opportunities.

Dominant Matriarchs and Remedial Education

The majority of the black women come within the larger mid to late 30s group. Of these five women, however, only two experienced schooling in Britain, arriving to join their parents as children, having had at least some schooling in the Caribbean. The other three emigrated from Africa or the Caribbean as young women after completing their schooling, where they all gained some qualifications to O-level standard. Ideologies of the black family in Britain and the USA have been termed 'pathologizing' (Phoenix, 1987). Black women were viewed as over-dominant and independent matriarchs — fitting neither picture of the complementary or symmetrical family. Black women, often working full-time in paid jobs throughout their lives, were said to emasculate their male partners, and thus cause the destabilization of the 'natural' nuclear family structure. The black mature women students did indeed speak of their mothers, grandmothers and aunts, as independent women: 'My grandmother . . . she was a strong person. She never depended on anybody, you know what I mean' (Val). Some of the white working-class women, however, also spoke of their mothers as 'wearing the trousers' within the home. In fact, those black women who, as children, came to Britain to join their parents (four women) all came to a traditional two-parent nuclear family. They had been brought up in the Caribbean by godparents, grandparents or aunts while waiting to join their parents, and the two Caribbean women who came to Britain later on had also been brought up by grandmothers. The only African woman had been brought up by both parents, but she, along with all the others, stressed the importance of the extended family in their countries of origin. All their female carers had worked full-time (those 'at home' in the Caribbean, mainly on the land). They also usually carried the responsibility for bringing up the children and for the domestic work in the home, in the same way as most of the white women's mothers, even where some involvement of men in childcare was mentioned.

For the four black women who did experience schooling in Britain, including the two women in the third cohort, their secondary schooling took place at a time (1960s to late 1970s) when education policy with regard to race had moved away from a colour-blind assimilation/integration approach. The move was towards an approach that identified and pathologized black families as 'culturally deprived' (Coultas, 1989). The education system was regarded as a way of re-socializing black children to the 'acceptable' values that their 'inadequate' families were not providing for them. All four of the black women who were schooled in Britain attended comprehensive schools. Only one of them left without any qualifications, and two went on to take A-levels. On the face of it, the lives of the black women in this study, in terms of educational outcomes, appear not very different from those of the white women. They went into the same kinds of paid work as the white women, although two of them (as was the case with two of the white women) became pregnant immediately after finishing their secondary schooling and had never held a paid job. As with the white women, they had their own perceptions of the way their opportunities had been constrained and the reasons for this.

The Meaning of Family and Education in Childhood

As writers on both white and black families are now pointing out, there is no such thing as 'the family', completely fitting any racial or class stereotype (for example, Gittins, 1985; Dominelli, 1988). Nor do girls and women completely and passively accept the gendered, class and racial identities offered to them socially and educationally (Amos and Parmar, 1981; Anyon, 1983). It is, therefore, important to look at what the women regarded family and education as qualitatively meaning for them in their childhoods, both separately and in relation to each other.

In the women's recollections of family life are notions of the home as a private and separate sphere, a haven from the public world that revolved around women's caring. To a large extent these ideas coincide with the ideologies and common understandings outlined in the previous chapter. Moreover, where the women's childhood lives did not fit this picture, there was a sense that they should have done so. The women's family lives in childhood had been built around routine and the minutiae of everyday life:

> In the summer holidays from school we used to go to the park. You know them Quality Street tins or biscuit tins, she'd make two of those tins full of sandwiches every morning and then we'd go to this park. And we used to go to this one particular place every day. And my mum would get a deckchair . . . And then we'd all come home, trail home together at about half past four, five o'clock, so mum could get the tea ready at night for dad to come home. (Alexandra, a white working-class woman).

Women, as mothers, grandmothers, aunts and so on, were overwhelmingly the caring centres of family life, responsible for this detail and for its process, whether or not they worked outside the home as well. If families, and the women within them, were not then it was felt that they should have been. Three women referred to unhappy childhoods in which they were abused physically or mentally. Helen, for instance, who came from a white working-class background, said her mother in particular had been cold and uncaring towards her, and occasionally physically violent. There had been no 'family atmosphere' (that is, a woman's caring) in her home. She and the other two felt, however, that home and their female carers should have been a warm retreat for them. Additionally, two of the four black women who had come to Britain to join their parents after many years apart, spoke with regret about never regaining a close relationship with their mothers, rather than with their fathers.

For these few women the home, and their mothers or grandmothers, were not a respite from the outside world. Helen spoke of it almost the other way round, with school and the streets becoming a haven from home. As far as the rest of the women were concerned, however, the home was there to come back to from school. Conventional family life was understood as something distinct from the public world. By the time they were at secondary school, over a third of the women (twelve) said they had hated school. For the most part their mothers and their homes represented a refuge:

> I was very, very unhappy at school, and there was always this feeling that come four o'clock it'll all be okay, you know. It was back with mum, which was nice . . . that very strong kind of, you know, that sigh of relief, oh mum's there like (Michelle, white working-class woman).

The home and family life served, or should have served, as an escape from the stresses of life outside it.

Families were important and, moreover, obligations within them were different from those outside them:

> For the family you did anything and everything at the drop of a hat, but friends, that was something different. They were outsiders (Jackie, a white working-class woman).

The women, while not actually talking in terms of a boundary around their separate, private spheres, often seemed to recognize an invisible wall around their families. 'Outside' was a word often used in the accounts of people and places in relation to family and home, or even 'outside world'. What was presented to the outside world was important to keep control over, and only certain aspects of the outside were allowed inside. Mothers and other female carers were the ones who signalled this separation to the women, as children, in various ways. Five white women from working-class backgrounds specifically mentioned that nobody but family entered their homes: 'They didn't have a lot of friends, it was mainly family I think. They didn't have sort of — friends didn't call round' (Cathy). On the other hand, the few white women from middle-class backgrounds talked of their parents socializing with friends at home quite a lot. In fact, many studies have suggested that access to the private domestic sphere of the home was, and is, more limited in working-class homes because it is regarded as an arena reserved principally for the family (see Allan, 1989).

In particular, the outside world should not be privy to certain details of the women's family lives. There is a strong belief, discussed in the previous chapter, that what goes on inside the family, especially if it reflects badly, should not be broadcast outside it. For Helen, this meant that she could not speak to anyone about the way she was being ill-treated at home:

> We knew that things weren't right but as children you can't do anything about it. 'Cos if you say anything to a relative their immediate reaction would be to question your parents. And then your parents get angry and say, "What are you talking to them about our business for", and things like that.

For the majority of the women, privacy was to do with presenting a respectable face to the outside world. There is, as six of the white women with working-class childhoods mentioned, 'class within class' and status was important. For example, illegitimacy in the family was hidden and not to be talked about, or a pregnancy in later life was felt to be shameful. As children, the women were aware not only that they should keep certain details of family life to themselves, but also that they should behave differently outside the home. The private and public spheres were thus also marked off in terms of the styles of behaviour thought appropriate to each. Being 'decent', 'presentable' and 'behaving properly' outside the home was mentioned by seven of the white women. Three black women from the Caribbean talked of the respect their grandmothers or other female carers were given in the communities in which they lived. This respect was bound up with social distance and a lack of familiarity with personal details. People addressing their grandmothers or aunts by their title and surname only was pointed to particularly as an illustration of the respect in which they were held. Irene was one of the only people from the small farming village in which she lived who could read and write:

> And because I could read as a child and there are people who can't read all the people used to bring their letter to me and I used to write their letter. You know, like read people's letters. So that mean I would know what's going on in the district, and people would call me Miss Grant.

While seventeen women mentioned that they were surrounded by others who lived the same lives as they did, there was also a sense that there was something different about their families that held them a little apart from the rest. For the white women from working-class backgrounds having a telephone or a car or a father with a slightly higher status job and/or income were mentioned as source of status. These things, however, were not to be used in an overt way to set them apart from the community: 'And I remember saying to a friend of mine, "We've got a telephone". And my mum overheard me and said, "Yes, but you're not to boast about it"' (Alexandra). There was thus a tension in many of the women's accounts between having status and the idea of not setting oneself apart by 'getting above yourself' (something which will find echoes in their descriptions of the meaning of gaining a higher education in this and future chapters). Five of the seven black women felt that their families had a higher status within their communities in the Caribbean, which was lost when they came to Britain. One aspect of status that cropped up quite frequently in the white women's accounts of their working-class childhoods was their choice of friends. This was another area where they were particularly aware of their mothers' drawing boundaries: 'I mean my mother always had this idea that, you know, there were certain people you didn't mix with because they were common, kind of thing' (Angela). Only four of the women (three white and one black) felt that their families had a lower status in their communities.

Up to a certain age friends were played with in the street, not in the home: 'We didn't really have friends in the house that much as small children. It was different when we were teenagers, but when we were small children . . .' (Jackie). It was around the age that friends began to enter the home (and they entered others' homes as well), in early adolescence, that the white women also reported that they became aware of larger social class differences. This was particularly so in the case of the white working-class girls who went to grammar schools. Gillian's account of how social class differences came to her attention is fairly typical:

I didn't fit in at all with the school. My friends were at the secondary modern . . . There was one other girl who lived quite close to me who went to the same grammar school, and she came from a big house and was extremely snobby. We didn't relate to each other at all. And I mean my mum used to sort of get nervous if we went past their house, you know . . . They had warm houses, you know, and they didn't have to go outside to the loo! I used to bring kids home from school occasionally, but when I went to their house, you know, they went to the toilet inside, upstairs or downstairs. It wasn't an easy thing to ask people to cross the yard. No, it wasn't, it wasn't a nice — I mean it exposed me to a lot of snobbiness . . . And it's so easy to get alienated at school because of that.

Again, getting above yourself, this time through their own education, was a theme and is one of the reasons given by the women for their lack of educational attainment.

Low expectations of them on the part of their teachers was also mentioned by nine women as a reason for lack of achievement. The black women schooled in Britain saw this entirely in terms of race, but the white women felt it most often in terms of sex but also in terms of class. Five white women from working-class backgrounds spoke of their schools being 'dumping grounds' for working-class children, or being organized for the benefit of the boys and their interests. Looking back, Judith felt angry about the sex and class assumptions on the part of the school, which affected the course of her own schooling:

I don't ever remember any teacher saying to me, you know, 'You could go and do O-levels' or, 'Have you thought about talking to your parents?' or — but that never came into it . . . I think if I hadn't gone to that school and they hadn't trained us so much like that [as office workers], perhaps I might have gone off, you know, into something else that would have been more suitable for me, I think. Because, you know, that was my destiny as far as they were concerned! Just fodder.

These attitudes were mirrored in Judith's parents' expectations of her, too. Education for their brothers was mentioned by ten women as being regarded as more important by their parents. Even for those who did not have brothers, their parents expected that girls would marry and have children, and therefore needed only enough education to get them a job that would fill in the time until this happened, and which they could pick up again later on. Indeed, most of the white women did this and were quite happy to do so at the time. While the black women also mentioned that their parents and other carers expected them to find a man and have children, without exception they all stressed how much importance was attached to getting a good education by their parents or other carers: 'I mean they've always wanted me to achieve, you know. I mean being West Indian parents, you know, education was the thing' (Maureen). Being 'pushed' or 'not pushed' by parents to achieve educationally, either as a good or a bad thing, was talked about by all the women.

All but one of the women from middle-class backgrounds felt they had been pushed, but the pressure was too much for two of them. While four white working-class women spoke of their parents' disdain for education beyond that which was absolutely necessary, most of the white working-class women felt that their parents did value education and had pushed them up to a point beyond which they were either not encouraged to go, or it was left very much up to them. The encouragement usually stopped at minimal qualifications because that is where their parents' own understandings of the possibilities of the education system ceased (and teachers did not appear often to hold out alternative scenarios for them). Very few of the women's parents had stayed on at school beyond school-leaving age, and most of their parents had few, if any, qualifications. It was not that their parents were unintelligent. Eleven women stressed that their mothers and/or their fathers had been bright and could have gone on to better things if free and universal education had been available to them and/or the second world war had not disrupted their schooling.

'Educated' people were often an unknown factor, outside their own social circles, and a quarter of the women (eight) mentioned how their parents regarded teachers as people with authority and power — to whom they were not quite sure how to relate:

> She wouldn't have known her way — how to manage sort of rela-
> tionships with school. She wouldn't have known how to go into the
> school and create the right impression (Jennie, a white working-class
> woman).

As will be explored in Chapter 5 (see also Edwards, 1993b), the women's own understandings of the education system as students in higher education led them to feel a different placing to that of their parents in relation to schools and to other public institutions.

The women's memories contain notions of what family life is, and of what education is about and who it is for, which run through into their present understandings. Their accounts of their family lives in childhood contain images of the maintenance of physical and mental boundaries separating the domestic sphere from the outside world. Within what should have been a private haven, women were held to be responsible for its everyday routine practices, and for caring and nurturing. While many of the women felt their families held some sort of status in their own communities there were tensions attached to holding this position. Moreover, the 'outside world', and education in particular, was a differ-ent sort of status-bound world where class and race played an important part. Education was, in the main, a world into which the women and their parents fitted uneasily. The ways in which these ideas and images run through into many aspects of the women's perceptions of what family and education were about for them as adults will now be addressed.

The Women in Adulthood

Acting in concert, family and education had placed the women in the situations they inhabited when they made their decisions to return to formal education. Having set up their own homes and families, the women had decided once again to have both family and education in their lives. The social context in which they

Table 3.3: Partner relationships

	Married (second marriage)		Cohabiting (previously divorced)		Live-out (previously divorced)	
White women:						
Working-class	9	(3)	1	(1)	2	(1)
middle-class	5	(1)	4	(4)	1	(1)
Black women	2		1		4	(2)
'Mixed' race women					2	(1)

were doing this and its implications for them are examined in the next chapter, but for now it is important to consider the meanings the women attached to family and education in adulthood in order to set the background for the examination of the interaction of the two in the women's lives. Together they provide an indication of the issues the women had to deal with as mature students.

Family Structures

Most of the women were married, or living in cohabiting relationships that were akin to marriage when they started their studies. Several of them, however, were in long-term relationships where their partners did not live with them permanently. A summary of the women's relationships is shown in table 3.3. Overall then, upon starting their courses, the white working-class women were more likely to be married (and also less likely to be divorced), the white middle-class women were mostly evenly split between marriage and cohabiting relationships, and the black and 'mixed' race women were slightly more likely to be in 'live-out' relationships. All the non-cohabiting women referred to themselves as lone parents, even though four relationships had been in existence for five years or more, and in two cases their partners had fathered one, and in another case both, of their children. However, one white, working-class woman's marriage was conducted on a similar basis to the non-cohabiting relationships because, for most of their twenty-seven-year marriage, her husband had worked away from home during the week and only came home at weekends.

How the partnership profile of the women fits with any larger picture for mature women students is impossible to tell as the statistics are not available. In Britain, as in many other Western countries, female lone parenthood is increasing as a result of rising marital breakdown and unmarried motherhood. In 1990, lone mothers made up 18 per cent of all families (OPCS, 1991a). The rate of lone parenthood is generally higher for Afro-Caribbean than for white and Asian women because the former tend to delay marriage (Brown, 1984). Cohabitation rates overall are also rising, although usually as a prelude to marriage (Family Policy Studies Centre, 1988). In 1988, approximately 6 per cent of non-married women aged 25 to 49 were cohabiting (OPCS, 1989b). Class, race, relationship breakdown, or parenthood figures are not collected for cohabiting couples, although it is known that the proportion of births outside marriage registered by parents living at the same address is high (OPCS, 1991b).

Fourteen of the mature women students (just under half) had been divorced, while the national rate is one in three marriages ending in divorce. It would be fair to say that upon entering higher education the women appeared more divorce-prone than the general population. This is an important point when considering the possible effects of studying upon partner relationships. The working-class women being less likely to be divorced then the middle-class women is, however, in contradiction to national class patterns (Murphy, 1985) — although of course it must be borne in mind that the women assessed their own social class rather than it being ascribed. Nevertheless, the lack of information of this type for mature students generally in higher education means it cannot be assessed, whether or not the women are representative in terms of their partnership circumstances. Thus no firm conclusions can be drawn about whether or not women with families who enter higher education are different from women generally in the way that the partnership details of these women would seem to suggest.

The majority of the women had between one and three children of various ages, but six women (three white working-class and three black) had four children or more. Three women had not actually had any children when they started studying but had become pregnant and given birth to a child during the course of their degrees. Additionally, two women who already had one child had another while studying, and two women with children, interviewed during their first year of study, were pregnant again by the end of the year. The children all originally lived permanently with the women, except in one case where care was shared with an ex-husband. With so many of the women divorced or having had previous unmarried relationships that produced children, in many cases not all, if any, of their children were fathered by their current partner.

The Meaning of Family

In similar ways to their childhood accounts, the women saw families in adulthood to be about women's emotional caring, whatever the variations in family structure and circumstances — but this time their family relationships were their responsibility. On the other hand, the extent to which their own families existed as a separate haven from the outside world and its inhabitants and concerns was more uneven than in their retrospective accounts.

Fourteen of the women, again talked about outside the family and about private lives. The family as a separate unit, into which intrusions from those outside of it were not wanted, was referred to:

> It's funny really because we're quite — we don't worry too much about other people. You know what I mean? We don't have many contacts outside the family . . . You know, I quite like not talking to neighbours. I find it irritating to have people around you you don't want. It irritates me. I haven't got that privacy . . . I think I'd quite like that. To have that, to have that privacy, you know (Michelle, a white working-class woman).

Two women who had rented out a room in their houses in order to supplement their grants spoke of how much they disliked having somebody who was not a member of their family living in their homes. Furthermore, as will be explored within the next chapter, six women indicated that they felt that their family should be able to function as an autonomous unit. A quarter of the women (eight) assured me, when asked how they felt about being interviewed, that I had not been 'intrusive'. Their very reassurances indicate that boundaries were there and could have been violated. My potential intrusiveness, it seemed, was also of concern to some of the women's partners. Four white working-class married women remarked that telling me about their family lives had been viewed with some unease by their husbands. Six of the women who had been divorced mentioned, among the reasons for their marriages ending, that their ex-husbands had not liked them doing anything outside the family except, perhaps, an undemanding job, or regarded the family as the woman's sphere and showed little interest or accommodation to it.[3] There were also stories about officials asking 'impertinent' questions about the women's family lives. The women were not only working with their own sense of where boundaries around the family lay, but also with their partners' and with those of people from the public world. Nine women articulated a sense of their homes and families as in some way being refuges to come back to from the public world. Paula (black) described this as epitomized for her by a slogan that she had seen painted on a wall: 'Modern life is shit'. She said that the world outside her family threw up situations in which she felt required to 'perform' and which intimidated her. Anne (white working-class) disliked the values she viewed her children as picking up from the outside world — acquisitive, competitive and hierarchical. Irene (black) remarked:

> It was nice that when I come home I'm coming home to somebody. There was somebody there waiting for me . . . I'm glad I come home and I have them. It's like I have something to hang on to.

Irene, however, did not hold an autonomous view of her family. She had little in the way of relatives in Britain, not coming to join her parents but arriving here with her (now ex) husband. She had annexed friends as members of her family, for example, by making them godparents to her children. Other women also conveyed a more open view of family and home life than some of the women discussed above. For instance, Lynne (white middle-class) spoke of her friends almost as if they were family. Lynne kept an open home:

> The house is always full of, full of people. Constant. I've got my daughter's boyfriend lives here and his friend has just moved into the house . . . This place is like a walk-in coffee house anyway. Sort of people are always here.

Inviting people into the home does not necessarily involve a greater willingness to divulge personal information, but it is indicative of a looser boundary (Allan, 1989). Indeed, what goes on inside the family was felt to be less a matter for privacy by a quarter of the women (seven). For example, June (one of the white working-class women whose husbands had felt uneasy about what they might be telling me) described herself as an 'open' person who did not keep to herself personal details that might reveal the family as not the cosy unit it could otherwise appear:

You see I think, I think like if the boys got in trouble at school or anything I'd say, 'Well, you have to look at this, why they're doing it'. Other mothers wouldn't admit it. And things like that. Or with my mother-in-law, I'd say, 'She's an old cow' you know. You couldn't help it! Whereas other people wouldn't say anything at all about what's happening in the home. They'd like everyone to believe everything in the garden's rosy or whatever, when you knew probably it wasn't.

Sandra (black) had frequently asked priests, her husband's employer and friends to intervene in her marriage and to back her up in her efforts to get her husband to stay at home and be more involved in family life — unsuccessfully, both in terms of getting some of them to do it and in having any effect upon his behaviour.

The sense of family and home as a separate private sphere varied between the women and thus differed from the more bounded images in their childhood accounts. Some drew the boundaries tightly around their families and the details of their family lives, while others had much looser ideas with regard to access and privacy. Historical time, along with social mobility (most of the white middle-class women having come from working-class backgrounds) may explain this shift in their accounts. Due to social and economic factors, the physical and mental privacy of the home has become much less important for working-class families now than in the past (Allan, 1989). What all but one of the women did share, however, was a sense of the importance of their role as women who were mothers and partners within their families, the personal commitment involved in caring, and the need for attention to the concrete and the particular as part of this. Once again, the women's accounts of their families were filled with personal details about partners' and children's tidiness or untidiness and so on, as well as anecdotes about who said or did what to whom and when. As with childhood memories, their family lives were, to borrow a phrase from Dorothy Smith, 'a local and particular world' (Smith, 1987, p. 6). For instance, in the few cases where I asked women questions such as, 'What does being a mother/wife/partner mean to you?', I was usually met with an initial bewildered silence. Their own family lives and relationships were difficult things for the women to conceptualize and talk about in abstract terms. Sarah Ruddick (1989) has termed this concern with, and attention to, particularity and detail 'maternal thinking'. She argues maternal thinking is grounded in ongoing experience rather than instruction. Other, empirical, studies also reveal a common concern with detail and process in mothering, rather than goals, on the part of women of various races and classes (for example, Mayall, 1990).

Only Val (black) felt herself to be emotionally distanced, notably from her extended family but also to some extent from her children and partner. She particularly resented being expected to provide physical caring 'simply because you are the woman of the house'. While there were variations in the division of domestic labour in the women's households, the women overwhelmingly felt responsible for caring *about*, not just caring *for*, their families, with the latter reflecting the former.[4] Paula, along with the other black women, felt that women within the family 'back home' shared both caring for and caring about among them. Talking of how life as a mother of two small children would have been for her in the Caribbean, Paula commented:

> Family is much more more united. There's a lot more support. If I had two children, I mean goodness me, I could go out tonight, Saturday night. My granny, my auntie . . .

Jackie (white working-class) regarded herself as responsible for holding her extended family together. The majority of the white women, however, middle-class and working-class, saw themselves as important within the narrower sphere of their partners and children. Michelle (white working-class), for example, saw each woman in her extended family, as a mother, as the focal point within their own separate domains:

> It's something to do with mothers being the centre, the centrepin of families, I think. I think they really are. Everything revolves — I mean if I go over to Jeff's [my husband] parents' house, if his mum's not there the house is empty. There can be five other people in it but if she's not there it's empty, you know. And it's the same even with my mum and dad . . . you're the one — you hold everything together.

All the women (except Val, quoted earlier) held themselves responsible for the happiness and contentment of the other members of their family, especially their partners and children — in other words a sense of connectedness as described by Carol Gilligan (1982). These responsibilities for the well-being of the members of their families were felt by the women whether their partners lived with them permanently or not, and whatever their children's age. Occasionally, though, their concern with the well-being of others extended far beyond their families. Four of the women mentioned that one of the reasons they filled silences in seminars or spoke up and asked questions of visiting speakers at the polytechnic or university was because they did not want the lecturers to feel hurt by lack of interest — a feminine psyche in operation?[5] Within their families, happiness was to be achieved by the women investing time and attention physically and emotionally, and in the details and routine of everyday life.[6] There may be disagreements among feminists over whether this sort of care-giving is oppressive to women (as for Barrett and McIntosh, 1982), or humanizing (as for Gilligan, 1982; Ruddick, 1989), or both (Abel and Nelson, 1990), but there is no doubt that it forms the focus of many women's lives. Jane Ribbens (1993, forthcoming) has also noted and explored the theme of feelings of responsibility in mothers' accounts of family life — also accompanied by varied notions of boundaries between the home and the outside world.

Living their lives in this way meant that many of the women perceived themselves to have a different outlook and different concerns and priorities to that of men, in a similar way to Gilligan's (1982) and others' conception of difference. Six women specifically mentioned their partners not finding it easy to express their emotions, and women's general abilities to deal with and to talk about feelings and related issues were remarked upon. The common-sense wisdom that men can compartmentalize their lives was reflected in thirteen women's comments. They saw themselves as unlike men in that they carried their attachments and responsibilities for caring about the happiness and well-being of others, particularly with regard to their children, around with them all the time:

I think men divorce sort of work and home very much don't they? I think women — it is true because I mean everything that I do, my children are in my mind. I don't mean that I'm necessarily worrying about what they're doing, but if I find out something I think well, yes, you know, Natalie ought to know about this or Lara ought to know about this (Jackie, a white working-class woman).

I found it very hard to leave Patrick [son], which I've said. And it was, it was upsetting when he was happy somewhere else and when he was sad at someone else's. It didn't seem to matter which way, it upset me! I think that, I think that I often felt that sort of Roger [my husband] didn't understand how I felt about that, and I'm sure that's because men are used to leaving their children so much more than women. (Madeline, a white middle-class woman).

Motherhood was a particularly intense emotional commitment for the majority of the women. This commitment was one that the women themselves valued and in the main enjoyed, even if it was at times draining and frustrating. The time and energy the women expended on motherhood was, however, declared by six of them not to be respected or valued within society generally — mainly white middle-class women. There are links here with the discussion of the conception of identity on the part of mothers from different classes and races in the previous chapter. White middle-class women may also be unused to being dismissed in adulthood because of race or class in the way other women might be, and thus feel it more with regard to motherhood. However, Kim ('mixed' race) shared their view. Talking about employers' attitudes she said:

You spent your time with the kids, you've spent your time developing your family, but that's not taken into consideration. It's like that year I took out, it's just like it never existed, like it was never there. I mean that's only a year, people take fifteen years out. And they've brought their family up and they've done their bit for society and yet it's like well, what have you done?

Motherhood had literally changed the women's lives in a myriad of ways. Twelve of the women referred to the way in which the birth of their children had matured them because they had taken on the responsibilities mentioned above. Additionally, and significantly, the women spoke of being a mother changing not only the way they thought about things, but also the things they thought about. Politics, the world environment and so on, now became of interest and importance to them because they had children. Jenny, a white working-class woman who was 30 when she gave birth to her daughter, described the whole process graphically:

I suppose it was having a baby that made me rethink my life, that I'd spent most of it in a bubble. And I think from that time I started to mature . . . and it wasn't that kind of maturity of being able to do things. I think just mentally. And I often think now, what did I do with those first thirty years of my life? What did I used to think about, politically or anything? I just, I just don't know. I just used to — I went along . . . Oh, I think having a baby definitely changed me completely. There's no doubt — or it started me on the road to rethinking.

One of the starting points for learning and thinking about things were their lives as mothers.

The Return to Education

The women had returned to formal education by various routes, and these tended to be differentiated according to their race and, to a lesser extent, the white women's class. None of the white middle-class women had taken Access courses, whereas all but one of the black women had done so, as had just under half the white working-class women. The white middle-class women had, in the main, studied for A-levels at evening classes, which enabled them to enter higher education, or had A-levels from their initial schooling, and/or sat a mature students' entrance exam under schemes operating at the institutions they planned to attend. A summary of the women's qualifications is shown in table 3.4. The women could be said to mirror the national mature student picture in that they were studying social sciences and three-quarters (twenty-three of the women) were attending polytechnics, rather than universities. Here again race and, to some extent, class played a part. All the black and 'mixed' race women were studying for their degrees at polytechnics. Of the white women, nine white working-class and five white middle-class women were attending polytechnics, while five white middle-class and three white working-class women were at universities. Only three of the sixteen non-traditional entry students (that is, coming via routes other than A-levels) were at universities.

Part of the reason for the preponderance of the white working-class, black and 'mixed' race women (linked with unconventional entry) in polytechnics may be due to the perceived status of universities compared with polytechnics. All the women at universities talked of degrees from this type of institution carrying more status than those from polytechnics. While four of them said they had only applied to universities 'tongue in cheek' and were 'terrified' at the thought of attending such prestigious institutions, this had not deterred them from applying. On the other hand, the perceived status of universities had deterred six of the women who went to polytechnics from even attempting to apply to them. Additionally, the fact that most Access courses feed onto particular courses in particular polytechnics had a bearing. The idea that they could choose another institution or course, other than their feeder polytechnic and course, occurred to only three of the women from Access courses. Doing a degree had been a 'wonderful' or 'unrealistic dream' in the eyes of most of the women anyway, and only five had consciously planned and worked towards it over many years. For the most part the women had suddenly discovered the dream could become a reality only after they had enrolled on A-level or Access courses.

The institutions 'chosen' were overwhelmingly those that were nearest to the women, so that attendance could 'fit in' with their family commitments. 'Nearest', however, could mean a ten-minute walk or an hour's journey. Nevertheless, being near in order that family life was disrupted as little as possible was the

Table 3.4: Qualifications for entry to higher education

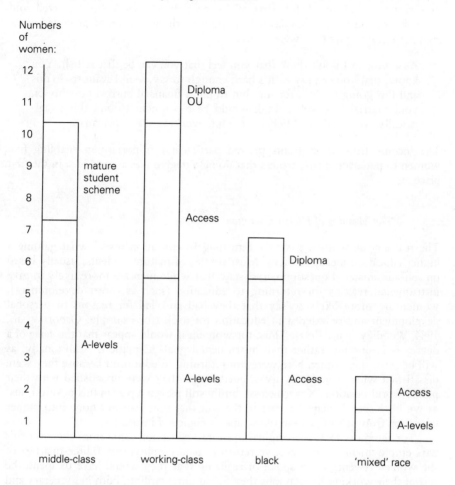

Numbers of women:

criterion applied. Thus the women living within ten-minutes' walking distance of a particular institution would rarely consider having a half-hour journey to another polytechnic or university and thereby enlarging their choice. (Access courses had been studied at colleges local to the women for the same reasons, so the polytechnics they were channelled into were also local.)

Obviously, unlike many mature students, none of the women had decided to pursue part-time degree level study in order to perhaps manage their attendance at institutions and their family commitments with more ease. Studying part-time for a degree was viewed as a commitment over many years and the women were unsure they would be able to sustain the self-motivation needed over such a long period alongside all the other things demanding their attention. It would mean at least five years of having to fit home and study as well as paid employment into their lives because they would receive no maintenance grant and would have to pay their own fees. Receiving a grant[7] was important for several reasons.

It provided an income of sorts — although nine of the women had to take term-time part-time paid work for parts of, or throughout, their courses as well, and most did so during the holidays. Importantly, though, a grant provided some legitimation for what they were doing:

> As a woman I don't think that you feel that you can be that selfish. You know, that you can say — it's hard enough to say, well I want to do this and I'm going to do it for me, but to put a financial burden possibly on your marriage as well I think would be too much. I don't think real-istically you can do it (Michelle, a white working-class woman).

The income from their grants proved particularly important in enabling five women to persuade their partners that doing a degree was a good idea in the first place.

The Meaning of Higher Education

The reasons the women gave for returning to education reveal what gaining a higher education meant to them. Most studies of mature students, usually based on self-administered questionnaires, state that while men are more likely to give instrumental reasons for returning to education (such as career development), women are more likely to say that they had enrolled for reasons of personal development and/or interest in education for itself (for example, Osborn *et al.*, 1984; Woodley *et al.*, 1987). Thus, for women, it would appear that the *doing* of a degree is important, rather than instrumental goal-orientation. Additionally, as will be seen, the women here were not returning to education because they were dissatisfied with their family lives, but because they were dissatisfied with their public world position. Nevertheless, family still played a part in this position, just as we have seen it played a part in the fact that they had not gone into higher education from school, and in the women's choice of institution.

For the most part, the original push into education came from the women's paid employment, or prospective return to paid employment. Three-quarters of the women (twenty-four) spoke of realizing that they would have to spend the rest of their working lives in jobs they found unrewarding, both in monetary and personal satisfaction terms:

> I mean that's really why I applied for the course, because I suddenly thought when I'd been there about, full-time, a while, it would be over a year. And I suddenly thought I've got to go on doing this for another twenty years. And I thought it's crazy (Cathy, a white middle-class woman).

Eight women (half of whom were black) also stressed how their children pro-vided an added impetus to study and to gain qualifications so that they could apply for better jobs. They saw themselves as ultimately providing their families with an improved standard of living in material terms.

In a couple of cases, bad experiences in their initial schooling meant that the women viewed their return to formal education as an unpleasant necessity. Having made the move to do an O-level or Return to Study course, however, they found that they actually enjoyed education and wanted to continue. By the time the women came to do a degree then, while job opportunities in better paid and more interesting work were still a goal, the desire to pursue 'education for education's sake', as Paula (black) put it, was of importance. Later on, towards the end of their degree courses, job opportunities naturally came to the fore again. In the main, though, the process of becoming educated was the women's main concern.

All the women spoke of wishing to extend their understanding of society in general. Apart from wanting knowledge because they were interested in the subject, the women could also feel that higher education would give them status in the eyes of others and would lend more weight to their opinions. This could be linked to job opportunities. Gillian (white working-class), who had been involved in voluntary work, was attempting to give some weight to her views and to place herself in a different position in the job market:

> This sort of anger drove me on you see. 'Cos I got involved in the Community Health Council, and then you get involved in the planning teams, and I was a school governor. And everywhere I went I still felt as if they didn't really believe me because they didn't think I knew anything. So to raise my status really I decided that right, if I can't persuade them that things ought to be different I'll have to join them. So I applied for a degree for reasons like that . . . I want to get into the decision-making.

The women recalled how nervous they were upon beginning their courses (those interviewed at the beginning of their first year giving an immediate sense of this). Eight women mentioned that they had been unsure whether they were really capable of degree level study. They had visions of every other student being 'cleverer' than they were and feared that they alone would be unable to cope. Gayle, a white working-class woman at a university, described her feelings:

> Anyway, I got my interview and, yeah, I got offered a place! I couldn't believe it. And I think it got to about September when I thought I can't go. They'll discover I'm really stupid . . . I mean I spent my first year thinking I was going to get found out! I only came for the cleaning job really!

Higher education was thus viewed as conferring prestige, related to it being for 'intelligent' people. The women also talked of doing the degree for their own 'self-esteem' in order to 'prove' themselves, occasionally adding that they felt 'stupid' in the company of educated people who appeared to be so much more knowledgeable. As discussed earlier, when the women referred to their initial lack of educational attainment they spoke of the effects of the low expectations their parents and teachers held for them based on race or sex and/or class. Yet when they came to recount their return to formal education, seventeen women mentioned how they had 'missed out' or felt 'lacking' educationally in terms of 'wasting' their opportunities. The women individualized their earlier failures when they came to speak about themselves as adults in relation to higher education in a way they did not when they talked of their (removed in time) childhoods. This was so even for those black women who held some mistrust of the education system and were wary of the institutions they attended (see Chapter 5). This sense of personal fault appeared to have ramifications in terms of the way the women regarded themselves as students in higher education, and may well also be linked to their ideas of what higher education and academic knowledge were about.

The women felt that education gave them a different way of looking at society and social life. Two-thirds (twenty-one women) referred to academic knowledge as a particular way of knowing, a way of 'getting above' the social that was abstracted from their own everyday lives: 'You're actually looking on the world now, you know, rather than in it. You know, a bit like the, a bit like the greek gods sort of looking down' (Jenny, a white working-class woman). Chapter 5 will address the differing extents to which the women felt insertions of the subjective, emotional and particular into academic knowledge and institutions were permissible. It should be noted, however, that even if they did this, the women always stressed the broader view and objectivity on which academic knowledge lays such emphasis:

> We are able to, I think, as mature students, to be able to put more reality into an academic piece of work. We can actually absorb it and then relate it to reality. We're able to look at it more objectively as well, much more. Cos everything's very subjective beforehand (Helen, a white working-class woman).

Academic knowledge and studentship was also about individual achievement. This was not only because the women wanted to prove themselves capable of degree level study, but also because formal education generally, and higher education in particular, often individualizes academic achievement. In higher education there should be no 'spoon-feeding'; students should discover knowledge themselves and work as individuals. Along with a conception of objectivity, the women also imbued this autonomy:

> You only get like, like a very small number of people who actually exchange work. Actually I don't know whether the lecturers like it as well. I don't think they do because I think they think we ought to do things for ourselves (Lorraine, a white middle-class woman).

Success or failure was seen as in their own hands: 'You can attend lectures but I mean when it comes down to it, you know, you've got to do it on your own' (Michelle, a white working-class woman). It is ironic that as part of their social science degrees the women were learning that success or failure in schooling was aligned to sex, race and class, while simultaneously a hidden curriculum contained the notion that success or failure in higher education depended on their individual merits and application, regardless of sex, race or class.

As we have seen, the women talked of the intellectual status they, and others, accorded to educated people, especially those who had degrees. There was a recognition that a degree education was not available to all, and a sense that gaining one would somehow place them apart from the general population: 'Doing a degree, it's like joining an exclusive club' (Jackie, a white working-class woman, first year student).

Because having done it, then you feel like you've accomplished something, especially like it's only 10 per cent of the population. I say here I go again, I'm in the minority! But positive, in a positive way (Irene, a black woman, graduate).

Becoming a student was, therefore, potentially shifting their status in some way — and five of the women said that just being a student in itself gave them a prestige that had not been accorded to them previously, either as mothers/partners and/or paid workers: 'I mean it gives you status being a student. I mean people — from housewife to student in one leap' (Jennie, a white working-class woman). While feeling those with degree qualifications were respected, however, three women observed that students were generally derided as having an easy time. Either way, though, gaining a higher education somehow set the women apart, be it in positive or negative terms, from others. It particularly set them apart from mothers in general:

Perhaps when they're [my children] older they'll think, 'Oh well, mummy wasn't like somebody else's mummy and just watched sort of all the soaps all day long'. Which I must admit I'm very tempted to do 'cos I love them! But maybe they'll think back then and think, 'Well, I think it's really good that mum was different' (Victoria, a white middle-class woman).

Being one of the minority who have reached higher education, and doing something very different from other mothers/partners, meant that the women felt that few people could understand the pressures degree level study put them under:

I don't think they know anything about what's involved at all. I mean, you know, the two girls I see each week, I'd be saying, 'Oh, I've got all this classwork for a seminar'. I suppose they knew what I was doing each week but I don't suppose they thought much about it (Carol, a white middle-class woman).

This feeling of difference is a feature of being in an unusual position noted by other researchers (for example, Homer *et al.*, 1985, with regard to battered wives, and Brannen and Moss, 1991, in the case of women returning to paid work after the birth of their first child).

In addition to being set apart as mothers and as people with a certain level of education, the women were also set apart from what being a student in higher education *should* mean, as well. A third (eleven women) referred to what could be regarded as a traditional view of higher education. They had dreamed of oak-panelled common rooms, cosy tutorials in lecturers' studies, and an atmosphere of studious learning infused throughout the institution. Higher education was viewed as a 'whole experience' involving social relationships and other activities apart from academic learning. While the women quickly became disabused of particular aspects of their conceptions of higher education, including the realization that other students were not necessarily intellectually superior, their ideas of higher education continued to include the social life they saw students as indulging in. This social life was something most of them felt unable to take part in to any great extent because of their family commitments and their age. Fourteen women mentioned that they wished they had been able to go to university or polytechnic at the 'proper' time:

> I mean it must be just so kind of a wonderfully self-indulgent thing to do, for three years to leave home to go and take part in the whole experience. 'Cos I think the thing of doing a degree with a family is that you can't take part in the whole experience (Michelle, a white working-class woman).

For the women, higher education meant present or potential status (in terms of social prestige rather than social class mobility). It was about becoming knowledgeable in an objective way and about individual achievement, but it also meant being different — as students in higher education, as mothers, and as members of the population generally. This can be counterposed with the overwhelming meaning of family life as grounded in the local and particular, in emotions, subjectivity and in the women's own caring about and for other people, although perceptions of mental and physical boundaries around the home were variable. These contrasting understandings of student and family life had ramifications for the women's having both coexisting in their lives. The women's understandings of 'family' and 'education' for them, alongside the themes identified within them, formed a base for separations and connections of the two in their lives as mature women students.

Notes

1 From the introduction of universal free secondary education in the late 1940s until the late 1960s, children at British state schools sat an academic test at the age of 11 (the eleven-plus). If they passed this test they were selected for entry to grammar schools — intended for academically 'bright' children. White middle-class children formed the bulk of these schools' intake. Those who failed went to secondary modern or technical schools. The system was then integrated into a unified comprehensive system.
2 Until 1987, a two-tier system of national public examinations operated, taken towards the end of compulsory secondary schooling at the age of 16. O-levels were taken by 'brighter' pupils, while CSEs were taken by children regarded as academically less able. Those remaining in education after the minimum school leaving age are able to take the next level of public examinations, A-levels, at 18.
3 Other reasons for the breakup of previous relationships included disagreements about money, and violence from the men to them and/or their children.
4 'Caring about' and 'caring for' do not always have such a linked quality, however (Ungerson, 1983; Graham, 1984).
5 Another example of the women's responsibility for the well-being of other people may be seen in the concern many of them expressed about identifying details of their lives being changed when I was writing up the research. This was not necessarily to do with protecting their privacy alone, but often also because they said they did not want others (partners, mothers, and in a few cases, lecturers) to read what they had said about them and perhaps to be hurt by some of their comments.
6 The idea that partners, and children particularly, needed time and attention was held by the women whether their partner lived with them permanently or

not, and whether they had stayed at home full-time when their children were young or had worked either part-time or full-time during their children's early years. Making their children their first priority and caring and thinking about them was not seen as synonymous with full-time motherhood only, just as caring about their partner's happiness was not synonymous with full-time (live-in) partnership alone.

7   At the time of interview, student loans had not yet been introduced in Britain. The women knew loans would be introduced shortly. Most of them felt that they would not have been able to enter higher education if they were going to build up debts to pay off in the future, alongside all the other financial commitments their families had.

Chapter 4

'Greedy Institutions': Straddling the Worlds of Family and Education

Family and education together had shaped the course of the women's lives from childhood into adulthood. They also shaped the pattern of their lives as women with their feet in two worlds — in the public sphere of higher education and learning and in the private domain of 'the family' and domesticity. This chapter looks at the ways in which the meanings and values the women attached to gaining an education and being a student, and to family life and their part in it as mothers and partners, as examined in the previous chapter, led them to hold particular expectations of themselves. These meanings and values shaped the women's abilities to meet the requirements of the two institutions, and played a part in constructing the pattern of the routine of their everyday lives. These expectations and patterns — and indeed the women's understandings of student and family life — did not arise in a vacuum and are not only the result of individual women's investments in each sphere; they acquired their ascribed meanings in socially constructed contexts. Internalized self concepts, attitudes and values converge or conflict with external expectations, standards and ideologies that support particular practical and emotional responses.

As Sandra Acker (1980) has remarked, both family and higher education are 'greedy institutions'. Louis Coser has termed greedy institutions as those seeking:

> ... exclusive and undivided loyalty, and they attempt to reduce the claims of competing roles and status positions on those they wish to encompass within their boundaries. Their demands on the person are omnivorous ... They exercise pressures on component individuals to weaken their ties, or not to form any ties, with other institutions or persons that might make claims that conflict with their own demands (Coser, 1974, p. 4, 6).

Greedy institutions, Coser contends, mainly rely upon non-physical mechanisms to separate the insider from outsiders, erecting boundaries between them. They also rely upon voluntary compliance and evoke means of activating loyalty and commitment that appear highly desirable. In an essay co-written with Rose Coser he argues that families are greedy institutions for women, requiring their constant allegiance and availability to cater to all physical and emotional needs in a way that is not required of men. The Cosers argue that many women accept the cultural mandate of committing themselves to their greedy families even when engaging in paid work, making themselves psychically available full-time even if they are not continuously physically present. Indeed, as will be discussed, references to both physical and psychic time permeated the women's accounts of combining family and education in their lives. The mandate of constant loyalty to greedy institutions also meant that any non-compliance, even mentally, could evoke the sense of guilt (a means of ensuring voluntary compliance) that was also an element in their accounts. As has often been pointed out, it is easier to stop doing than to stop being: women may *do* housework but they *are* mothers or wives. Similarly, entry into higher education can involve taking on not just studying as work but also an identity as a student.

As Coser observes, however, for those who take on the demands of another greedy institution — in this case, following Acker, higher education — the conflicts that arise do not simply result from participation in two different activity spheres whose claims on time allocation are incompatible; they derive from the fact that the values underlying the claims are contradictory. Higher education demands the commitment that the 18-year-old 'bachelor boy student' (Robinson, 1980, p. 4) is able to meet, and values separation and objectivity. Conventional students' lives can be encompassed totally within the institutional set-up (e.g. eating, sleeping, leisure activities, friendships) — the 'whole experience' to which the women referred. Full-time mature women students are required to give as much commitment to study as bachelor boys at the same time as they are normatively required to give priority to their families, based on values of affiliation and subjectivity. There have already been some indications in the previous chapter that the values the women ascribed to education and family were dissimilar, and future chapters will take this further by examining how the values underlying the types of knowledge generated in each sphere might conflict. The counterposed values and meanings also resulted in a particular channelling of certain of the women's emotions, including the feelings generated by the prioritizing claims of each world.

Women are under pressure to achieve success in each of the two greedy spheres by showing that neither suffers because of their participation in the other. They must show that their educational work is not affected by their family commitments, and that their family lives are not suffering because of their studies. Women cannot meet public world obligations without being accused of neglecting their duties in the private domain. Moreover, it is often argued that the qualities associated with the competent performance of roles in one sphere are deemed inappropriate for success in the other. Dorothy Smith and David Cheal, for example, respectively address this issue in terms of 'opposing modes of organizational consciousness' (Smith, 1987, p. 66) and 'moral' and 'political' economies of 'social organization' (Cheal, 1991, p. 118). Bernice Fisher and Joan Tronto (1990), however, state that this dichotomous view of separated, differentiated sets of value consciousnesses within the spheres needs to be challenged and replaced by an emphasis on the integrated and connected core of human activity across the spheres. These differing conceptions of the nature of values and activities are, in fact, reflected in the accounts of their lives given by the mature women students. Yet, whatever the women's conceptions, in trying to meet the demands of both family and higher education, and in their belief that this was possible, they strove to organize themselves and others to this end. In doing so they were attempting to meet standards which, while ostensibly set by themselves, are in fact socially constructed.

Serving Time

Inequalities in the use of time and the ability to pursue and develop personal interests may be posited as characteristics of the power relationships between men and women. Woman can be termed 'time poor', and this poverty is argued to relate to their material and relationship situations (Millar and Glendinning, 1989). When women become partners and mothers this is said to be accompanied by a diminution of their control over the personal time and space available to them. Rosemary Deem (1986) and others writing in the field of leisure have shown that women rarely have time for 'themselves' when at home with their families. As the discussion in Chapter 2 indicated, however, the concept of time for oneself is not without problems, at least in terms of an identity apart from being a mother or partner. As will become clear in later chapters, not all the mature women students had this sense of a self that separated their own needs, or their education, from their family life and relationships. Moreover, time is not a unilinear and/or a continuous resource, nor does it just concern the physical dimension that can be implied by the conception of leisure as something one does when one is not occupied by paid work or unpaid housework.

As Karen Davies (1990) has pointed out, we tend to lose sight of the ways in which time is socially constructed, and its use is imbued with social meaning and value beliefs. Women's time within their families, in particular, needs to be seen as being constructed in relation to the time requirements of others' daily lives and needs (their partners, children, parents, friends and so on). Additionally, as Davies (1990) argues, the amount of time to be allocated by women to others' requirements is defined by the length of the task they have to perform itself, not by clock time, as is the case with paid work, and this gives it a particular rhythm of its own.[1] Studying is also task-defined. The women could thus be said not to be attempting to manage clock and task-defined time, as are many women with family responsibilities who undertake paid work, but to be attempting to combine two sets of task-defined time, both of which had large amounts of apparent flexibility and autonomy, but which in concert were restrictive and individualized the women's time management problems. Even the clock/task distinction, however, leaves other dimensions of time allocation unaddressed. Neither clock nor task-defined time capture the allocation of psychic or mental time, nor do they address the forms of consciousness required within different allocations of mental time.

Questions of when and where the women felt they should give priority to spending more time on one part of their life rather than on another — on family or on education — were not simply quantitative questions about how long they should spend doing this or that particular task. Their time allocations, on both physical and mental dimensions, were shot through with qualitative beliefs and assumptions about what it meant to be a mother/partner — responsibility and subjective attention to detail — and to be a proper student in higher education — the whole experience and objective overviews (see Ribbens, 1993, forthcoming, on the meanings attached to time in family lives).

'Doing Physical Time'

All the women in this study did indeed feel a lack of time as a practical, material resource with which to meet all the commitments that both education and family, as they saw it, rightfully laid claim to and which they had a responsibility to fulfill. As Irene (black) put it, 'Everything is timed, you see. The time was my master.' Others spoke of 'rushing around', of 'being on overdrive', and of 'doing everything at breakneck speed' in an attempt to fit in all their commitments. Despite their efforts, the majority of the women explicitly mentioned that they often felt that they did not properly meet each of the sets of requirements of family and higher education; only two did not refer to this problem. The women's families needed time and their education needed time. Both were regarded as having legitimate claims upon them because the women felt that they had chosen freely to have both in their lives. Yet the amounts of time that both seemed to require appeared never-ending. The women were unable to keep 'on top' of all the things that needed doing for their families in their homes:

> I would come in and the house would be in a state, you know, and I'd think oh my god, and I'd race — you know, I'd get really depressed, you know. I'd wake up early in the morning and clean before I leave. Because I do the dog as well, you know. And then, you know, I mean like when I'm at college sometimes the bed will disappear, you know, beneath these books and everything and clothes and the whole work (Beverley, a black woman).

Moreover, the women rarely seemed to feel that they were ever on top of their studies:

> And the reading. I mean like all these reading lists that you're given and these huge numbers of books. I don't think I read any of them because there just doesn't seem to be the time. You know, I mean little snatches so that you vaguely know what's going to be going on in a seminar or something someone else is presenting. But the lists and lists and lists and lists of books that you were supposed to read (Lynne, a white middle-class woman).

Both family and education were indeed greedy for the allocation of the women's 'doing' time.

The women's feelings about the use of time within their families and homes, in terms of giving priority to the needs of others, and in terms of their sense of their own relationship to and responsibility for others, worked to place the family use of time, organized around others, in opposition to the long stretches of time studying takes up, which was regarded by many as time use organized around and for themselves. That education was perceived by them as individualistic, abstract and as something which made them different fed into this, and led several of the women to mention that they felt they were being 'indulgent' or 'selfish' in requiring and making space for so much time in which to study. Five of the women who graduated felt that they could have achieved a better class of degree if they had been able to apply themselves more fully to their studies:

I mean I know that if I hadn't've had the kids maybe I could have got a first. I know that. But I would have had to have really been in the poly all the time and do nothing else, and I had so many other distractions I couldn't (Marcia, a 'mixed' race woman).

I feel that what I did, I did well considering how much work I had to do. That I wasn't just — I couldn't either just be a mother, housewife or a student, I had to combine everything. And I think considering the things that happened to arise in those three years I did do well. But at the other end I was very disappointed that I didn't achieve the pass that I felt I was able to . . . After my first year, which was very hard and stressful, and I came out with marks which I was very happy with, but I knew there were problems at home because of what I was putting in, the amount of time I was putting in (Janice, a white working-class woman).

They believed (like Marcia) — or came to believe (like Janice) — that totally immersing themselves in study, however much they might want to, was un-acceptable because their families would 'suffer', or were suffering. This percep-tion could be so even for the women who talked of gaining an education to eventually improve their families' standard of living and prospects.

Taking time for study was, in the main, viewed as taking time for them-selves and therefore as taking it away from others. Time spent studying at home was seen as time *not* being available to the family:

You know, there are some people at college that say, 'Oh god, you know, I can spend all day Sunday'. But I mean you can't do it. *I* can't do it, not with kids and a husband, because I don't think it's fair to sort of lock yourself away (Michelle, a white working-class woman).

On the other hand, the women wanted to do well educationally in order to prove themselves and to enhance their future job opportunities — and education demanded of them the same totality of commitment as did their families. Time spent with the family, therefore, could also be seen as time spent *not* studying:

Well, the main thing is time, to get away, to be able to study. Just me studying without constantly having to come back home or have family concerns (Paula, a black woman).

As a result, whichever way the women prioritized their time they often did not feel completely at ease with their decision. Most of the women wanted to fulfill all the commitments generated by the family and by education to the full because both were so important to them. This feeling was particularly so in relation to time for their studies and for their children:

I just think that I'd like to have been able to do both, you know, at the same time. Devote my whole life to college and somehow have this other person looking after my child the whole time. I felt I did feel very torn (Madeline, a white middle-class woman).

You know, you have your work to do but the time you spend with him [your son], you know, is just as important, you know . . . Because they are two very important things to me, you know. I don't want to drop one and concentrate on the other (Maureen, a black working-class woman).

Women are, however, not just regarded, and regard themselves, as responsible for their children, they are often regarded as responsible for the conduct and success of their relationships with men. Partners, as well as children, were important to the women and thus generated time commitments. Indeed, Heidi Hartmann (1981) and Nicki Thorogood (1987) report that it is having a male partner, rather than children, which decreases the time available to women. While they put this lack of time in terms of the increased domestic labour men (both white and black) appear to generate, the women interviewed for this study most often saw having a partner as constraining their time in terms of attention. Indeed, later I will argue (in Chapter 6) that this is a crucial aspect of the effects of studying upon the women's relationships with their partners and is related to power. Yet, as will be shown, this consuming familial responsibility was not necessarily regarded as a bad thing when placed alongside the greediness of higher education; family could be regarded as a balancing influence in relation to education and its required form of consciousness.

While many authors writing about women with a double burden of domestic and paid work have noted that they have rushed schedules, being a student as well as a partner and mother could have different implications for the women to those of combining paid work with family life, quite apart from the financial aspects. Although five of the women referred to combining family with education as being easier than they had found combining it with paid work, this was in terms of their physical availability to their families, particularly their children. As mothers, being a student was far more flexible in terms of staying at home with a sick child or leaving earlier to meet a child from school, getting to the shops, or whatever, than the often inflexible hours of paid work — a flexibility of hours and home-based work that Janet Finch (1983a) argues can lead to a more rigid sexual division of domestic labour. In the case of women it makes them appear even more available to perform these tasks, but in the case of men it operates to make them appear less available.

Because of the need for at least some time and space at home in which to study, education intruded on family life in ways that paid work did not, particularly with the types of jobs the women had held or were holding, in shop, clerical or secretarial work. Not bringing 'work' home was not an option in the way it previously had been:

Somehow the university was an ongoing thing. You brought it home at night with you. You had things to study, you had things you wanted to plan and things that you were going to talk about the next day or whatever. But going to work, you come home and you're finished (Stella, a white middle-class woman).

Combining education and family therefore threw up different problems for the women than did combining paid work and family. These dilemmas, however, were not only in terms of actually doing their studies.

'Doing Mental Time'

Education did not just come home with the women in a physical sense, in terms of books and essays to write, but it could also do so mentally. Seventeen women related how the subjects they were studying were constantly in their thoughts — in the same way it has been previously noted that many of the women said their families were:

> I went to sleep thinking about things, particularly essays, and woke up in the middle of the night thinking about them or woke up in the morning. So I mean it did take over my life really (Cathy, a white middle-class woman).

Even one of the women who had her first baby during the degree and took a year out found she could not always mentally put aside education, even if she did so physically:

> The constant feeling that perhaps I ought to be reading something from the reading list, and I really should start my dissertation now and, you know, get ahead a bit . . . And I don't think I ever let college go in that year off (Madeline, a white middle-class woman).

Similarly, none of the women, even if they wished to do so, could entirely keep out the other, domestic, side to their lives when in the academic environment. Domestic chores and responsibilities never totally left their minds. Shopping needed to be remembered; they had to remember to be outside the school gates at a certain time. They might worry about whether or not their partners had managed to sort out a particular problem they had at their workplace, or if their children were happy at school or with the childminder. Anna (black) described how these worries about her children were so intense during the first few weeks of starting her course:

> That was the first time I'd actually left them by themselves with someone else, especially the youngest one. And I just could not think. It took me a month to get used to that. Right, she's at a childminder; there, I have to do this work.

The time and space both education and family could, potentially, constantly take up mentally created the same sorts of dilemmas and pulls that the women felt with regard to the physical allocation of their time, particularly when in their own family homes. In most cases it was their families who won out in terms of what actually got done because the women felt that they were the ones who had taken on education as well as their families and so it was up to them to ensure their family lives were disrupted as little as possible. Yet families did not necessarily win out in terms of their preoccupying thoughts. Thus it was not just a question of the physical allocation of time according to the women's beliefs about what their priorities should be, it was also a question of beliefs about their mental preoccupations:

You do have to switch off from other things. I mean, you know, when I come home in the evenings and I cook the dinner and listen to what the children have been doing during the day, and — and I'm doing the degree for myself not for them and so there's no reason why they should suffer because I may be bad-tempered because, you know, I can't work something out, or I've had a horrible morning on the train or evening on the train, or whatever. So you have to pretend everything's hunky dory. And then, you know, bath time and reading story time and so on. And I'm dying to get down and do some work and open some books because I've got a class in the morning! And you can't rush, you have to pretend, you know, you've got all the time in the world and you're ever so patient. And again, you know, when I come and sit down here with Ian [husband] and we have a cup of tea, I listen to what he's done at work, you know. It's his time really (Gayle, a white working-class woman).

Because their families and their education required the women's time and attention on both physical and mental levels, the women were faced with an inherent strain that needed to be addressed, and a pattern of daily living created which could absorb it. When with their families, and particularly their children, some of the women seemed to feel that their whole attention should be taken up with them, and they should not be thinking about their studies. Similarly, while studying, and particularly when attending lectures and seminars, these women seemed to feel that their families should not be in their minds and their whole attention should be directed towards their studies. As will become apparent in later chapters, however, while some of the women worked towards achieving this state of affairs, others did not see or want such a distinction, and still others did not want such a separation but came to feel it was necessary.

The now voluminous feminist and other social science literature on women within 'the family' has documented the ways in which power imbalances between men and women are reflected in the division of domestic labour within households and the management and control of household finances. In her extensive overview of the literature, Lydia Morris calls domestic labour and household finances 'the critical areas' (Morris, 1990, p. 21) when it comes to examining relationships between men and women inside families and households. As will be explored in detail in Chapter 6, there is, however, another 'critical' area: how women believe their time should be spent, not just physically but also mentally, has had relatively little 'attention' paid to it. Who gets time, attention and emotional support is also an area where power imbalances between the sexes can be noted. While thinking about someone or asking how their day was and then listening to the answer in an interested (or disinterested) manner is a more elusive dimension to chart than who does the washing up, writes the shopping list, goes to see the teacher, or decides to buy a video recorder. It is an issue that needs to be addressed. Although there has recently been an increase in time-use studies to chart power in relationships, these are not able to capture the complicated emotional caring work that women carry out for their families. They do not begin to address the fact that many women appear to see the giving of time as an end in itself, a symbol of caring, rather than just a means to an end (to do housework, childcare and so on). The implications of women's caring as part of their identity cannot be accommodated within such studies. Moreover, they adopt a framework that is simply not present in the relations of a woman to her family and housework. A work/non-work concept is utilized that stems from the social organization of men's lives (Smith, 1987). Giving members of the family attention and emotional support — being interested in them — was regarded by the women as a crucial part of being a partner/mother, and had particular ramifications for combining family with study.

The Channelling of Emotions

Women have often been found to feel guilty about holding paid jobs when they have families (Brannen and Moss, 1988, 1991) — although black women are less likely to feel this way (Mayall, 1990). White women at least are said, when at home, to want to compensate their families for their absence. Their time and attention, when at home, should be directed towards their children in particular. As I have argued, however, education is not quite the same as paid work for women. Studying might perhaps be seen as closer to leisure in that it was often spoken of as 'for myself' even by women wanting to improve their families' prospects. With regard to leisure too, Deem (1988) notes the guilt that many women feel in spending time on themselves at the expense of their families. Education, however, is also not quite the same as leisure in that the mature women students could feel guilty about *not* studying. In fact, nine women, both white and black, referred to a sort of cycle of guilt that spiralled out of a combination of the two, although over two-thirds actually spoke of feeling guilty over both family and education separately:

> I'd feel guilty if I had to take time off to take them to the hospital or doctor's appointment, because I had to ask for time off from the poly. And thinking well, I'm not quite one of the other students 'cos I can't totally give all my attention to it. And then I'd feel guilty about the kids because I'd think well, really I'd prefer to be over there studying and I've got to take them somewhere. And then I'd feel guilty for feeling like that. It's just one big mess, isn't it? (Janice, a white working-class woman).

These feelings are arguably one of the means by which greedy institutions evoke voluntary compliance and commitment to their requirements. The women saw compliance to the needs of each as something desirable, and held a sense of loyalty to each. They felt guilty over their inadequacy to meet these needs. They rarely believed that they did enough studying because of their family commitments, and they did not feel they were giving their families enough attention because of their studying commitments. Beverley (black), for example, had felt 'god, what am I doing?' when her children had said to her: 'Oh, you're not mum anymore!' You know, because I suppose your priorities changes . . . naturally I've always worked, but I've always worked around them'; and Judith (white middle-class) had thought 'Oh god, I shouldn't be doing this, you know' when she gave up reading her son a bedtime story because she felt so pushed for time in which to study. Giving up their courses because of the guilt they sometimes felt over the ways in which they were prioritizing their time had entered half (sixteen) of the women's minds at one time or another, however fleetingly or unmeant.

Eleven women also voiced feelings of frustration and/or anger about the amount of concern and attention they were supposed to give their families:

> It was a bit unfortunate because during my finals when I was just going to start my revision, you know, just about a month before the finals, and Roger [husband] was really bad, very ill with some mystery virus, and not particularly well-timed I suppose. But I was more concerned with him getting better. No! I was actually basically quite cross he chose to be ill at that time! (Victoria, a white middle-class woman).

> I do sort of resent them [my husband and son] sometimes, you know. If there's something I want to do I think god, not nastily, but you know, I think I've got to get back for them, you know. I don't know whether that's natural or whether that's just me (Wendy, a white working-class woman).

The women could, however, also feel guilty about the anger they felt as well. It was regarded as 'irrational' and 'unfair' to put the results of their tiredness and inability to cope onto others within their families when they were in a situation of their own choosing.

Guilt was also a facet mentioned by thirteen women in talking of their feelings about their studies. If they were not attending to their families' needs and wants then they felt that they should be studying. Any form of relaxation that had nothing to do with being a mother/partner or being a student appeared to be out of the question. Being and feeling so pushed for time in these two areas of their lives meant that the women felt that they should not 'waste' any moment of this precious resource. Reading a novel was often referred to as a source of guilt in this context. The women felt that any reading that they did should be from one of the 'lists and lists' of academic books, or at least related to their studies in some way, rather than anything so frivolous as, say, romantic fiction. Watching documentaries on television was regarded as acceptable because this might be useful educationally, but merely watching for relaxation was not. Jenny (white working-class) made a typical comment: 'I used to really feel guilty when I used to watch television. I'd think I shouldn't be sitting here, I should be studying. I should be upstairs reading'. A couple of the women seemed to regard housework and shopping almost as a form of relaxation from study because they could feel justified in doing these in a way they could not over light reading or watching television. This situation could also operate vice versa — studying providing a legitimate reason, to themselves at least, for not doing housework. Excuses were needed for not meeting each of the needs of the greedy institutions of family and higher education.

The amount of attention education required rarely turned to anger with lecturers or education institutions, as it could do within their families, no matter how 'irrational' or tired the women got. Arlie Hochschild (1975) has argued that feelings are linked to the distribution of power in the ways that they are targeted. Negative feelings, in so far as they are deflected at all, tend to be deflected 'down' into relative power vacuums. They run in channels of least resistance (the 'kick the cat' syndrome). Conversely, more positive feelings tend to run up the socio-political hierarchy. As shown in the previous chapter, higher education and all that is connected with it had great status in the women's eyes. In the main their feelings were channelled inwards (in terms of guilt), targeting their feelings at themselves being the line of least resistance. When their feelings occasionally did turn outwards, however, in terms of anger, it was within their family that this surfaced. The women would lose their tempers, or feel cross with children and partners because they were under such stress from their family and educational commitments. Getting cross with lecturers or administrators was regarded as pointless because the women were such little cogs in an enormous and powerful public world machine, to which they accorded status. Gayle (white working-class), who had a second child during her degree course and took a year off, was speaking about this particular period:

> [I] did my first year exams a year later, which was — I remember feeling very cross about that. I ended up getting three Cs and a D, and I was ever so disappointed. Because I'd been getting like Bs and As again for my sort of essays during the year and I really thought my exam results would be, you know, more or less the same. In fact one of the papers, the course had changed and I had to make it up. That's the one I got the D for. And it was just awful. Anyway —
>
> RE: Didn't they let you know the course had changed?
> No. Anyway, it's my own fault, I should have enquired.

The fact that she was 'very cross' was not directed towards the institution or its personnel. At the same time Gayle was experiencing problems in her relationship with her husband over what she saw as his expectation that she would continue to bear the domestic workload in the same way that she had during her year off. Yet she was not prepared to take such a 'reasonable and adultlike' stance with him: 'Instead I was oh, you make me bloody sick!'. Two of the other women who had taken time off to have children also experienced problems and frustrations created by a lack of communication from the education institution, but similarly never spoke of their anger being directed at its personnel in the same way they talked about getting cross and 'irrational' with partners and children. The women, and to a lesser degree their families, absorbed the costs of coping with two greedy institutions and all which that entails, and left the education institution unchallenged.

There is an underlying assumption that women can avoid conflict and can avoid 'bad' feelings if only they are 'good enough'. Women tend to interpret such feelings as signs of a unique personal inadequacy and to internalize any difficulties experienced in combining two worlds as personal failings (Brannen and Moss, 1988). Meeting the responsibilities of being a proper mother/partner and a proper student, was a tall order and six of them mentioned that they never felt 'very effective' at doing both at the same time — although all but two referred to not being 'very good' at fulfilling the needs of either their families or education separately. For women with family needs to meet there are the insoluble dilemmas of reaching perfection in imperfect circumstances. Yet, women are the subject of censure if they cannot cope, however difficult the task. Hilary Graham (1982) argues that women try to expand their personal capacities to meet the needs of a situation whatever the costs to themselves. The mature women students were convinced that they should be able to be good enough and felt that being organized would enable this to happen.

Organizing a Happy Medium

Laura Balbo writes that women feel 'a sense of guilt when problems are not successfully resolved' (1987, p. 53). She argues that this feeling of guilt is because it is women who are responsible, and who feel responsible, for piecing together and coordinating the fragmented nature and strands of the demands of life in contemporary society. Balbo uses the images and words of patchwork quilting to describe:

> The servicing, the pooling and packaging of resources, the self-help activities, emotional work and survival networks; how women keep at their endless tasks, how they put vision into the planning and design of their own and others' lives whose responsibility they carry (1987, p. 46).

Women plan, organize and create orderly patterns around others' individual needs and wants.

Three-quarters of the women (twenty-four) said that the answer to the problem of combining the all-consuming commitments of education and family successfully was to be organized.[2] The lack of boundaries to the requirements of both meant that the women had to try to create their own structures. Organizing themselves, their lives and the lives of their families, as they viewed it, would mean that they could do everything. The women were often teetering on a knife's edge with a finely-tuned structure of arrangements that they had constructed for fitting family and education into their lives. Additionally nine women (mainly white working-class and black women) tried to fit some part-time paid work in during the term as well as education and family. Four of them found this was too much to cope with and, despite the financial constraints and pressures thus imposed, decided to only undertake paid work during the holidays. Not only did the women have to organize care for their children as and when necessary, and by whom and when the shopping was done and so on, they also had to organize time and space for themselves to study within the home. A few of the women even tried drawing up timetables of when they would study and when they would shop, clean and pay attention to their families, or household rotas of who was cleaning the bathroom, washing up, preparing a meal and so on, for themselves and their families to follow.

The majority of the women felt that they organized their studying around their family lives, but six said that family life was organized around the requirements of their studies. In the end, though, whichever way round they organized it, their accounts of the ways this organization happened appeared to boil down to the same thing. Domestically they did the 'essentials' of either doing, or arranging for, the feeding of children and partners, and making sure there were clean clothes for everyone. They let the housework go to the extent they felt that they could live with and then had a major clean-up when they had time during term breaks. Clean socks and shirts (even if unironed) and some sort of meal on the table was the bottom line most often mentioned. As many others have noted (including Pollert, 1981; Porter, 1983; Finch, 1983a), even if women do not do everything themselves, they are the ones who must organize and worry about them. The psychological division of labour is often left intact. Some conceive of this division as due to the continuing power of the ideology of the all-responsible mother/female partner and the privileging of paid work for men (for example, Brannen and Moss, 1991); others have argued that women themselves do not allow encroachments upon their own defined territory of domestic labour (for instance, Eichenbaum and Orbach, 1984). Women's protestations that men do not do the housework properly, or as quickly as they themselves do it are said to be the protection of areas where women feel some sense of power and control. This may well be true, and seven of the women did mention this sort of feeling:

> But I just don't think they [the children's packed lunches] would be done, you know, if I didn't do them. I'm sure, because my husband just wouldn't be able to get everything sorted out and together in time . . . Yes, I mean the times my husband's gone shopping I've said, 'Now remember this for the packed lunch and remember that for the packed lunch'. Otherwise I think they'd just probably get a packet of crisps or a chocolate biscuit or something! He wouldn't have thought about it, because he never has to, you see. That's the thing (Judith, a white middle-class woman).

Yet, as has already been indicated above, there is an additional dimension to both arguments. It was not just the doing of the domestic task itself by their partners that was problematic for the women. It was often the lack of any emotional commitment invested in such tasks by men which meant that men did not do them properly and the women retained responsibility. Paradoxically, it is men's ability to perform domestic labour without this — to *do* without *being* — that leaves women feeling an unreciprocated type of powerlessness.

The women usually attempted to organize their studying so that they did it in the evenings when the children, if young, had gone to bed, or if older, after the evening meal, and/or got up early in the mornings before their children were up, or during the daytime when the children were at school. Their attendance at the education institutions, for the most part, was organized around the necessities of attending lectures and seminars alone. They usually had little space or time for anything other than 'Just go in and do it and come out again. Literally. Go and get it done and come home again' (Paula, a black woman). The women mainly also tried to keep weekends free for their partners and children to have their undivided attention and for their families to do things together. Plans like these often went to pieces when they had an essay to hand in at the beginning of the week or around exam times. The organization and the routines upon which the women depended were so fragile that the unexpected crises that are a part of family life, such as illness (to which father-in-laws seemed to be particularly prone around exam times), adolescents' traumas, or partners' problems/problems with partners, could throw their carefully laid plans into confusion. The women felt everything had to be dropped and rearranged around allowing everybody else's lives but their own to proceed as usual. In ensuring order remained in others' lives the women could pre-empt any sense that their studies were negatively affecting their family responsibilities. Victoria (white middle-class) announced right at the very beginning of her first interview: 'The children come first before anything. That is the — that is my main concern. And so really I adjust everything accordingly'. Women attempt to take on extra burdens as they arise and work to make the lives of others smooth, leaving the effort involved invisible (Graham, 1982; Ribbens, 1993, forthcoming) — indeed that is its purpose. It is not even recognized as work. As Val (black) said when she was describing how she had organized her life around her first husband, 'I think it's called love!'

Organization was seen as a self-imposed matter — something that could only come from, and was down to, the women as individuals. This notion is closely related to the women's conception of making a personal, and a different, choice to have both family and education in their lives, rather than having any right to have both. They viewed themselves as having to take on and deal with the consequences of their decision. It also has links to the self-sufficient, autonomous and private view of family life held by some of the women noted in the previous chapter. For example, Janice (white working-class) was particularly against having to resort to employing a cleaner because she felt between them her family should be able to cope alone, and Maureen (black working-class) did not like to lean too much on her extended family because she was 'proud'. Julia Brannen and Peter Moss (1988, 1991) also note how self-reliance pervades the language of working mothers. They argue this is due to working mothers having to juggle diverse responsibilities that they see as essentially their own because they too define a dual earner lifestyle as their individual choice. Seventeen of the mature women students said that their partners had, initially at least, been 'encouraging' or 'supportive' of their pursuing a higher education, but the women usually still couched this in terms of their own personal, rather than a joint, responsibility. For example, Paula (black) said of her boyfriend's reaction to her wanting to do the degree course, 'Oh, he was brilliant, you know. A hundred per cent. He was really behind me'; but a little white later added: 'You can't get all, I mean a hundred per cent support. You realize that. You've got to do some things on your own. You can't ask for too much, can you?' The other women's partners had not been enthusiastic but had done nothing to actually prevent them, so again studying was viewed as their own choice. As Alice Lovell (1980) suggests, it is likely that women whose partners are actively against their entering education do not get that far — at least not while continuing their relationships.

Women have to draw upon their own practical and psychological resources in order to cope both because there is little help available to them and because in their own and others' eyes it can be normatively unacceptable for them to seek help. With echoes of the Puritan work ethic the women talked of being 'firmer', 'strict', and of 'disciplining' themselves. As discussed above, in their efforts to be organized and their attempts to rush around meeting the greedy requirements of both family and education any relaxation for themselves seemed to be a sin. Not only were the women unable to join in with many, if any, of the social events that they regarded as a part of what being a student was all about, but the social lives that they previously enjoyed tended to disappear almost completely, or to be severely curtailed: 'I mean my day consists usually of going in, coming back, slumping around for a while and then getting on with things. I really don't go out that often' (Cathy, a white middle-class woman). The patterning of the demands made upon the routine of women's lives affects the time they have for interaction with friends, the effort they are prepared to make and, consequently, the form that their friendships take (Allan, 1989). Sometimes the women felt they were becoming 'anti-social' because they were not so welcoming to friends who came to their homes as they had been previously. Reducing previous social activity due to lack of time is also something working mothers tend to do (Brannen and Moss, 1988). In the case of mothers who are also students, while the time available to them was a component of this reduced socializing, other factors, linked to their identity, were also at work here and these are discussed in Chapter 7.

Several of the women, however, questioned whether or not, if they had unlimited time to devote to study, they would use this time so purposefully as they did because they were under such pressure. Carol (white middle-class), one of the women who had her first child halfway through her course, contrasted how she used her time before and after she had her child:

> Having only a short time to do work in made me a bit more concise about things I think. And I think knowing that I only had those certain times made me get on and do things in those times. Whereas before I had him I would just let things drag on and then do everything at the last minute, and know I could stay up at night to get something done, you know, if necessary.

Indeed, some even felt that so voracious was the desire to study generated by the requirements of their courses, that it was just as well they had their families there in order to stop them going 'over the top'. Family life was viewed as providing them with a sense of proportion and reality which they could easily have other-wise lost in a conceptually-ordered, abstract world of textbooks and essays. Living on campus and thus in the unusual position of being almost totally immersed in higher education and surrounded by the institution itself, Angela (white middle-class) found this particularly so:

> I used to find a sense of Sam [my son] coming home from school at the end of the day, or Tony [my boyfriend] coming in at the end of the day, like the real world coming back in, which was quite nice. So there was resentment about that, about the time that that took up. But there was also the knowledge that without it I think I would've gone round the bend.

The organization the women strove for was viewed as necessary in order to achieve the need for the balance between family and education that is implicit in Angela's words. Yet, because the giving of time and levels of importance were linked, balancing family and education in their lives, or finding the 'happy medium', was in fact rarely done to the women's own satisfaction. The simul-taneous but divergent cultural forces and natures of the institutional values that worked against this remained hidden from view. The women rarely questioned whether or not what they were doing was attempting the impossible. The balance they were seeking appeared to be the ability to do everything as if other things did not exist. This, coupled with their belief in organization, meant that if they were not 'on top' of all that needed doing in and for home, family and their studies they felt this to be their own fault for not being properly organized:

> My mistake is to, it's not being organized, i.e. you know, the reading lists that they give us? I'd have to like skim through most of the books to see which ones I could actually relate to, right. That's time consuming. I know I should have time to do that but still! . . . And I don't really like using him [my son] as an excuse really, you know. I think a lot of it's to do with me, you know, being disorganized and stuff like that (Maureen, black working-class woman).

> I'm behind. I'm trying to work at the weekends and that, and they [the children] do lose out a bit, I mean there's no doubt. You know, it was a lovely day yesterday and we [myself and my husband] should have been out with them and I wasn't, I was working . . . I suppose if I was better organized it might not have happened (Jennie, white working-class woman).

Moreover, when the women did achieve this balance they tended not to attribute it to their own successful organization or to other personal qualities, but to providence:

> It's like the whole package is really — I wouldn't want to get rid of any part of it. You know what I mean? I'm very lucky, 'cos it's like having your cake and eating it really (Michelle, a white working-class woman).

Attempts to maintain equilibrium are more often affected by social expectations than by personal disposition. The women were placing themselves as the crucial centre of a scenario that had, in fact, externally placed them.

Balancing 'Standards'

Although women with their feet in two worlds are unlikely to be able to comply fully with the demands and ideals of full-time self-sacrificing motherhood, companionate partnership and self-sufficient domesticity, they often still see their part in family life in such terms. Similarly, while unable to meet the demands of full-time studentship, totally engrossed in the social and educational undergraduate experience, they measured their own experience against such an image.

Hochschild has concluded that the wives/mothers she interviewed who worked a 'second shift' at home after they came home from their paid work, redefined their roles and their standards of the needs of their children and domesticity so that they could cope with both home and paid work. She is implicitly arguing that they 'lowered' their standards: 'Many women *cut back* what *had* to be done at home by redefining what the house, the marriage and, sometimes, what the child *needs*' (Hochschild, 1990, p. 259; my emphasis). This would seem to beg the question of what they were 'cutting back' on? What 'had' to be done? Social

standards and ideologies are not static. They have, in fact, expanded from the
second half of the nineteenth century, when they were concerned with the meeting of physical health needs, to also embrace emotional and cognitive development (Lewis, 1986).

A superficial listening to what the women in this study had to say might
have shown that they appeared to do the same as Hochschild's respondents; to
redefine their standards of what was required to run the home and meet their
children's needs. Beverley (black), for instance, remarked:

> For the little one, you know, in the morning she say, 'Mum, I ain't got
> nothing to wear to school', so I say, you know, 'Find something'. And
> that's changed. I mean at first I used to say to her, 'Well find something,
> leave it on the ironing board and I'll sort it out later', just so that I could
> do something else. But if I leave it she start doing it herself. So that's
> changed, you know.

This might be seen as an example of redefining what needed to be done and by
whom it needed to be done. There were, however, contradictory messages in
what some of the women said. Jenny (white working-class) at first announced:
'I've never been sort of houseproud so I was quite happy to just have an excuse to
skip housework and not to do it, to do my studies'; but a little later commented:
'I'm sure if I hadn't kept things [housework] up to scratch, things [husband's
views on her studying] wouldn't have gone so well'. Kim ('mixed' race) stated:

> I mean I explain to people when they come in the door, sorry about the
> mess. I don't do anything about it 'cos I hate housework, but I feel I
> have to explain it. And the thing is I don't give a shit about the house-
> work, but I feel I've got to explain why it's always messy.

The women were often still working with the actual or presumed acceptable
standards of others, be they those of partners, relatives, visiting researchers or
society in general. Even in private they were under the sanction of the public
scrutiny they carried in their minds. They attempted to redefine their standards
on one level but were unable to do so on another.

The women, as Kim's need to explain away her messy flat showed, were
aware of these socially defined standards and were uncomfortable over not meeting them. Moreover, they usually attempted to meet them fully as soon as they
had space and time to do so. It may be that, unlike Hochschild's analysis of
women and paid work (an ongoing commitment), the knowledge that studying
was a temporary, three-year commitment with breaks, contributed to this difference. Indeed Kim, despite her hatred of housework, when she graduated and had
a few months of unemployment took on more housework during this period.
Weekends were often, as has been mentioned, devoted to partners and children —
and also to the housework. In particular, there was an expansive movement of
one greedy institution (family needs and domestic chores) to fill the vacuum left
by the retreat of another greedy institution (education) at the end of the academic
year or upon graduating:

> You're exams, exams, exams, exams, and then you come out, you've
> finished the last one and oh, well, what do I do now? I haven't got to

read a book tonight, I haven't got — funny feeling. I had a couple of days sort of sitting about doing nothing and then the next week I started on the house. Blanket washing, curtain washing, lampshade scrubbing, cupboard emptying, you know (Anne, a white working-class woman).

I mean what I'd intended to do [after finals] was to have a rest. And then Tony's [my boyfriend] house sale was dragging on and dragging on and I thought I'd really better chase it up. Because he wasn't getting back until solicitors and estate agents were shut and he couldn't make phone calls from [work]. So my time then got taken up with being constantly on the phone . . . I thought I'd cook a lot of meals and just go — but I'd completely forgotten how to cook! Even that got messed about because Sam [my son] was having a really bad time at school as well . . . and I had to go and sort that out (Angela, a white middle-class woman).

That this movement happened shows that the women did not really redefine standards at all; they just held them in temporary abeyance.

Moreover, it was very difficult for the women to cut back on education and the requirements of studying, although they could, and did, when it came to being a student. Essays must be handed in and exams sat at certain times, but joining student societies and so on can go by the board. There are, though, similar questions about standards to be asked here. As has been pointed out previously, they are the standards of bachelor boy students. The women could suffer the same guilt in not meeting these standards as they did over failing to fulfill their family and domestic responsibilities.

The time limits on their attendance created by the responsibilities of family life meant that the women could never totally immerse themselves in being a student in the ways that they felt other students without such responsibilities could:

I'm watching for the last lecture to finish to rush out, you know . . . [My daughter] finish school like ten to four . . . So like the last part of the lesson anyway, you switch off anyway and start to watch the clock. So if there was 'Any questions?' I never have time for a question. *I'm the one to have to pack up*, you know (Irene, a black woman; my emphasis).

Such feelings of failure were compounded by their ideas of the status of higher education, their acceptance of higher education's hidden curriculum of achievement based upon individual merit and application, and notions of the 'whole experience':

I like being a student. Yeah, I do . . . I'm not a good, particularly good student. I don't sit in the library and read books, which I know I should do . . . I mean I stood on the outskirts of the demonstration. They had a demonstration last week . . . I was there but I was completely away from them. So I suppose I'm not really a proper student in that way. Don't get involved in anything particularly (Victoria, a white middle-class woman).

The categorical character of the greedy standards of educational and family life took no account of the actual practicalities of the contexts and conditions under which the women attempted to meet these moral or normative paradigms.

Shifting Consciousness

Each woman considered that she had made an individual choice to have education as well as family in her life and had to make her own decisions about how to prioritize and organize her time accordingly. Yet, as has been shown, this prioritizing took place in particular social and institutional contexts and had symbolic meanings attached to it. The social organization of both family and education underpinned and gave shape to the women's understandings and experiences. Moreover, even the possibility for women with families to make the individual and different choice of a return to education is situated in the context of policies that encourage mature women into higher education and to the provision of routes, such as Access courses, which specifically channel them in the direction of higher education. The conflicts and feelings of frustration and guilt the women experienced in their attempts to fulfill each of the expectations and requirements of family and education were felt to be their own problems alone, and the women therefore blamed themselves for their own individual lack of ability to organize themselves properly. Yet each woman appeared to experience very similar tensions and emotions. Feelings, such as those of guilt, were organized by the institutional practices and paradigms of family and higher education. These made no reference to, and were not modified by, the actual context and conditions in which the women were both mother/partners and students.

As Balbo (1987) suggests, the difficulties that women experience in their endless task of patching fragmented needs and demands into a whole quilt expose the contradictions and inequities in the nature of social systems. The possibility that the demands of family and higher education were unreasonable or incompatible in terms of the amount of time each laid claim to was occasionally mentioned by the women themselves, in particular material time. That their conceptions of the requirements — or indeed, the actual requirements — of their ways of thinking and being in each institution might have also been incompatible was not considered. Yet within many of the women's accounts of their lives there were indications that this was indeed the case, that they addressed these incompatibilities in the concrete experiences of their daily lives as mature students. When they talked of the difficulties of breaking off from studying in order, say, to cook a meal, they spoke of the way in which they would lose the threads of the topic they were concentrating on and how it would take them a long time to think themselves back into their studies when they returned to them.[3] Some of the women spoke of their shifts from the concerns of one world to those of the other on arriving at the education institutions or on arriving home:

> You'll be there [at the polytechnic] talking politics or something in the paper, you discuss that, but when you come home, you know, you have to switch that off, and nobody want to know about what Marx said or

what Weber said. Who the hell is Marx and Weber to them, you know! They want, 'Where's my dinner' or 'I fell today at school and somebody not talking to me' . . . and then when you are at college you can't talk about it [home] 'cos nobody want to hear all about four kids and their — you know, what Sonia [my daughter] did such a wonderful thing yester-day! Nobody wants to hear that, so you have to stop yourself from saying it (Irene, a black woman).

The shift from the local and particular to the conceptually ordered with its required shifts in modes of being and acting was felt, often unconsciously, by many of the women.[4] As Smith describes it, they were often operating with a 'bifurcated consciousness' (Smith, 1987, p. 6). However, their ways of being mother/partners and students within this situation were not all the same, and were not static. As will become clear within the following chapters, it should not be thought that the women were the passive recipients of the values and ideologies of higher education and family life. These did form the social and institutional context within which the women conducted their lives, but they were also able to negotiate them in varying ways. The following chapters are concerned with detailing the different ways the women attempted to manage the shift between family and education — through separations and connections — and with how others, especially within the educational institutions and within their families, reacted to their attempts.

Notes

1 See also Tamara Hareven (1982) on interactions between 'family time' and 'indus-trial time'.
2 Here there is another reason why some of the women chose to attend polytechnics rather than universities (see Chapter 3). Polytechnic degree courses were regarded by a few of them as more 'structured' than university courses. They felt that they needed this structure in order to help them to be more organized in the rest of their lives.
3 The shift from academia to family and back is one that even some experienced academic women can find problematic. See, for example, Dorothy Smith's (1987) and Hilary Land's (1989) accounts of combining motherhood and academic life.
4 This was another difference Irene and some of the other women found between combining family and education and family with paid work. At work they felt there were no drawbacks to discussing children's achievements and so on, and that people were interested in that part of their lives, particularly as they often worked with women of the same age as themselves who also had family commitments. Hochschild (1990) mentions that home and paid work are different cultures, between which mothers often feel poised. It would seem, however, that in their paid work there was at least some room for this kind of insertion of domesticity. Higher educational culture appears to be even further removed from home and family than is paid work.

Chapter 5

Women and Family Life in the Academic and Public World

Mature women students entering higher education are, as many feminists have pointed out, entering a world of male-defined structures, values and knowledge (for example, Spender, 1981, 1983; Belenky *et al.*, 1986). This chapter considers whether the women made connections between their family and student lives and selves within the higher education setting, or whether the two parts of their lives and selves were kept separate. In exploring this issue, it is important to examine some of the circumstances, such as institutional sexual inequities and compart-mentalizations, under which these connections or separations operate.

Both governments and individual educational institutions promote a positive view of the life experiences that non-traditional students bring to higher education. In Britain, for example, a leaflet directed at mature students by the Universities Central Council on Admissions stated:

> Mature students are welcomed in universities. Their high motivation and experience are valuable assets to the life of the university and to the course they follow.

Ostensibly, then, mature women students should be able to connect their family life experiences into their academic learning. Yet many feminists have argued that within higher education institutions there is a separation of formal educational knowledge and knowledge acquired through living. Public, objective, detached institutional knowledge is regarded as being given validity over and above private, subjective, emotional, personal knowledge (for example, Spender, 1981, 1983; Belenky *et al.*, 1986).[1] Within higher education, women students have to learn to treat experience as a faulty representation of theory, and theory as the 'real reality', as do all those outside the category 'white, male, middle-class'.[2] Jenny Shaw (1986) makes the additional point that the orthodox disciplinary 'ideas' approach to social science, in particular, distracts and detaches teaching from problems of evidence, and this too denies students a sense of competence.

Kim Thomas (1990) has documented the ways in which the culturally avail-able ideas of masculinity and femininity reproduce sexual inequality and marginalize women students. Other studies of how students perceive and receive bodies of knowledge in the higher education environment have found that mature students, both male and female, express disappointment over what they regard as the denial of the voice of their experience (Martin *et al.*, 1981; Weil, 1986). There appeared, however, to be differences in which particular experiences and skills, brought to higher education by the mature women students, were felt by them to be regarded as valuable assets by the institutions. Moreover, while some of the women regarded their life experiences as having also given them something to offer in an overt way to other students and to lecturers on their courses, others were, as will be seen, for various reasons, less willing to share particular facets of their lives.

There are aspects other than the curriculum also to be considered, including the ethos and organization of higher education itself, and the women's interactions with others within it. The relationship between the women's family lives and their higher education is thus considered here in several ways and in different dimensions. As well as looking at the ways in which family life experiences and local and particular ways of knowing were, or were not, drawn upon in the women's formal studies, the extent of insertions of their family relationships and responsibilities is examined both emotionally and physically. These also give certain meanings to facets of the women's relationships with lecturers and with other students. The discussion is then widened out to look at the ways in which the women felt that higher education had affected their interactions with others in the public sphere. As will be seen, there is a tension between the view of higher education as masculinist knowledge received in a masculinist environment that emerges from the women's accounts of their experiences within higher education institutions and the women's views on the ramifications of their gaining admittance to this knowledge and environment for their ability to operate in the public world generally.

Valuable Academic Assets?

All but one of the women said that aspects of their life experiences had made them interested in studying for a social science degree in particular. They also felt, as Jane (white middle-class) did, that the subjects they covered could not be treated 'as a dry set of facts, you've got to be involved'. The women had looked forward to being able to explore their interests further within their degree courses. Their life experiences (including, as noted in Chapter 3, motherhood) were starting points for thinking about issues and wanting to learn about them: 'I think a lot of my knowledge, with the degree that I was doing, has come from home and come from my interests' (Janice, a white working-class woman).

> I think as a black person actually going on to it (a degree course), is because you want to know. Right. You want to know. You want to be able to put — you've had all this experience, all this knowledge, and you want to be able to put it in perspective (Beverley, a black woman).

The majority of the women (twenty-seven) mentioned that because they had not gone straight from school to higher education they had gained useful experiences and wide perspectives. This experience could prove an asset in seminar situations. Half the women (sixteen) said that they were often looked to by tutors to keep the discussion going when younger students just sat in silence:

> I found that the mature students were more good at discussing things
> than the younger ones, which was really — I thought the younger ones
> with A-levels would have, would know a lot. But actually, when you've
> worked and you've experienced life more than the younger ones, you
> seem to know more than them, which was great. 'Cos they actually kept
> quiet during seminars and discussion, things like that, while the mature
> students were like leading the discussions and knowing more about
> things. Which was quite surprising actually (Anna, a black woman).

Studies of mature students often state that they are lacking in confidence and
some say this is particularly so for mature women students (for example, Martin
et al., 1981; Woodley *et al.*, 1987). These women, however, while they felt less
confident of their examination or essay writing abilities, regarded themselves as
more confident than younger students in the seminar situation.[3]

In the main, the women talked about their experiences in the public world,
of paid work and/or voluntary work in the health service, personal social
services, adult education and so on, as being regarded as useful both by themselves and lecturers when it came to understanding the social science issues they
were studying and feeding into seminar discussions. When the women did choose
to discuss these more public aspects of their lives in the formal academic setting,
they mostly felt it was acceptable for them to do so. On the other hand, the
women's private world experiences as mothers bringing up children and running
homes were rarely felt by them to be valued. This perception is despite the fact
that often their public world roles as, for example, nurses or secretaries, could
also be termed caring work. Helen (white working-class) spoke of the feeling that
family life experiences were somehow inferior even where they might have been
relevant:

> We felt that by bringing in sort of our home life, what was going on, we
> would be sort of demeaning the conversation that was going on about a
> particular problem or Freud's theory or something like that.

Family Life: An Invisible Experience

The women who did use their experiences of family life had a sense that this was
not really permissible. Twelve accepted, or after a period came to accept, the
view of family life experiences as not being valuable assets. Victoria (white
middle-class), for instance, said she rarely used any examples of her mothering
experiences when she was discussing issues:

> I don't like to ever harp on about having children. Not because I'm
> ashamed of it or anything, but I don't actually think people want to hear
> about — you know . . . I don't think people would want to know about
> that.

Michelle (white working-class) had, at the beginning of her first year, talked of
how she fed her life experiences into her learning. By the time of the summer
break between her first and second years, however, she had shifted to a viewpoint

more akin to that of Victoria's, saying that her experiences were not relevant and that she kept them out of her academic learning. Another twelve of the women, however, said they did, to varying extents, speak about their family life experiences because they felt that these revealed an important perspective on issues (even though four of them did not always think this was well received because it was not always perceived as academically valid). The rest of the women (seven) spoke about certain aspects of their experiences in particular ways. They and the women who said that they had overtly used aspects of their life experience in academic discussions, were careful to add that they recognized the need to place these experiences 'within a wider context'.

For the most part, the women's perception of academic study as to do with objectivity and with the removal of personal bias made them very wary as to how they drew upon their experiences:

> I think we're more prone to sort of personal explanations for things. But I mean I think I'm aware that they're not always valid as, as ways of explaining things, especially in social science (Jennie, a white working-class woman).

> In terms of necessarily, not personal examples, but in terms of your personal experience giving you an understanding of the issues, I think I relate to it more that way rather than necessarily saying, 'My experience of this was . . .'. So it's a little bit more indirect. I mean you tend to try and feed it through the sort of *acceptable academic channels* maybe (Angela, a white middle-class woman; my emphasis).

The 'acceptable academic channels', the ways of knowing within higher education, were thus set apart from, and were not constructed upon the same bases as those the women used in their everyday lives. Indeed, the former also involved a different means of verbal and written communication:

> It's so abstract, isn't it? It's just so removed. And using all these, all these really difficult words, not the commonplace words that people understand. And like, you know, they're talking about the proletariat and like the proletariat don't even know what they're supposed to be! It makes no sense (Kim, a 'mixed' race woman).

> I used to think, and I still think, that anything anybody writes is legitimate, and the fact that the educational institutions want a specific way of writing makes me angry because I think it's totally unnecessary (Janice, a white working-class woman).[4]

Local and particular knowledge thus had to be represented in a certain way. These forms of communication perpetuated the marginalization of the women's family life experiences.

The apparent incompatibility between the women's everyday family life experiences and academic knowledge also held other implications for them. Stella (white middle-class) felt that acknowledgment of the mothering side of her was difficult for lecturers and others because it was often seen as irreconcilable with being able to do academic work:

> One thing sticks in my mind that one particular person that I knew quite
> well, and when he taught me for the first time I happened to go along to
> his room when he was marking one of my essays and he said, 'This is
> really good, you write really well', and he sounded so surprised! And I
> said, 'What did you expect then'! So I think maybe sometimes people, if
> you are a mother people define you as that and they don't really consider
> that you can do anything else! And that wasn't, that wasn't because he's
> a particularly insensitive person or whatever. But I do remember the
> note of surprise and I've never forgiven him for that!

The mental sense of mothering and mothers not being valued by the education
institutions was reinforced in various practical ways. A lack of freely available
childcare provision and administrative arrangements that took no account of
their domestic responsibilities could make the women feel that they were not
really considered by the institutions in the way that students without such
responsibilities were, particularly the conventional 18-year-olds. Anne (white
working-class), for example, was told changes to her seminar times were only
allowed 'for academic reasons', which apparently excluded the reason of easier
childcare arrangements; although others found the institutions they attended
understanding in this respect. Five of the eleven women who attended one
particular institution mentioned the way they were not easily able to bring their
children on site (a physical aspect to the integration of themselves as mother-
students that is discussed below).

Being Different

In addition to a sense that family life experiences were not academically acceptable, thirteen women also felt that they had to be careful generally in any overt
use of their life experiences for other reasons. The ethos of the institution overall,
combined with a realization that particular sets of experiences that formed an
important part of their identity were not really admissible, reinforced the sense
the women had of being deviants within a system with the norms of the white
middle-class bachelor boy student. Four of these women were so aware of this
that they worried about 'standing out', or being seen as different:

> I didn't want to be treated differently because I was older. I would have
> resented that far more had they treated me differently. Had I been picked
> out, she's mature, then I would have felt different (Jenny, a white work-
> ing-class woman).

As well as feeling that they could be 'set apart' from the other students, there was
also the danger of being seen as 'dominating' seminar discussions just because age
meant the women had more experiences to draw upon. Three black women
voiced a fear of any revelations rebounding on themselves. Maureen (black and
working-class) commented:

> You tend to think that even if you sit down and you speak to the group
> about it, you know, you just have this idea that, you know, they're
> trying to suss you out, you know.

There was also awareness on the part of six women that if they talked about family problems this could be construed as 'making excuses' for themselves.

The overall motif running through many of the women's accounts was that mothers should not really be studying at a higher education institution at all, and that any problems that resulted from their being there would tarnish all other women students with families. The feelings the women expressed were similar to those described by Rosabeth Moss Kanter for situations where women are operating as numerical minorities — as 'tokens' — in a male world: 'Visibility tends to create performance pressures on the token' (Kanter, 1977, p. 212). The mature women students were tokens in the bachelor boy environment.

For black women the understanding that they were in a masculine-oriented institution where female, domestic, experiences were not valued was, as indicated briefly above, transformed by their race. The sense that if they talked about their lives they could be 'sussed out' was part of a feeling that they were under scrutiny as blacks. Val described how this had led her to feel a responsibility for all people of her race on her course:

> The first thing I looked to see how many coloured students failed to the proportion of white students . . . 'Cos I always think they would tend to think well, we did try with the coloured students and we had a 5 per cent failure, you know. Its amazing how you can find yourself with these type of responsibilities . . . Because I always believe that we are under constant scrutiny. Probably we are not. I don't know if we are. But constantly I have that feeling, you know. I don't know why I feel like that. I think the onus on you is to do even better to be accepted at their standard, you know what I mean?

The black women's sense of tokenism tended to be as black rather than as women with families — although black women have been described as 'double tokens' in academic life (Reid, 1990).

While the black women's experience of mothering and others' valuation of it was significant to them, within the education institution it was issues surrounding race that most often became central. They could, however, be left with the feeling that the subjects that were central to their lives and perceptions were not tackled deeply enough. Anna commented on this sense of being unable to pursue things:

> Well, we're found it's very conservative. Especially the lecturers, you know, they don't really want to touch — even if its something about race or women, it's just like they're just touching the surface of it 'cos they don't want to get down to the, you know, the roots of the problem whatsoever. They just want to touch it and — like it takes half an hour for them to discuss it and that's it, its finished, you know. But when you tackle them to going into it more they say no, you know, we just want to talk about this particular area and that's it. So what I find is that the lecturers don't really get into the things as well as I thought they would have.

Moreover, for six of the black and white working-class women there was a sense that what was presented to them was not their experience. This led two of the white working-class women (but none of the black women, perhaps due to their embeddedness in 'Afrocentric' communities, Collins, 1990) to feel that because, as Jackie put it, 'If I ever heard someone with a really middle-class voice speak then I'd think oh, they're cleverer than I am and I'd shut up', that where their own experiences did not fit what was being taught then they, as working-class people, must be wrong rather than the middle-class knowledge they were receiving being wrong. Michelle's comments on what she was learning are an example of this sense of being in error:

> There have been things that have just like — I've thought no, that's absolute rubbish because I — you know, my experiences are very different to that. But I mean I don't know whether I'd actually say that's absolute and total rubbish or whether I'd sort of say well, maybe for other — I think it all again comes down to this fact of thinking that other people do things properly, you know, and if it doesn't apply to me then it's because I haven't done something properly! You know!

Privacy

In addition to any feelings that mothering and family life were not valid experiences upon which to draw academically, and a sense of difference, tokenism or 'wrongness', there were other reasons why not all the women would have wished to talk about certain experiences within the formal academic setting, even if encouraged to do so. The idea of the privacy of family life was mentioned by a quarter (eight) of the women: 'My personal experiences I expect is my private experience, you know. My private affair as they say, you know' (Maureen, a black working-class woman).

> Sort of low wages and that, you know, I've used my experiences. I've got a lot of them concerning that, you know, and that sort of thing. But it depends, I will draw the line. I won't sort of, you know, let out sort of things that — you know, I've got things that I want to keep private and I wouldn't sort of bring them out in that sort of situation (Wendy, a white working-class woman).

Thus, while what was regarded as acceptable academic knowledge in itself drew boundaries around the use of life experiences, there also appeared to be boundaries that the women drew around aspects of their domestic and family lives.

Childrearing, being homeless and/or being a lone parent might be experiences some of the women were willing to feed into discussion where appropriate and accepted. Their relationships with men, however, were often regarded as the ultimate privacy:

> I mean, you know, your married life with your husband, things like that, I don't bring that up in the class. That's my business. On the other hand, things like unemployment or being on sickness benefit for a long time, the fact that I was divorced before I married Ivor and I spent some time as a single parent, you're talking in very general terms. You're just skimming off the top I suppose (Anne, a white working-class woman).

In the main, only a minority of the women wanted to feed relevant points about all aspects of their family lives into academic discussion. The details of their family lives, and their relationships with their partners in particular, were felt to be private.

The Mental Presence of Family

As has been shown in earlier chapters, the women's part in their families was organized around emotional caring in the form of thinking about them, responsibility for their happiness and for domestic tasks and the details of everyday life. It was also shown that this concern ran alongside different views on how separate their family lives should be from the rest of the public world and (in this chapter) different views on how separate from their educational ones in terms of learning. Additionally, as referred to in the previous chapter, thinking about their families while in the education institution could lead the women to feel themselves to be a 'student, housewife in brackets!', as Sandra (black) described it.

Seventeen women, however, also felt that to a large extent they either had always, or eventually came to be able to, 'shut off' their family lives when attending the education institution — even though, as we will see in later chapters, not all of them would ideally have wanted to do this. Eleven of these women, though, positively enjoyed the chance to be what they described as themselves alone, an 'individual' and 'independent', when they were in the polytechnic or university. Despite acknowledging that time limits and domestic responsibilities did mean that they never really 'escaped', they valued the way that they were not responsible for others and the different way of being and thinking that education required of them. Nobody could interrupt them or make demands upon them in the way they did at home, and their thoughts turned to 'big' social issues rather than detailed domestic ones. Some also spoke of enjoying the feeling that people within the education institution did not necessarily know they had families:

> I mean it's really nice to be 'I am a student' sometimes. I quite enjoy going to college and being a student. I mean okay, I wear a wedding ring so I suppose there's — that says something about me I suppose, in that I mean I'm slightly older and I think things like that do show. But there are a lot of older people so it doesn't make you feel different. But I quite like being a student because you do lose some of your — I mean, you know, people don't know you have a baby unless you say anything, and that's quite nice sometimes (Madeline, a white middle-class woman).

Fourteen women, however, did not feel they ever mentally separated themselves from their family and domestic selves. They remained connected to their family lives and responsibilities:

> I just couldn't separate it, it's funny that. I couldn't put on different coats, you know what I mean? Be a student and then come back and be a mother. I was always — I was there and I'd be thinking about what I had to do [at home] (Marcia, a 'mixed' race woman).

These women were quite happy to be students who were mothers and partners, rather than one or the other. They had not even considered the possibility that their family status might not be apparent to others, and did not look for the opportunity to feel an independent individual, unencumbered by other's demands. They felt comfortable with the existence of their family lives in their minds when they were within the education institution; shutting it out was felt to be impossible:

> It isn't something you can split off into a different sphere, if you like. It's not something you can define separately to the rest of your life . . . It just seems part of you, being a mother. I mean it's something I'll always be, isn't it? Once you've started to be a mother that's just — it's just a fact (Stella, a white middle-class woman).

Yet even the women who mostly shut out these aspects could not always do so. Some types of problems at home were not so easy to dismiss from their minds, even if they were given advice to do this:

> I was really angry that I didn't get straight Bs in my final year. That was Malcolm's [my boyfriend] fault. I'll never forget or forgive him for that, 'cos that was my best option. I mean nobody, you know, nobody would have denied me a 2.1 out of that because, you know, they'd been to the seminars that I'd presented, you know. There's no way I should have slipped that one, and that's what happened. And I didn't miss it by much, about three marks. But when you're under tension — my mind, I could not undo my mind when I got into that exam. I was still so screwed up from the arguments that we'd had (Gillian, a white working-class woman).

> I did in fact go to see Harry [my tutor] because I also had a — my son got into a lot of trouble . . . Harry was sort of quite understanding about it. But he in fact firmly said that I should *put myself first* sometimes. Which is okay to say, but when you've got, you know, something like that, it's quite hard to put it out of your head (Cathy, a white middle-class woman; my emphasis).

Moreover, as has been shown, for some of the women putting themselves as students, rather than as mothers, first would not have been conceptualizable because their 'self' *was* a mother as well as a student. For others the difference was easier to envisage.

The Physical Presence of Family

Bringing in the family, either via experiences to be fed into their learning, or as responsibilities in their minds, were not the only possible ways in which the women's domestic life could enter into the higher education institution. There were situations, or opportunities, where there was the possibility of their families' physical presence. Partners and/or children occasionally could, or had to be, brought along to the place where the women were studying. For example, rather than stay away if childcare arrangements broke down they might bring their children into the polytechnic or university with them.

Fourteen of the women were unenthusiastic about their partners, and another two about both partners and children, coming to their place of study. The feeling of being an independent individual, mentioned earlier, would be shattered by the physical presence of their families: 'It's something I'm doing and I want to do it on my own . . . The poly is my little domain. I don't want the others coming in on it' (Helen, a white middle-class woman). The feeling that they were students, and the ability to cut off from family and its demands could not be sustained if 'the family' was physically in the institution. Sometimes, however, bringing their children in particular into the education institution could not be avoided. For the women who enjoyed keeping their two worlds separate, even if they did not mind their children coming to the institution a few times, this physical meeting of the two aspects of themselves, the student and the mother, could feel very strange: 'I've had to bring the youngest one in once or twice and that's a really weird feeling, because this is like the meeting of the two lives' (Jennie, a white working-class woman).

Partners rarely had to come to the institutions in the way that children did. Five of the women's partners were, however, not happy to be kept out of this particular aspect of the women's lives:

> It's very, very strange, you know, taking your partner to places like that. For him as well as me. Because I live almost a totally different existence at [university]. I'm almost a totally different person. And, and you sort of arrive with one half of your life linking into another half of your life and it gets difficult marrying up the two. Sitting on the bog for half an hour trying to work it out! Yeah, yeah, I find those occasions quite awkward really. I like him to share it because otherwise he gets all ratty. It sort of pays (Gayle, a white working-class woman).

For the most part, though, the women who did not want their partner's physical presence at the institutions were not challenged in this by their partners.

Unlike with partners, the women mentioned no instances where their children wanted to be involved in their student lives when they themselves did not wish this to happen. Indeed, only two of the women wanted the physical separation of motherhood and student life to be total. Even some of those who valued their independent life as students could see some positive aspects in their children coming to the institutions with them, if only once or twice. The benefits they saw in their children coming to their place of study were shared with those who wanted to bring their children along, and who actively made efforts for this to occur. An ability to visualize what the women were talking about was the main reason for taking their children to the education institution at least once. When they told their children that they were off to the university or polytechnic for the day, or spoke about things that had happened at the institution, they wanted their children to be able to picture where they were. The inability to do this, in the case of those attending the one institution that did not easily allow children on site, caused the women not only practical inconvenience, but also went against what most of them felt was an integral part of being a mother to their children — that their children should concretely know where they were:

It's terrible. 'Cos sometimes there are a lot of Baker days and things like that, holidays or — I mean it wasn't too bad because sometimes the childminder had them all day, but sometimes she couldn't. I would take them there just to go and get a book from the library, something like that, and you had to leave them by the door if you haven't got a pass . . . But I would love to take them there like, you know, maybe one of the days I'm off, just to walk into the library and walk round, but you can't do that.

RE: Why do you feel like you want to do that?

'Cos I say I'm going to poly. They only hear me say that, they don't know where I'm going. So I like to show them, "This is where mummy comes when I leave you at the childminder's," or whatsoever. But I would like to take them in there a few times so they could actually get used to this place that I'm going to, you know (Anna, a black woman).

Another reason four of the women gave for taking older children particularly to their place of study or even into lectures, was that they hoped that their children would themselves go on to higher education and they saw this as a good introduction to what it was like.

Although fewer women said that they wanted their partners to come to their places of study than wanted their children to, a substantial number (seventeen women) did, and for some similar sorts of reasons. They wanted the mystery of where they went removed — for their partners to see, and to get a feel of, the place where they spent many of their days and which generated the work that they spent so much time on at home. They wanted them to meet the friends, and occasionally the lecturers, who were part of their lives and whom they talked about at home:

It was quite nice because it was the café at lunchtime and he [my husband] met the people that I particularly go around with. The little crowd that I — yeah, he met them and one thing and another. And then we went back again. We've been up there during the holidays actually . . . I wanted him to meet some of them, yes. Sit round and have a quick cup of tea together and talk (Anne, a white working-class woman).

Not all of their partners (five), however, would agree to the women's suggestions that they should come to the institution. They were said to be 'not interested' in seeing where the women went and what the building was like.

The women who actively contrived for children and partners to visit their place of study did not talk of the strangeness of the meeting of their two separate lives in the same way as the other women. They wanted some connection in the form of their families knowing the institution and the people in it. Part of this wanting their families to get a feel of higher education may well be linked to the way the women felt about the amount of time and attention studying took up. If their partners and children could know the institution on that physical, visual level, to connect into and become a part of it in some way, then they would have an understanding of what was behind all the work the women did at home.

Moreover, spending time studying at home would, perhaps, not seem so much like time taken, and spent separate from their families, because their families were a connected part of their student lives. The other women's ways of dealing with this could be said to revolve around trying to keep the two worlds separate. Some women, as will be seen in Chapter 7, tried one way first and then tried the other.

Pregnancy

A physical manifestation of family life that could not be kept separate from the institution, even for those who wanted this, was to be pregnant. At the very least 'the lump' eventually became noticeable, and lecturers had to be informed if the women were taking time off from the course. As mentioned in an earlier chapter, seven of the women interviewed became pregnant during the course of their degrees (three of whom did not have children previously), and additionally another became pregnant but miscarried early on in her pregnancy. Mature women students becoming pregnant would, then, seem not to be such an unusual thing, given that a quarter of the women did so.[5] For all of these women, however, there was some sense of incongruity between being pregnant and being a student. The two did not appear to go together. Being pregnant seemed to make the women feel they were definitely different from proper students — a 'contaminated student', as Gayle (white working-class) described herself. When women are pregnant they are incontrovertably sexual and — in this society — 'natural' rather than 'cultural' beings. They are thus viewed as, or feel themselves to be, incompatible with the 'serious' work of the public world because this side of them cannot be ignored.

Five of these women mentioned that some lecturers had shown a lack of understanding of their position and of the effects of pregnancy (or indeed miscarriage) upon their studies. Even for those who spoke of lecturers as being understanding and helpful, there still seemed to be a sense of the unacceptability of being a pregnant student in what they said:

> Luckily I had no — nobody was overtly unpleasant to me in any way. That was all very easy. People were very sympathetic towards that. I had no problems at all. It was a bit funny because [another student] had decided to do the same thing, so that made it a little bit worse for both of us. Only from the point of view that, you know, it's okay for one person to just *get away with it* (Madeline, a white middle-class woman; my emphasis).

Relationships with Tutors: Accessibility and Availability

The women's perspectives on their relationships with the lecturers who taught them reflect facets of, and links into, their images of what higher education was supposed to be like; their views on what caring about someone actually means, based on their ideas of their own roles within their families as organized around accessibility and availability to them; and their feelings about how separate their educational lives should be from their more personal lives. Higher educational knowledge was seen as impersonal and holding high status, with the keepers of that knowledge consequently 'like Plato, they're sort of up there', as Maureen (black working-class) put it. Yet there was also some sense of the possibility of there being a more intimate relationship with tutors. Cathy's (white middle-class) image of higher education had led her to expect more personal attention from her lecturers:

> I mean all you've got to go on are sort of films you've seen of personal tutors having long conversations with their tutees about everything. And that doesn't seem to happen, does it?

While eighteen women had expected, but as in Cathy's case did not always get, a more personally-based relationship, thirteen women said they did not look for this from their lecturers at all: 'There are very few that I would ever get involved with' (Victoria, a white middle-class woman). The women who held this latter view often saw their lecturers as very different people from themselves. They felt their lecturers had academic knowledge but a lack of life experience as they knew it. Lecturers were regarded as not living 'real life' in the way that the women had done and did. Their race and their class might be seen as the basis for this, and as what held them apart from the women:

> My first tutor was very middle-class . . . she'd had a successful middle-class family life. She wouldn't understand what it was like to be working-class, dependent on your husband's income. She wouldn't understand that (Gillian, a white working-class woman).

Up in their 'ivory towers' there was no sense for these women, and for five other women who had wanted more personal relationships, of lecturers suffering the same problems as they did — or therefore being able to understand their problems. Lecturers could thus only be approached for help for purely academic reasons, which the women felt was, after all, what they were there for. They were not regarded as interested in other, more personal aspects of the women's lives. This was mostly seen as acceptable because the women wanted to keep the private side of their lives separate, and could feel uncomfortable discussing personal problems with their tutors even where they affected their studies.

A quarter of the women (eight), however, viewed the academic staff as similar to themselves. The lecturers were often the same age as them, and these women felt that they were their peers. Lecturers too, for example, would have families and would suffer the same stresses and strains as the women did in trying to combine academic and family life:

> And David [a lecturer], he's a black, so I could relate to him being a black person, and he could help me. And Martin [a lecturer], who had family, I relate to him about family . . . because he is a governor, I'm a governor, and he have children and I have children (Irene, a black woman).

These perceived similarities and equalities meant that these women felt they could easily go and talk to their tutors about academic problems, but often also felt that they could discuss personal worries, however small the effect might be upon their studies:

> I mean when my second son played up I said to my tutor, 'Oh, he's finding his feet, he's gone to live with his friends in a flat and he's come home now because he ended up eating tinned peas and Oxo', you know! . . . This was in the summer holidays. And Kath [the tutor] said, 'Did you have a nice summer?', and I said, 'Well, one son left home and came back', you know. And she said, 'It wouldn't have done him any harm' (June, a white working-class woman).

The women spoke warmly of some of their lecturers as interested in their family lives, and as taking time to seek them out and find out how they were coping. The academic staff were thus regarded as knowing the women on a more intimate level.

As indicated earlier, however, not all of the women who looked for a more personal relationship in which lecturers cared about them as individual people felt that this was forthcoming, and this was a disappointment to them. It seemed to these women that their lecturers did not really know them, and therefore care about them, and it was down to them to go to their tutors rather than academic staff approaching them. These women were often surprised (as, indeed, were even three of the women who were not wanting a more intimate relationship) at what appeared to them to be the contractual nature of their contact with lecturers:

> I was thinking just now that I think one of the disappointments has been, how shall I say, that lecturers don't really — I expected them to get much more involved with their students. But of course, on reflection, their time is pressed all the time as well. Their time is precious. And they don't really — they just give you the minimum, what they have to, like personal tutorials. All right, they say they're there and you can go any time, but I think, you know, in reality I don't think that you could do that to them . . . Although they say that, there isn't really that feeling that, you know, yes, come and have a chat or whatever. Well, I suppose if you were in desperate trouble, you know, they'd make the time. But I think that has been a disappointment. There's no — it doesn't seem to flow as it were between the students and the lecturers. It's very much on a contract basis. They do the lecture, they do the seminar, and then that's it. Gone (Judith, a white middle-class woman).

It was a shock for the women to think that academic staff were just doing a job of work. Their lecturers, they felt, should be enthusiastic and committed to sharing their knowledge with students. They should make time for their students, and not give them the impression that they would rather be doing something else (rather like the way that the women tried to treat their children and partners).

The women's accounts of their relationships with, and how they saw, their lecturers were thus all organized around accessibility and availability (having time for them) — which their lecturers either were or were not. For some of the women, however, this accessibility and availability (or its lack) was, and should, only be related to their formal academic performance, and should not spill over into other areas of their lives. For others, though, their ideas of accessibility and availability were more closely allied to being cared about as individual people on both personal and academic levels. Again, it can be argued that while certain elements of the ethos within higher education gave a portrayal of this intimacy, other elements discouraged it, and some women accepted or preferred the latter. Interestingly, only four women referred to the sex of lecturers as part of their accessibility and availability, or its lack. Two women felt that women lecturers were more accessible, while two felt that they were even more remote than the men. In the main, lecturers were regarded as academics *per se*, rather than as male or female, an attitude that was not so for the women's relationships with other students.

Relationships with Other Students: Similarities and Differences

As has been noted, many of the women often regretted the way their family responsibilities prevented them from fully joining in with the social aspects of being a student. Half the women (fifteen) referred to this limitation as the main difference between themselves and other students, particularly the younger ones. Some felt, however, that there were other things which held them apart as well. The lighter attitude younger students displayed towards studying as against mature students' more serious approach was mentioned by six women, and a quarter (eight) spoke of how their age separated them off in other attitudes and ways. For example, Jackie (white working-class) felt that the younger students may have been 'a bit dubious' about the mature women students at first because 'it was like having their mother sitting in there.' She felt, however, that this had passed and that she had settled down to getting on with them quite happily as 'sort of Auntie Jackie! You know, somewhere between a maiden aunt and a grandma!'

The friendships an individual is involved in are not independent of other facets of her life. Friends are often drawn upon for support and assistance in handling contingencies, and the social position each occupies is important (Allan, 1989). The aspect that the majority of the women (twenty-six) singled out as most valuable in the friendships they developed as a student, or would have wanted to develop, was relationships with other women who were in similar positions to themselves as mothers at least, if not also as partners. The really close supportive friendships they made with other students tended to be based on their shared understandings of the difficulties involved in being a mature woman student who had family responsibilities; although in three cases women mentioned this was cut across by race or class. Sharing the worries they had about leaving their young children with others in a similar situation was frequently mentioned by those experiencing them as making them feel better about it. For the women like Judith (white middle-class), who found themselves on a course with few other women in their position, this was an aspect of peer group support that they felt they would have liked and which was missing:

> I suppose that's a slight disappointment, yes, that I haven't met up with
> a group of other women, which would have been very nice. And I sort
> of look at the other years we've got now which have got quite a few

mature — I don't know, it was very odd in my year . . . I would have enjoyed that I think, yes, having a group of women to share the experience with, discuss with them and things.

For the most part, though, those who developed supportive relationships with other mature students with whom they could identify felt that this was an opportunity within the institution to talk about the private side of their lives. They could share their personal situation with people whom they felt they could 'trust' and who would be sympathetic — and for which there was often felt to be no acceptable outlet academically either in learning or to lecturers, or for which they did not wish to have such an outlet. Three women, however, while still valuing these relationships as supportive, kept a separation between these aspects of their lives in the relationships with other mature students:

> You tend to gravitate towards people who think very similarly to yourself. You're just with a little crowd of friends, seems terribly quaint doesn't it, but there's sort of about, there's about five of us who are on a fairly, you know, the same wavelength. We're all very different but we're all mature students . . . I think *we sort of all respect our own private lives*. But then we all get on very well. I suppose that's why we're all together. We boost each other up when we feel we can't cope with things, all the work (Victoria, a white middle-class woman; my emphasis).

Unlike most of the women, however, a smaller group of five women perceived little difference between themselves and the younger students. In the main, these women felt they were friends on the same basis with an age-mix of students, and could view themselves as in the same position as younger students. For three this sameness with other students was based upon this common bond of studentship in higher education:

> I mean a lot of the things you're going through are exactly the same as them anyway, so the age thing doesn't really matter. I mean when I went up to get my exam results . . . I don't think there's any difference between the way we all felt about going and looking at the noticeboard really. So that's all the same. It's just the outside things that I suppose are different for us (Cathy, a white middle-class woman).

The support and empathy they felt between themselves and the younger students stemmed from their shared difficulties in getting to grips with certain concepts, pressures of sitting an exam, the ability to compare essay grades, and to sit in the canteen together and moan about certain lecturers because the other students knew them. For two others, the similarity was felt to be based upon something else; for example, in Alexandra's (white working-class) case, their shared sex:

> I mean I have the same problems as all the girls on this course . . . you know, do you get a lot of pain when you bleed each month, and having a period, does it affect your concentration and, you know. Oh god, I mean the talk's the same as it ever was . . . 'Cos we're all struggling for

the same thing in a way. We're struggling to find ourselves, we're struggling to learn what we're doing. No, I feel very much on a par with them.

These women often rejected any attempted placing of themselves as mothers or aunts by the younger students:

I think I was accepted, really accepted, really well. Just the odd occasion when they sort of made me feel, you know, like their mum. I said, 'I'm not your mum'! I made it quite clear I didn't want to be anybody's mum! (Jenny, a white working-class woman).

The separations and connections with other students, in terms of perceived differences and similarities with them, therefore, operated in several ways. The women might either see themselves as very different from other students without family responsibilities, or as similar to them. They might feel themselves as very close to other women in their position, or as separate even from them. Any perceived similarities with other students, of all ages, could be based purely upon discussing the common experience of higher education or upon talking about more personally-based, private, aspects of their lives. The women who had a more intimate type of relationship with other students tended to be those who invited their student friends home, perhaps to become a part of their family lives, where they could. Those women who felt that there was a separation between the academic and the personal aspects in friendships rarely extended these relationships into their lives at home. Their only contact with other students on their courses was within the education institution.

Reworking Education

As noted in Chapter 3, many of the women had mentioned factors surrounding sex, race and class as responsible for low expectations of and by them educationally during their period of initial schooling. It would seem that once more in their lives the women's perceptions of the value placed on particular aspects of their life experiences could make them feel that they did not fit into the education system. This was especially so with regard to their domestic life experiences. For the women who wished education and family to connect and feed into each other in their lives, in terms of what they were learning, their was thereby made a particularly difficult task. For those who wished to keep their family life experiences separate from their educational learning experiences there was less difficulty because both the ethos and the practical ways of operating of higher education institutions encouraged this approach.

Nevertheless, this is not to say that higher education was a complete disappointment to the women. Mary Belenky and colleagues (1986), borrowing terms from Carol Gilligan's (1982) work, make a distinction between 'separate' and 'connected knowing'. The former is an orientation towards the detached in learning and the latter is towards the relational. They see higher education itself as concerned with, and rewarding, separate knowing, and as having the authority and power to require adherence to these 'agreed-upon ways for knowing'

(Belenky *et al.*, 1986, p. 134). Belenky and colleagues, however, state that some of those in their study of women in learning situations were able to rework, to 'jump outside' of, this frame of reference. They began to integrate personal, 'real life', and academic knowledge — a state that comes at the pinnacle of their 'women's ways of knowing'. Many of the women did indeed rework their educational experience, although this tended to be outside of formal academic requirements.

Learning about race and racism as part of their social science degrees was mentioned by five of the seven black women, and one of the women of 'mixed' race, as giving them a wider understanding which enabled them personally, if not academically, to put their own experiences in context in a way that was important to them. Additionally, while most of the women had felt that their life experiences prior to doing a degree had widened their perspectives when it came to studying social issues, a third of them (eleven), mainly black or white working-class, felt that meeting other students had brought them into contact with groups of people from different cultures and/or different social and sexual orientations, whom they would not otherwise have come across. It was the personal relationships with such people, rather than an abstracted learning about them, that these women felt really broadened aspects of their outlooks:

> I made some really good friendships from it. And I learnt not just about studying about people, particularly about things like racism and homosexuality. And I really began to understand it, whereas before I — you know, like racism, I had a very narrow view of it. And homosexuality, I didn't talk about it. I mean 'cos I've got a good [student] friend who is gay and, you know, we sort of talk about it in depth. So I feel I've gained a good understanding of it in a completely different way (Jenny, a white working-class woman).

Gayle's comments (below) illustrate the reworking undertaken by many of those interviewed. Nine of the third year and graduate women mentioned, as she did, how important their dissertations were to them, often choosing topics that related to aspects of their own life experiences:

> It turned out at the end not to be what I thought it was about, which was sort of encouraging creative thought and, you know, bringing your own life and experiences into, you know, your studies, and, you know, making parallels and links. And it wasn't about that at all. I mean it was training to be an administrator basically. But then I don't actually feel cross about that anymore, because I think I gained an awful lot from doing that. I mean if they didn't give it value, well, you know, okay. I mean I actually developed my own ideas and, and that was one of the most valuable things for me on the course. I mean I loved doing my dissertation. I really — it was the best thing I've ever done. To actually go away and research it all and just produce this stuff, you know, that I'd written.

Thus, despite the feeling that their life experiences had been asked for in the promotional literature put out by the institutions, but was either not used or was misrepresented (explicitly mentioned by seven women and implicit in what others said), the majority of the women valued and enjoyed studying for a degree.

For some of the women, however, it was this very removal from the personal and everyday that they found satisfying. The opportunity to discuss issues on different terms, and to a depth that they would not normally do in everyday conversations, was something five women mentioned as particularly enjoyable. Jennie (white working-class) was reflecting on her recent graduation: 'You miss most the opportunity to talk about things that you don't talk about in everyday life. That's really what you miss, sitting around theorizing'. Indeed, it was this ability to take an academic overview that gave many of the women confidence when dealing with others in the public sphere.

Confidence in the Public Sphere

All but one of the women remarked that what they gained from higher education was confidence. They spoke of a generally increased ability to express their views, both in informal and formal public world situations. The white middle-class women were more likely to stress the former and the black and white working-class women more likely to mentioned the latter; this difference may be because white middle-class women have already learnt the ideological coordinating relations that those in authority operate with (although this does not mean these relations are unproblematic for them; Ribbens, 1993). As many of those analyzing and explaining women's lives have pointed out, it is principally women who hold responsibility for linking and coordinating the physical and emotional needs of family members with the varying requirements of public world organizations and agencies (for example, Graham, 1984; New and David, 1985; Balbo, 1987; Ribbens, 1993, forthcoming). The mature women students felt that they now occupied a different position in this mediating work with state agencies and so on:

> I suppose in certain situations I know what to do in some respects. I can put on a front when I want to get on with it, whereas before I might just have not done anything. Even simple things like going to the doctor, you know. I might have thought I should just take the doctor's word and not question anything. You know, just accept what they say. But right now I don't really feel that way. If the doctor tells me something and I'm not happy I'll tell him I'm not happy (Paula, a black woman).

> We're also able to, if we do have to use, have to go to, say, local authority or something like that, we can also use our knowledge what we've gained by manipulating the situation. Instead of you being the client and them being sort of the employee or whatever, you can now manipulate that situation where it's a one to one basis. 'Cos in the past, specially with social security or something like that, you were there [finger pointing down], and this is much more one to one. You negotiate, you know, what's going on. You get more confident as well in handling authority and in handling people in authority as well (Helen, a white working-class woman).

Seventeen women (mostly black and white working-class) felt themselves to be much more confident, particularly in their dealings with their children's teachers and with the education system generally. The whole area had been demystified for them, particularly on the level of who loses out within the education system (both areas the women had pointed to as their parents having a lack of understanding of, and knowledge about):

I mean when my first, my two big ones went to school, I mean I didn't have the sense where education, you know, where I would sort of — you know, you go to like open day and school and the teacher fob you off with all sorts of cock and bull stories. Before time I believe them . . . But now I don't give a damn. When people talk about West Indian children in this country not learning it's got nothing to do with the children . . . They [the teachers] weren't interested in whether the kids learnt. They see them walk through the door, oh a black face, another problem (Val, a black woman).

I mean I'm very interested in the sociology of education and things to do with class, social class and stratification and things like that. And I think a lot of it is you think, Christ, you know, they're [my children] not in with much of a chance in the education system as it is [Michelle, a white working-class woman).

The women saw themselves as being able to talk to teachers and others in 'authority' on more equal terms than previously, with these people respecting them and their opinions much more (even if they did not like the values behind this change of attitude particularly):

I've been up [to the school] on parents' evenings and they really look down their nose at you. Really offhand. In fact one of them was downright rude and turned his back on me . . . [now it's] 'oh, she can read, she's worth talking to'. It makes me really cross (Anne, a white working-class woman).

The women could use the education system in ways they would not have had either the confidence or the knowledge to do prior to their own forays into higher education. Janice (white working-class), for example, pushed a reluctant local education authority to provide special tuition for one of her children who had learning difficulties in a way she felt she would not have been able to do before, and Paula (black) was able to ensure her child went to the particular school she wanted her to attend.

A third of the women (eleven), however, (again, mostly black and white working-class) were careful to add that while their new confidence and knowledge of the workings of 'the system' meant that they were no longer 'down there' in their negotiations with those in authority, it did not mean that they were now 'above' these people:

I think I'm more confident. I do things, you know — it's like I used to be nervous about sort of phoning up people, you know, sort of complaining about things and that sort of thing, whereas now I do it anyway, you know. It doesn't worry me anymore that sort of thing. I think I always thought sort of before, you know, God they're better than me. I mean I don't think I'm better than them by any means, but now I think that they're not better than me (Wendy, a white working-class woman).

Conclusion

The women's private world understanding of the meaning of their caring within their families could lead them to want to carry their family lives into higher education in their learning, and mentally and physically. It largely structured their understandings of the role of their tutors. On the one hand images of, and the invitations of, higher education and studentship within it could feed into this understanding, leading the women to expect a particular commitment from lecturers and to be able to integrate their life experiences into their learning. On the other hand, the images and reality of higher education also countered this feeling. The women's perceptions of appropriate, objective, higher educational knowledge, and higher education's response to any attempts at integrating the personal and the academic, could lead them to keep the two separate in their learning, and in the mental and physical presence of 'the family'. Another facet of their understandings of family life — its privacy — could also reinforce this.

Those women who accepted and valued the separation of family and academic life and learning were more easily able to pursue this course. Those women who wished to exercise the preference for the personal as a basis for knowledge usually had to rework their educational experience in particular ways. This involved a more personal evaluation of the benefits of education, outside of formal achievement. Yet, another contradiction surrounded the status that even these women still attributed to higher education. The image and reality of being a student within higher education, as well as its perceived status, could make the women feel like deviant tokens within it because they had family responsibilities, and particularly if they were black and/or working-class. The presence of other mature students in similar circumstances could prove supportive in this respect. The very image and status, and the supposed objectivity of academic knowledge, however, allowed the women to perceive themselves as holding, and to view others as perceiving them as holding, a different and confident place in their mediating work with the public world, as compared to that which they had previously occupied. Yet, once again, within the women's accounts there was a tension between the status of higher education and not getting above themselves or viewing themselves as better than others.

Notes

1 This view does not necessarily totally dismiss theory in itself. It is the social conditions in which intellectual life takes place that produce the élitism of theory, rather than theory itself (Evans, 1983).

2 Indeed, there are links here with Gilligan's work. Gilligan (1982) also says that when the inter-connections women try to make are dissolved by hierarchical

orderings they come to question whether what they know from their own experience is true. She argues women usually interpret a moral choice within the context of the historical circumstances that produced it (personalize it), whereas men usually abstract that choice from its particulars and analyze it in abstract (impersonalize it). Therefore encouraging students to discuss hypothetical, theoretical abstracts rather than actual situations, is teaching them a male pattern of reasoning.

3   Unfortunately for the women, as they were well aware, contributions to seminar debates were not valued in a concrete way because they did not count towards assessment. The areas where the women did feel they lacked confidence, in essay writing and exam techniques, are the very areas higher education values and assesses.

4   Many of the women who held similar views on academic language to Janice and Kim, like them, received good degrees. Lack of sympathy with academic jargon was certainly not related to an inability to use it.

5   While three women, two third-years and one graduate, who had not had children when they first started their degrees were interviewed, women with a partner but no children who were just starting their degree courses when originally contacted were not. Thus the proportion of women who became pregnant during degree study may have been higher.

Chapter 6

Power, Interest and Support: The Effects of Education on the Women's Family Lives

Feminists have long been concerned to deconstruct the privacy of the domestic sphere, to break open the 'black box' and to reveal what is inside and its links with the public world. Much feminist research has demonstrated that 'the family' is not a consensually operating body with common interests. In particular, relationships between men and women have been revealed as a site of power struggles: 'The household [is] seen as the theatre of many aspects of the relationship between men and women' (Morris, 1990, p. 2). The research documenting this 'domestic politics' within the private sphere has mainly concentrated upon certain practical and measurable areas, such as the domestic division of labour, household finances and decision-making, and domestic violence.

Numerous studies (for example, Oakley, 1974; Boulton, 1983; Brannen and Moss, 1988, 1991; Hochschild, 1990) suggest that while men may be increasing their involvement in the more play-related enjoyable aspects of childcare, across the social classes there has been little in the way of a substantial increase in their involvement in other areas of childrearing, or in the doing of and/or taking responsibility for housework tasks. Men are regarded as wishing to avoid domestic labour and as having the power to do so. Other studies have shown that women's financial dependency on men has meant that women have less control over resources and decision-making than men (see Morris, 1990, for a review of this literature). The distribution of the fruits of paid labour and decisions as to how it is to be spent and to other decisions made within the home are argued to be closely related to who earns them. Moreover, behind the 'power of the wallet', ultimately, is the 'power of the hand'. It is men's distance from the private sphere, their access to and place in the public world, which is often argued to underpin this state of affairs (New and David, 1985).

The mature women students have been shown to hold varying attitudes towards the extent of the autonomy and privacy of their family lives with their partners and children, and the extent to which they wished their domestic worlds to feed into their education on various levels within the public academic setting, albeit aided or constrained by higher education's ethos and values. This chapter explores the women's attitudes with regard to bringing higher education into the private sphere of the family and their perceptions of the effects of this upon their relationships with their partners, children, and also extended family, and the ways that these are related to power.

Empirical investigations attempting to measure power relations between women and the men with whom they live have relied heavily on resource theories. Under the resource theory view of power and its derivative models, a woman's power within a relationship can be assumed to increase as her resources (personal attributes as well as possessions) increase relative to her male partner's. Women's entry into the public sphere, it has been surmised, would loosen their association with the private sphere. Giving women access to public world resources (such as education and wages) would mean a more equal sharing of power within the domestic sphere. Yet, even where there is less financial dependency and women have entered (or always been in) the public world of paid work, sharing their partners' provider role or even being the main provider, they have not as a result seemingly divested themselves of the responsibilities of the private sphere (Morris, 1990). Julia Brannen and Peter Moss's (1987) work shows that however much women earn in relation to their husbands' earnings, the women's contribution is mostly defined as peripheral — a protection of the male ego and breadwinner status which signals that something else is at work here. There is evidence from some studies that black women have more power in their relationships with men (for example, Willie and Greenblatt, 1978; Stone, 1983), yet other studies (such as Pleck, 1985) find the opposite. Most studies however, admittedly usually of white women, show that women with male partners who enter the public sphere to take up paid employment do not radically change the unequal balance of power in terms of domestic division of labour and so on within the private sphere, especially if they work part-time (again, see the review of studies in Morris, 1990).

Gaining a degree level education may be thought of as a different resource for power from a certain amount of financial independence. The ability to define issues and to formulate and evaluate arguments that would be skills developed within higher education might better enable the mature women students to renegotiate the division of household labour with their partners. Constantina Safilos-Rothschild (1976) has particularly pointed to educational level in power balances between women and their male partners (although she places emotional commitment as of greater importance — on which see below). Similarly, Gerald McDonald (1980) posits educational status as relating to power because it reflects interpersonal skills, expertise and competence brought into 'the family' from the outside. In other words, education is a form of power from the public world that can be used as a power resource within the private sphere to renegotiate and shift the division of domestic labour and decision-making.

I have already argued that the women were juggling themselves between two greedy institutions (higher education and family), each requiring their attention and affiliation to the exclusion of the other. Within both spheres the women did little reassessment of the commitments each institution required of them. It might be thought that, if the women's own expectations and commitments remained unchanged, the power (im)balances within their relationships would remain unchallenged. However, I will show that this was not necessarily the case. The women's expectations of others, particularly their partners in terms of emotional support, but also their children and their extended families, as well as these people's expectations of them, could be thrown into sharp relief by the process of being a student in higher education. Moreover, the women's ways of enabling family and education to coexist in their lives, their separations or connections of the two, also played a part. Their separations or connections of the two could shape, or were shaped by, the women's perceptions of their partners' actual or potential reactions to their studies.

The Practical Division of Labour: 'Sharing' the Domestic Load

Gaining an education did not appear to be a potential resource for shifting the division of labour within the home for the women, no matter what their race or class. Only three of them spoke of their partners having taken on substantially more domestically in the home since they had become students. For the most part women who had previously worked full-time had also carried the main burden domestically, so that more time at home as a student could in some ways lighten the stress they had felt. Those who had worked in part-time paid jobs previously, or not worked at all, tended to carry on with the same domestic responsibilities as well. In this sense studying, even if full-time, seems to be regarded as akin to women working in part-time paid work.

Most of the women (twenty-two) seemed to regard the domestic division of labour between themselves and their partners as reasonable. As was shown in Chapter 4, the women mainly regarded taking on education in addition to family as their own decision, and felt that they themselves should manage the two as best they could. Those women whose partners did not live with them permanently carried far more responsibility domestically and for childcare than did the women who were married or cohabiting. Their partners were almost guests within their homes, and so these women did not feel that they could carry many expectations of their partners.

Several studies (for example, Brannen and Moss, 1988; Hochschild, 1990) have shown that women may not perceive or be critical of inequality in the division of household labour or childcare, even despite normatively believing in sex equality, because it is masked by the ideological vocabulary of sharing used by themselves and their partners. At a time when the ideal of the egalitarian marriage is widespread, women are likely to present their relationships in such sharing terms, no matter what the reality, and to believe this sharing to be so. Madeline (white middle-class), for example, described how it was implicit between herself and her husband that the state of the house was not just her responsibility:

> I mean the ironing pile upstairs is absolutely huge, but he never sees that as my responsibility that it's so huge. He never says, 'Don't you think you ought to get on with this ironing pile?'. I mean it just sort of takes over the house and that's it. It just is taking over the house. I mean he's never ever said to me, you know, sort of, 'Why isn't the bathroom clean?'. He never assumes that it's my responsibility.

The end result of her husband's non-assumption of her responsibility was that Madeline eventually did these chores.

The women's entry into the public world of formal education, their gaining of a resource that might potentially be used as a vehicle for the renegotiation of power within their partnerships, thus did not appear to affect the practical division of labour within their households radically. Yet this domestic inequality was often not so much a source of conflict between the women and their partners as it might have been. Where it was a source of conflict, as will be shown, this was most often because of its links with another kind of lack of involvement on the part of their partners. The distribution of household labour does not in itself give a full insight into the relationships between the women and their partners, or the effects, if any, of the women's education upon these relationships. This is because emotional commitment as an aspect of power has been left out of the domestic division of labour picture. For the women who tried not to let their study affect their ability to service their families, this was linked to a demonstration of their commitment to their families. Even where partners, comparatively, helped a lot, the women might question their partners' commitment:

> There's difference between feeling responsible for something and to actually do it. And there was no sense of Malcolm being responsible for anything in the house . . . it's not just whether or not they can cook a meal but they actually share the importance of it (Gillian, a white working-class woman).

How much help was, or was thought should be, received was variable — the link between these differing perceptions is domestic labour as a symbol of emotional commitment, which in its turn is linked to power.

The Division of Emotional Labour: Interest and Support

Margrit Eichler has stated that, particularly within its decision-making mode, 'emotions are assumed to be irrelevant to the study of family power' (1981, p. 202). She suggests that 'positive sentiments may be an important resource and thus radically alter the overall balance of spousal power' (Eichler, 1981, p. 213). McDonald (1980) has also argued for examinations of power in terms of commitment, trust and reciprocity. Indeed, there is some evidence that these aspects do play a role in how women regard the balance of power in relationships. Brannen's long-term study of dual earner households has led her to argue that the women she interviewed 'placed higher value on emotional sharing and togetherness than they did on the practical division of labour in the household' (Brannen, 1990, p. 16).

The mature women students regarded their partners' emotional support and encouragement while they studied as very important. This support could, indeed, be signalled to them in material ways, by their partners taking the children out at weekends so that they could study, or helping with the housework. Yet it was also signalled in other, psychological and emotional, ways. To the women these ways could appear as more valuable symbols of their partners' support. Partners' pride in, and commitment to, the importance of their studies was referred to positively by seventeen women. An example of this could be that their partners would tell people about what the women were doing. Other demonstrations, for the women, of partners' commitment were that they would give the women verbal support to continue studying when the women felt doubtful about their own abilities, and that they took it upon themselves to find or draw the women's attention to information that would be useful for their studies:

> If we're discussing something one day, the next time he goes to the library he'll look around, see if he can find any books about what we've been discussing and things like that. Yeah, he's pretty good (Anne, a white working-class woman).

They also spoke of partners helping them to revise, reading their essays and dissertations through before submission, and listening to and commenting upon their seminar papers before presentation. All this attention showed these women that their partners were not just committed to them gaining a degree, but also knew about and took an interest in the subjects they were studying. It was, for them, a tangible demonstration of their partners' caring about them:

> In a way he's so incredibly proud of what I'm doing and he thinks I'm so clever, you know, and tells everybody how clever I am and everything, you know. And you think well, I'm not really, but it's nice to have someone that believes in you, you know (Michelle, a white working-class woman).

Being able to talk about what they were doing and learning was, for the majority of the women (twenty-six), a form of sharing their education. These women wanted some connections, in the form of being able to discuss their educational experiences with their partners, between their student lives and their home lives. A third of the women's partners (eleven) were willing for the women to talk about any and all aspects of their student lives. Michelle (white working-class) felt that she would have found the whole process of studying for a degree really difficult if her husband had not been disposed to discuss all the aspects:

> With him I don't feel any block there, which is good, because I think if he, if there was a block there then I think that would be very difficult. It would actually be very difficult to do it, you know, to actually continue.

A quarter of the women's partners (seven) were included to discuss only certain topics, in certain ways. This was often structured around a willingness to talk about the social side of their student lives and areas of learning which their partners felt that they knew about — and which did not impinge upon the men personally. Thirteen of the women's partners, however, did not want to discuss anything that the women were learning, or perhaps even to hear much at all about any aspects of their experiences as students. Most of these women (ten) felt distressed by their partners' disinterest:

> I felt hurt that what I was interested in wasn't being supported . . . I mean I used to come back from the poly in the first few months full of enthusiasm about what was going on, and I'd discuss it, and it seemed

to be Cliff [my husband] particularly didn't want to allow that in (Janice, a white working-class woman).

The connections these women desired, between their student lives and their home lives, were denied to them by their partners' unwillingness to discuss their educational experiences. Within their study of marital problems and helpseeking Julia Brannen and Jean Collard (1982) found that wives were far more likely than husbands to complain about their spouses' lack of communication and demonstrativeness. Partners' lack of interest, their lack of willingness to share the women's educational experiences with them, was linked in these women's minds with their partners not really caring about them:

> I'd like him to sort of take more interest than he does, you know. Sort of sometimes I think well, you know, you don't care anyway, you know. But, you know, I would — he sort of — he doesn't mind me doing it but that's as far as it goes really (Wendy, a white working-class woman).

These women, as will be discussed in the next chapter, could either continue trying to draw their partners into an interest in their education or could shift towards keeping their two lives separate.

Again, as with the sharing of a commitment to the carrying out of domestic tasks, the women who were in this position felt that their partners were not recognizing the importance of what they were doing. While the women regarded the giving of time and attention to their partners, as well as their children, as a fundamental part of caring about their families, they did not all expect this to be a one-way process. Janet Finch (1983a) has written of an implicit contract within marriage: wives will give their husbands moral and emotional support in the carrying out of their paid work. This would seem to be akin to giving men time and attention, taking an interest in their paid work and recognizing its importance to them. Linked with the ideology of the sharing marriage there could also be said to be expectations of some reciprocity from partners in the giving of this psychological support for activities wives consider important.[1] This is perhaps why other studies have found that women seem to be happy to have their partners doing less in the home than themselves, as long as the men showed an emotional commitment to its doing. Certainly the ten women who wanted their partners to share the importance of their education, but whose partners did not seem inclined to do so, appeared to have some notion of reciprocity in terms of the giving of moral support. This attitude could be expressed as having supported their partners through a similar experience in the past, or a willingness to do this in the future:

> He turned round to me and said something like, 'Oh, just because you're on this course it doesn't mean to say that you're more intelligent And I thought that was a nasty thing to say. And I said unto him, I said unto him clearly, I said, 'Because if it was you, I would be there for you. I'd be rooting for you'. You see, I'd never do something like that (Val, a black woman).

It was this lack of shared recognition of the importance of studying for the women (the lack of reciprocal support) and the women's inability to connect their student and home lives in the way that they would wish, which affected the women's perceptions of the equality or otherwise of the division of labour within their homes. It was this lack that brought to their attention inequalities within their relationships, rather than the practical division of labour itself. The men's exercise of power within the relationship could be to withhold interest and moral support. Partners had the power to be disinterested, and not to invest time and attention (although this is not such a simple one-way process as it would seems.[2] As long as emotional support and communication were present the women were willing to accept inequalities in the domestic division of labour. Only when interest and moral support from their partners were absent, and their desire for connections thwarted, was it obvious to the women that ideals about mutuality and sharing could no longer exclude domestic inequalities within their relationships.

Not all the women, however, had a desire for insertions of education into their relationships in this form. Three women did not perceive their partners' lack of interest in their studies as unfair or hurtful. Indeed, they shielded their partners from any effects studying might have, not just on a practical level but also on an emotional level: 'I didn't actually want him to feel threatened in any way so I just didn't talk about it much' (Victoria, a white middle-class woman). These women kept the two worlds as separate as possible because they felt that their gaining an education could somehow cause conflict between themselves and their partners, and could — at least potentially if not actually — put their relationships with them at risk. Additionally, all but one of those women whose partners did not take an interest in sharing their educational experiences but who wished that their partners would, and even five of those women whose partners did take an interest, either came to be or were aware of this potential or actual conflict. Michelle (white working-class) said, at the start of her first year of degree study:

> I hope that it won't alter, or threaten maybe, the relationship I've got. I
> mean I know that that does happen quite a lot with people. I mean they
> say there's quite a high percentage of marital breakups.

Directly before she had expressed worries about her education threatening her relationship with her husband Michelle had been talking about the way she had quickly noted that people in the second and third years of her degree course were able to 'make connections with, like with everyday life to what they're actually learning'. The idea of a threat to her relationship with her partner came spontaneously to her mind after that.

Perceptions of Education as Threatening to Relationships with Partners

All the women expressed ideas on what it was about gaining an education that could potentially cause, or indeed had caused, conflict in relationships with partners. These ideas or realities can be grouped into three main 'threats'[3] which, although dealt with separately, could link together in various ways. These threats were: partners' desire to have the home as a separate, private and unconnected sphere; partners' fear of losing their central place in the women's attentions and feeling that the time the women spent studying was taken away from them; partners' fear of the women's educational success and the potential ramifications of this in terms of independence.

Violating the Home as Separate and Private

The threat to partners' wishes to have the home as a separate sphere appeared to be demonstrated to the women by the men's reactions to their bringing education home on both physical and mental levels.

The privacy of the home could be violated physically by books and papers. Women have been found to have unequal access to individual private space within the home in relation to men (Deem, 1986). The material conditions under which the women studied in their homes varied, and of course this was to an extent linked to class and to race. At an extreme, Sandra (black), living in a two-bedroomed council flat on the eighth floor of a tower block with her six children and her husband, could only intermittently work in peace in the kitchen, usually late at night. The majority of the other women managed to find more space for themselves. Five white middle-class, two black and one white working-class women had a spare room in their home that was set aside for use as their study. Most of the women, however, studied in their living/dining rooms and/or in their bedrooms.

Studying in these places meant, of course, that the women were often disturbed by their children and partners (when there) wanting to watch television or had to clear their work off the dining room table in order to eat and so on. Not only were the women interrupted by their children and partners, the women interfered with their partners and children too. While children did not make much fuss about this, partners could. The women whose partners did not live with them were unlikely to speak of the men complaining over the practical intrusion of education into what were not, after all, their own homes (although they could, and did, express discontent over mental intrusions — see below). Three of the women who were married or cohabiting spoke of how much they envied lone women parents on their courses because they could do what they wanted to when they wanted to at home (an envy that would appear to have some basis; Hardey, 1990). Six of the eight women who eventually split up with their partners said that they found studying much less pressurized in these terms once they were without the men. As Stella (white middle-class) remarked, 'It wasn't a problem bringing the university into the home when he wasn't there'.

The privacy of the home could also be violated by mental concepts. As shown previously, a proportion of the women wanted to discuss what they had been studying with their partners and were either unable to, or could only discuss certain issues with them. These topics appeared to be subjects that the men felt fell within their province. In the main these areas of expertise centred around economics and some aspects of politics, including, in the case of the black women's partners, racism.[4] June's (white working-class) husband was happy to talk about some employment matters, but firmly rejected her attempts to introduce sociological or psychological dimensions to issues:

He used to say, 'I don't want any sociology talk around here'! I used to explain something psychologically, you know, and he used to say, 'I don't want to know'. He used to think it was partly intruding I think.

June's reporting of her husband's words reveal the idea that these particular educational understandings should not enter family life and relationships. They were *intrusions* upon it. Apart from not liking these sorts of analyses to be brought up within the home, June also mentioned that her husband was deeply shocked when she told him that she had talked about their relationship as part of a seminar discussion on 'the family'. Knowledge gained in the educational setting should not be used in certain, more personal and private, ways it seemed, and vice versa. Six white working-class women mentioned how their partners would react angrily to any supposed sociological or psychological analysis of their own actions, feelings or beliefs:

My husband thinks I've changed. He thinks I sit down — if I want to talk to him about anything he always says I'm analyzing him now, which is absolute crap but, you know. Whereas I wouldn't know where to start analyzing him. I don't know. I know I sort of think things through more now, you know (Wendy, a white working-class woman).

It would appear that there was a fear that the insights the women gained from their studies might give them a power over their partners because they would be able to understand the men's emotions and motivations. Partners were described by ten women (white working-class and middle-class) as generally unable to show their emotions or to discuss personal issues in the way the women themselves could and would wish the men to.

In these women's anecdotal reporting of such incidents, their own ideas about sharing and connections appeared to clash with their partners' beliefs about separate spheres and the mental privacy of the home. Thus the women whose separations of their family lives from their educational lives were stronger than their feelings about affiliation and connection avoided this overt clash. These women were not only protecting their partners' male psyche, but could also avoid a clash between their own notions of sharing within their relationships and what actually happened in practice with regard to their education. Through the process of compartmentalizing and separating their different worlds some of the women achieved a measure of integration between belief and practice. They therefore did not have to confront the inherent contradictions between the two in the ways that other women, who did not do this, had to. As will be shown in the next chapter, some of the women who confronted this clash moved towards separation for both the reasons of protection of partners and themselves.

Lack of Time for Attention

Living with men has been argued to decrease women's access to the resource of time (Hartmann, 1981). The time that men take up, the time that women spend with their partners, is not just a matter of servicing them domestically, but is also time spent servicing them emotionally. An American study concerned with the effects of wives' employment on their marriages suggested that the diminution of time couples spent together was a more important factor in marital instability as a result of a wife's employment than was her gaining an independent source of income from her entry to the public world of paid work (Booth *et al.*, 1984).

Studying has been shown to be a concern that took up much of the time and attention of the mature women students, not just physically but also mentally. Moreover, it was a concern that existed within 'the family' and the home but came from outside of it. All but three women mentioned that paying less attention than previously to partners might be threatening to the men. This concern occurs in the context of the women's belief that caring about people was linked to giving them time and attention. The men's 'security' could be threatened by too much of the women's time and attention being directed elsewhere, especially within the home. And yet one of the ways in which the women might try to alleviate this potential insecurity, by drawing their partners into their education, as we have seen above, seemed to them to often be rejected by their partners.

Four women had always studied in various forms since they had started their relationships with their partners, or for a long time before entering higher education. They felt that this 'preliminary' had helped to reduce their partners' conception of education as in competition for their attention. June (white working-class), who was one of these women, also felt that her husband was as encouraging about her education as he was because, despite his dislike of her connecting her educational knowledge into her home life understandings and vice versa (quoted earlier), he was away from home during the week. When he was home at weekends she could either not study or pretend that what she was doing was not important:

> It worked for me because I didn't work at the weekends on my studies unless I really got behind. And then I'd choose a time when he was really absorbed in the television and sneak a read, or 'I'm just reading this, it's not important, carry on talking', so that he didn't feel neglected. So I suppose I was lucky. I mean if he'd been home every night I don't think it would have worked.

Thus making sure that partners felt that they were still the centre of the women's attention was another form of alleviating education's perceived threat:

> At the moment he [my boyfriend] is more and more staying here now than before because I realize that when I was doing it [the degree] he was being seemed to be excluded. And the only way I could make him feel like part of it is to allow him to stay more and more so he would be part of it . . . So you have to make him feel like he wasn't out. You have to make him come within the family. Before he was wondering where does he stand, you know (Irene, a black woman).

Sexual relations were also a way in which the women gave their partners attention, and therefore could be regarded as an area in which they could neglect their partners. Along with 'communication and demonstrativeness', 'sexual activity' is one of the most problematic areas within relationships, and the latter is the one that men most often complain about (Brannen and Collard, 1982). The sexual side to relationships is also, as David Clark and Douglas Haldane point out, 'regarded as *the* secret, the most private element of the relationship' (1990, p. 136; their emphasis). Only four of the white women and none of the black or 'mixed' race women referred to this aspect of their relationships. Victoria (white middle-class), for example, only alluded to her sexual relationship with her husband as being affected by the attention education required of her:

> I wasn't very attentive in all respects I think. Not that he's, he's not one of those sort of men that expects you to give, you know, in all ways. He's not that sort of person. But I think, you know, I just couldn't even bring myself to, you know, give him a cuddle now and again. I just didn't have time. You know, I was thinking of too many other things. You know, he puts up with it, but in the end I know he does feel, you know, oh, perhaps she doesn't love me any more, that type of thing.

The other women were more direct about this, two of them feeling that their partners were the type of men who did expect them to be 'attentive in all respects'. In a quarter of cases (seven), partners were also thought to be threatened, at least potentially, by the time and attention the women might give to their friendships with other students. This could also be linked to sex, with partners being worried that the women might start a relationship with someone else.[5]

Women's Success and Independence

Other ways in which gaining an education was perceived by the women as a threat to their partners, referred to by thirteen of them, concerned the women's success with their studies. Achieving educationally meant that the women could potentially end up knowing at least as much as, if not more than, their partners about certain things, and might also come to be financially independent of them. The women could attempt to deal with this situation in various ways.

As has been noted, the women's partners could be willing to at least discuss topic areas in which they felt that they had some expertise and a greater understanding than the women. The women's education could, however, eventually begin to undermine this superior status with regard to knowledge on the part of their partners. Helen (white working-class), for example, felt that her boyfriend could not take any reversal in their respective knowledges, and their relationship ended because of this:

> He used to tell me about things 'cos he's, he was a coach driver. And he used to go to all these different places and tell me about them. And soon after I started the course, I started talking to him about things that I sort of learnt and discovered and what not. And I found that our roles were being reversed, that he didn't know about things that I knew about. I didn't know about things that he knew about, and I started to tell him things about different things. And I found him starting to switch off as soon as I started sort of talking about things that I'd learnt during that day or whatever, the lecture. Started switching off. You know, that sort

of glazed look . . . And when you can't talk to somebody about what you've just learnt or heard or read or something, you can't discuss it, then there's nothing left really, is there?

Maureen's (black working-class) boyfriend actually taught one of the subjects that she was studying as part of her degree. She found, however, that whenever she asked for his help he would explain things in such a complex manner that she could not follow him. As she learnt more as part of her course she felt that he was using 'jargon' to make simple things appear beyond her comprehension. She concluded that he was, in fact, threatened by the idea that she could end up as knowledgeable as him: 'I mean there's always encouragement there to go ahead and do this and the other, but at the end of the day I don't think they want you to achieve anything'. The academic jargon Maureen's partner used gradually became part of the women's own language, and two women felt that their partners could also find this threatening because they would not be able to follow what the women were saying.

In all, a third of the women (ten) mentioned this 'success' aspect of gaining knowledge as a conflictual factor in their relationships. Three of them came to keep their academic knowledge separate from their relationships for this reason, although in one case the woman had also felt the position of authority she would be in was unacceptable to herself:

> I mean you can't really discuss *Capital* if someone hasn't read it or doesn't know about it . . . I mean it would be dead boring. He might not find it boring actually. But I wouldn't be the best teacher because — and it would be like a teacher. It would be like teaching (Jennie, a white working-class woman).

Even three women who acknowledged the potential, but did not feel their partners were threatened by them becoming more knowledgeable about things, tended to make jokes around this issue, which may have indicated some underlying discomfort: 'I mean Bob would probably say he's lost [out] because he can no longer beat me at Scrabble! That's a definite loss!' (Lorraine, a white middle-class woman).

The implicit power balance (or imbalance) in the women's relationships with their partners could be disturbed if the women did not compartmentalize and separate off from family life their educational understandings and concepts. There are also links here with some of the partners' reported dislike of the women analyzing them with insights gained from their studies, and fears of the power this might give the women over them. Compartmentalization, the separation of their education from their family lives, could also be the case when the women's opinions were in conflict with those of their partners. The women felt they had become much more expert and confident about arguing their case. Five women mentioned that their partners could no longer casually dismiss what they said and so, if a subject was pursued, the result could be confrontation.

An ability to argue cogently was one element of the women's educational success that could underline another element. It highlighted the fact that the women were potentially gaining independence not only in thought, but also because their degrees could lead them to better paid employment. Even Judith (white middle-class), who felt that there had been to conflict with her husband at all because of her degree study and regarded her husband as supportive and interested in what she was doing, said:

> I suppose one of the things that might've changed is that he has a realization that I have an earning power, an earning capacity which I didn't have before, which could make me be independent, which I couldn't so much before.

Nevertheless, as a look at the literature shows, independence within a relationship on the basis of earning power seems to be elusive, whereas some form of independence outside of one seems more obtainable.

Finances were, in fact, what twelve of the women's partners had regarded as the main reason for the women doing a degree (ironically, in the three cases where women saw this as enabling them to leave their partners). While four women's partners also accepted and supported education for eduction's sake, eight women felt their partners held an entirely instrumental view of why they should be doing a degree course. Indeed, two of them spoke of being able to manipulate their partners to some extent because of this, gaining an acceptance of their studies that otherwise would not have been forthcoming:

> I mean to get to the poly, I mean, had been difficult, because he had been very much against it. And I used the fact, and in many ways I was blackmailing him in some ways, and saying that I'm doing it not only for myself, but I can get a job and I can have an income and we'll be better off financially (Janice, a white working-class woman).

This need to feed their partners' instrumental view of their education mainly affected the women who were married to or cohabiting with their partners. Although live-out partners could also hold this view of education as well, the women in these relationships felt that they were responsible for, and to, themselves: 'He's supportive. But how I look on it was it was my decision. I didn't need his approval because I was responsible financially for my children and here' (Irene, a black woman). The women themselves also saw their degrees as leading eventually to a better paid job, but they also knew that they were doing it for other more personal reasons, such as proving themselves. This, in conjunction with the fact that the women were enjoying what they were doing, could, particularly for the married and cohabiting women, feel like they were indulging themselves. Thus it was felt that partners might also perceive their studies as indulgences. As the previous quotation from Janice shows, however, this indulgence could be hidden by overtly agreeing to partners' stress on education being a means to an end.

On the other hand, for the married or cohabiting women, it was this potential financial independence from their partners through paid work, linked with an independence of spirit, which could threaten their partners. Sandra's (black) husband, for example, was quite disgruntled at the thought that she might indulge herself by continuing with more studying after completing her degree:

My husband, he doesn't want to hear that. He said, 'Look, three years you are not doing anything! Three years, you have to go and get yourself a good job. I mean we have to look for, you know, mortgage. We've got to buy a house. I don't want to hear anything you want to do something after three years. I mean what are you going to do with all these certificates, you know. You want to do everything. You don't want to work, just to be reading'.

He was also disgruntled when Sandra, fed up with arguments over his lack of support to her domestically and emotionally, feeling herself more confident and seeing financial independence on the horizon, suggested that if more input to the family was not forthcoming he could leave:

> I mean I can't understand them. They don't always like their wives to progress because they feel oh, if you achieve your academic end and then you start bossing them, you know. They want you always, you know, at the bottom. It's crazy really. You know, they can't carry on like that. No, no, not in this modern era ... I've told him times without number, I'm no more interested in this bloody marriage. Because I mean he is not doing anything.

RE: Do you think you will split up?

> Well, I always suggest that to him. He says I'm crazy, you know. You see this is why he never wanted me to go to school!

Power, Masculinity and Education

Education was, it seems, not just threatening to the women's relationships with their partners, but somehow was threatening to their partners personally, perhaps as men. The women's understandings of what exactly constituted this threat, outlined above, are their own perceptions. On the whole, however, their perceptions agree with much of the psychological and sociological writing on men and masculinity. Such analyses often point to men's desire to have the home as an idealized separate retreat (for example, Tolson, 1987; Jackson, 1990); their demands for attention and emotional sustenance from women, while at the same time having an inability to acknowledge emotions and a fear of intimacy (for example, Tolson, 1987; Blackie and Clark, 1987); and their attachment to their status as the breadwinner and fount of public world knowledge in a relationship (for example, Tolson, 1987; Seidler, 1989).

Moreover, that some of the women's partners felt threatened and reacted accordingly would appear to be real enough. Conflicts between the women and their partners, due in the women's view to partners' feeling threatened, in the main resulted in verbal abuse and arguments (reported by sixteen women). Three white women, however, also spoke of their partners resorting to the 'power of the hand'. Lynne (white middle-class) ended up with broken ribs, and Gillian (white working-class) with a broken tooth. Stella's (white middle-class) account of her boyfriend's almost total lack of domestic and emotional support, and his angry reaction to her studies (a reaction which also included violence) brings together all the factors identified as threatening to the women's partners:

He didn't like the fact that I could do it [the degree], and as it turns out I could do it quite well. And he didn't like the fact that I wanted to give it some time . . . I mean at one stage I was sort of hiding the fact that I was working at home because he was so antagonistic towards it. And he used to attack my books and things.

RE: You had to physically hide them?

Quite often I did, yes. I used to push them to the back of my desk and rush into the kitchen. The study door was opposite the kitchen, and I used to rush into the kitchen just to avoid a conflict when he came in.

Andrew Tolson (1987), and Kobena Mercer and Isaac Julien (1988) argue, respectively, that masculinity is differentially constructed along class and along race lines, arising out of the variations in their oppressions — although both accept some elements of continuity. While only white working-class women spoke of their partners' aversion to any academically-inspired analysis of their motivations, in all other respects the women attributed the same sorts of threats to the men whatever their race or class. Domestic violence also knows no class or race bounds (Hamner and Saunders, 1984; Pahl, 1985). It might, however, be thought that the level of partners' education would coincide with the women's partners' reactions to, and understanding of, their studies and to how threatened the men might feel. Some studies suggest that highly educated husbands are more likely to give help in the home and to hold more egalitarian ideals (for example, Farkas, 1976). Nevertheless, the educational level of the women's partners was not a good indicator of the distribution of power within their relationships as discussed here. All but two of the white working-class, one of the black and one of the 'mixed' race women did not have partners who had studied for degrees themselves, and neither did just under half (four) of the white middle-class women. In fact, many of the women's partners, like the women themselves, had left school with few qualifications. Partners' educational standing appeared to make no difference to their reactions to the women gaining an education (or indeed to their helpfulness within the home). Interestingly, over a third of the women (eleven) thought that it would make a difference. Six of those whose partners had no degree said that it would have been easier if their partners had gained one because the men would then be able to understand what was involved. These women partly attributed any conflict they had with their partners to the men's defensiveness over their lack of education. Two women whose partners had a degree, however, talked of a lack of understanding because those degrees had been gained as conventional students, benefiting from the whole experience. Yet the two white middle-class women and one woman of 'mixed' race whose partners had studied for degrees as mature students, felt that there was still a difference because, as women, they had carried the brunt of domestic and childcare responsibilities at the time in a way that was not fully reciprocated. Indeed, one of these women was Stella, whose partner had reacted violently to her studies. On the other hand, Michelle's (white working-class) partner, who had left school with only a few O-level qualifications, took an interest in her studies and supported her domestically and emotionally.

A quarter of the mature women students split up from their partners over the course of their degree study (discussed further in the next chapter). None of the relationships ended over the unfair division of domestic labour. The reasons the women gave were largely related to the more emotional effects of education upon their relationships outlined above. These were the areas where power battles were played out between the women and their partners. It was not necessarily education in itself that threatened the women's partners, and therefore their relationships with the men. Rather it was the disturbing power balance effects of any attempts to share their education with their partners. Sharing, and connecting, education with their children was a different matter for the women. It was not seen by them as a threat to their relationships with their children in the way that they perceived it as a threat, potential or real, to their relationships with their partners — and thus in some ways also a threat to their own ability to study. As Jenny (white working-class) said, 'Children can't stop you from doing it. It's the husbands rather than the children, in a sense'.

Children: Connection and Power

It is within the private sphere, through their childrearing activities particularly, that women are said to be able to wield some power, albeit constrained to an extent (New and David, 1985). Men have been shown, in the main, and despite their increased input into aspects of childrearing, to be marginal to it (Lewis and O'Brien, 1987; Ribbens, 1993, forthcoming). It has been argued, however, that overt authoritarian forms of power wielded by parents have given way to a marked move towards a closer identification of parents with their children and a more egalitarian relationship (Backett, 1982) — corresponding, it would seem, with the supposed move towards more egalitarian relationships between men and women within 'the family'. Separations or connections of their family lives with their educational lives were more possible for the women to conduct in the way they would wish with respect to their children than they were with partners. As with their partners, any connections were also viewed in terms of sharing their education with their children in various ways. Yet, as has been shown in the relationship between men and women, the language of equality and sharing can paper over and make more covert any exercise of power. Indeed, their children's help with domestic labour was presented by four women as an equal relationship through the language of sharing: 'They've got the feeling that they're contributing to the household . . . We're more of a team. They've got to pull their weight otherwise it's not fair' (Marcia, a 'mixed' race woman).

Children were generally spoken of as 'supportive' in terms of the women pursuing an education with regard to any domestic help, and if they did their best to leave the women alone to study. Once again, however, support and interest could be demonstrated in other ways. As with partners, their children's interest in what they were doing (if the children were old enough) could be signalled by the fact that they told people that their mother was a student and took some pride in their mothers' unconventionality. The process of studying itself could be shared with older children in particular, if they themselves were studying for GCSEs or A-levels: 'They do appreciate it for their own reasons and do understand the studying involved in it themselves . . . we sort of encourage each other' (Lynne, a white middle-class woman). Older children could therefore understand what was required of the women, and younger children were spoken of as relating to their mothers' study in terms of school: 'They say, "Oh mummy, can we go to your school", you know!' (Sandra, a black woman). Any lack of acknowledgment along these lines on the part of children was rarely interpreted by the women as their children not caring about them, as it could be with partners. Rather it was viewed as their children just not being interested because children have other concerns. Lorraine (white middle-class), for example, was talking about her graduation:

> I think somebody said to him [my son], you know, 'Oh, have you told your teacher at school?' or something, and he said, 'No' ... I think when he gets older I'm sure he'll appreciate it more. He can't quite understand, you know, its relevance.

Two women were quite happy to take this disinterest as given and not even start any attempts to directly discuss social issues and student life generally with their children.

All but three of the women, who had very young children, and the two mentioned above, however, said that they did at least try to discuss issues that they were learning about and what went on generally at the university or polytechnic with their children, even from an early age. The women spoke of how they felt their children had become much better informed because of the discussions, and mentioned that it might also have some effects upon their children's current and/or future education. Indeed, thirteen women referred to the way in which their own education had enabled them to help their children with homework. Eight saw themselves as role models for their children; because they went off to do their 'homework' within the home their children were encouraged to do theirs in the same way. Even in five cases, where children were too young to have homework, or to be at school, the women spoke of their children copying them:

> If I pick up a book, they'll want to pick up a book, which is quite good. So if I want to do some reading or writing I'll always bring up a book, 'cos I know they're going to run and get a book as well. Every time I get paper to write, they want paper to write as well, you know! (Anna, a black woman).

Educating their children was also seen as occurring more broadly through discussions of social issues. For example, five women mentioned that when they did sit and watch television with their children they would often choose to watch an informative type of programme so that they could discuss it with them:

> They did have a series about the life, you know, birth, talking about the miracle of life. And I didn't do any studies, I sit there with all of them. We all sit round the box watching babies born and all that! ... So I use programmes like that to discuss things. 'Oh, this is coming on, should we watch it tonight?'! ... Doing the degree make you more aware about how important parent involvement is. You see, it make you more aware (Irene, a black woman).

Only two women's children resisted and were said not to be interested in discussing issues in cases where the women would have liked to be able to talk about them.

In these ways the women's education could be integrated, directly or indirectly, into their everyday lives with their children, and was particularly stressed in the case of bringing up their younger children. Only one woman did not feel her own education had an effect on the way she brought up her children: 'You're in a rut by the time you've — you know, the age mine are, you've made your mistakes and go on making them I suppose' (Jennie, a white working-class woman). The rest of the women, however, regardless of the age of their children, felt that it did have some effect. Nine of them spoke of incorporating things they had learned about in the way they dealt with their children, or understood them:

> I try to show him [my son] the importance [of education] but as — I'm with the psychology teacher, and they say at a particular age the children never see the reverse point of view. They only see their point of view, they can't see your point of view. Yeah, from that, that's why I'm so patient in that respect (Maureen, a black working-class woman).

Others spoke of being more aware of the way they brought up their children, daughters particularly, in terms of assumptions or stereotypes on the basis of sex, and of the broader discussions referred to above.

Another way in which the women could feel that their education had affected their children's upbringing was, as we saw in Chapter 4, because they felt guilty about studying taking up so much of their physical and mental time. Nine women specifically mentioned making more efforts to give their children some undivided attention when they were with them. Making time to sit and watch television with their children and so on, was part of the women's efforts to give them compensating attention, 'because I don't want them to resent me doing it' (Judith, a white middle-class woman). Nevertheless, although these women did see some potential for education threatening their children in this way, this is as against all but three women perceiving some potential 'attention' threat when it came to partners. Moreover, only three women felt that their children had actually been threatened by their being a student and studying. For example, Jennie's (white working-class) eldest child had felt aggrieved at having to spend an hour or so with a childminder after school, and in her first year of study ran away from school one day: 'All he'd say was that, you know, he just didn't like me doing it because it meant me not being there in the evening for him, and things like that'. These sort of upsets for their children, all occurring upon the women starting full-time education, were mainly felt to have been quickly resolved, with any problems settling down rather than building up as they might with their partners. Certainly none of the women spoke of seriously contemplating giving up their degrees because of their children, or shifted the ways in which they had education and family coexisting in their lives because of children's reactions alone, as they did with their partners (see next chapter). They were able, through talking to their children, to impose their own definitions of the situation:

> I explained to them that I didn't have the chance to do it earlier, now I've got the chance to do it, it would be difficult for three or four years and

we'd be short of cash, and they wouldn't see me around and they'd have
to be quiet in the evenings, but at the end of it I'd be able to get a better
job and the long term prospects for them were a lot better if I was to do
the degree than if I didn't . . . And I think they understood it, that it was
better that they cooperated as it were (Marcia, a 'mixed' race woman).

Thus it was particularly in the broad area of their children's education that
the women could make links and connections between their own learning and
their home lives (see Edwards, 1993b, for further discussion of this point). Even
those women who attempted to ensure that studying did not interfere with their
family too much, and who separated off their educational lives from their home
lives, could make connections in this manner. There was less of an expectation of
reciprocity in terms of interest in, and support for, their studies from their children on the part of many of the women, than there was of their partners. Their
children's interest in what they were doing was not so closely allied to their children caring about them. The threat of education to these relationships was limited
because children did not have much power (and maybe no inclination) to define
the home as a physical and mental private sphere into which education should not
enter. Additionally, their mothers' educational success did not undermine their
children — or rather disturb the balance of power in the relationship. In fact, only
one woman mentioned this aspect as even a potential threat to her children.
Moreover, the time and attention the women gave their children was more easily
able to incorporate connections with their educational knowledge and lives where
the women desired this.

Censure and Censorship: The Extended Family

Many of the issues surrounding power relationships discussed with regard to
partners and to children are also to be found in the women's relationships with
members of their extended families. This point is particularly so with regard to
their own parents and the parents of their partners, although none of the women
actually mentioned the word threat in the way they were wont to do when
talking about their relationships with their partners. These issues in relation to
parents or partners' parents were not relevant for all of the women. For example,
two of the black women's and two of the white working-class women's parents
had died. Additionally, two women had been estranged from their parents long
before they started studying. The white middle-class women were more likely to
live further away from their parents (these women and/or their parents having
been mobile geographically as well as socially, a normal state of fluidity in
contemporary society; Payne and Abbott, 1990) than were the white working-
class women or the black women whose parents were alive and lived in this
country. For ease of discussion, in what follows the women's parents and/or
partners' parents will mostly be jointly referred to as 'parents'.

Little attention has been paid to the part extended family networks may play
in supporting, or not, unequal relationships between men and women partners.
This is another aspect to the view of 'the family' as a self-contained unit that even
much feminist work fails to challenge. Indeed, generally, the external constraints
that may affect power balances within families, other than women's access to paid

work in the public sphere, are rarely explored. Elizabeth Bott's work (1957) pointed to the embeddedness of couples in social networks as an area of importance, and showed that the extended family can have an effect on the segregated or joint domestic roles men and women may play in terms of tasks and obligations. Bott argued that: 'The degree of segregation in the role relationships of husband and wife varies directly with the connectedness of the family's networks' (1957, p. 60).[6] In other words, the extended family can exercise normative pressure on men and women who live together to sustain a particular form of relationship. Clark and Haldane (1990) suggest higher education may play a part in this situation, in that it allows working-class couples, particularly, to rise in the class structure and to feel they have little to gain materially or psychologically from remaining closely bound to their families of origin. Another indication of the importance of extended family occurs in some studies of women's experiences of mothering (for example, Boulton, 1983). These sorts of insights, however, are often not followed through in terms of any investigation of links to power relationships between couples. Nor are they often thought of as being power relationships in themselves. Jennifer Mason's (1990) work on the relationship between elderly parents and their adult children, from the perspective of the parents, shows the tensions there are in this particular relationship between privacy and access to their children's private sphere. If parents can have scruples about the privacy of their adult children's home life in relation to themselves then they may well have opinions on other things that might violate this privacy. Indeed, the parents of the mature women students, like the women themselves, appeared to see the women's education as in some way threatening their relationships with their partners, and also with their children.

Certainly ten white women, seven of whom were white working-class married women, talked of their parents, usually mothers or mothers-in-law, worrying over the women's supposed actual or potential neglect of their partners and children:

> . . . and Ollie is at a childminder's full-time and quite happy and settled, despite what my mother thinks!
>
> RE: What does she think?
>
> Not a lot really! She thinks I ought to be at home like she was and we can't agree about that . . . [My parents say] 'Ian [your husband] has really suffered whilst you've been doing this'. Poor man! (Gayle, a white working-class woman).

Three of these women mentioned that their own parents, particularly their mothers, would refer to how 'lucky' the women were because their partners put up with so much due to their studying and were so 'good'. Two other women just 'sensed' an unexpressed censure rather than anything being directly said to them. Parents could withdraw, or not offer, practical support to the women because of their disapproval:

> [My parents-in-law] would not sort of — if I said to them like, 'Could you pick Stephen up from school?', they would do it very reluctantly, you know. But they'd never go out of their way to sort of help . . . Paul's [husband] got a sister and she's got children. They'll go out of

their way to sort of help her out because she's at home all day. They used to be like that with me, you know, but not now (Wendy, a white working-class woman).

Five women mentioned that parents could not understand why they were not satisfied to either stay at home and look after their families, or to continue in the jobs they had held previously. Another three women also mentioned some disquiet on the part of parents because they were no longer as available to spend much time going to visit parents or doing things for them. While the women may have temporarily suspended the full extent of their domestic and familial responsibilities, the expectations of them by parents appeared to remain the same. In all, a third of the women (eleven) felt that no account was taken by parents of the demands and responsibilities of the other part of their lives, as students. How many women are deterred from entering higher education in the first place by expressed or silent pressure from parents can only be surmised.

Half the women (fifteen), however, felt that parents were pleased that they were doing something to improve their life chances, and once again there was mention of the fact that parents would proudly tell people about what the women were doing. If living nearby, approving parents could also be practically very supportive — something that occurred in nine cases. For example, Michelle (white working-class) had originally been urged back into education by her father, and her mother-in-law had minded her youngest child for her, while her mother had collected her eldest child from school and often went to Michelle's home during the day to wash up, do some ironing and so on: 'It would have been incredibly difficult for me personally to have done it without that kind of help and support'. Madeline (white middle-class), too, relied on her mother-in-law for some of her childminding, but felt that her own mother was not prepared to 'put herself out' at all to help. Nor was her mother interested in what she was doing as a student: 'You know if I asked her did she know what course I was doing I'd be surprised if she came up with the right answer!'

The disapproval of parents could also be signalled to the women by parents' ignoring the fact that the women were doing the course and were students. The censuring took the form of censorship. Thirteen women described how parents did not mention their studies or ask how they were getting on unless the women themselves brought the subject up. This emotional lack of support was experienced by white women particularly, regardless of class. All of the women who referred to parental lack of interest in what was, for them, an important part of their lives, found this sort of imposed separation of student and family life hurtful and uncaring:

I mean [my parents] never really, really said anything about the degree or what it meant to them. And it was all, 'Oh, well, that's nice dear'! You know, like the sort of response they'd say to anything really. I mean it didn't seem to have any significance at all . . . I am upset about it, that they won't recognize that, and frustrated because they won't praise me or acknowledge . . . They all thought that 'cos Ollie was born in my first year, that I wouldn't go back. And, and I think maybe that was the only time there was any flicker of acknowledgment or recognition that I was doing the degree (Gayle, a white working-class woman).

Parents thus appeared to attempt to cope with the fact that the women were allowing something important other than family into their lives by shutting out the women's education.

Nevertheless, only three women felt that they could discuss anything of what they were learning with parents, even if parents were willing, because the issues and concepts involved were just beyond them. Although the women could resent parents ignoring their doing a degree, they took as given an inability to discuss what they were learning with parents. One woman helped her parents-in-law to avoid the topic altogether:

> When my husband's parents come to stay for the weekend or something they don't know me as a student and they don't see that, because I never do any studies when they're here. And they don't really know what the course is about. They feel it's out of their depth anyway to ask me about it (Judith, a white middle-class woman).

Four women, however, spoke of attempting to overturn this, endeavoring to re-educate parents on issues such as racism, sexism, political affiliation and so on. Conflict and arguments ensured:

> And I said to dad, 'I'm glad you don't subscribe to this awful tabloid press idea of seeing women as objects' . . . and my mother, she said, 'How can you say that? Those girls have every right to earn money in the way they want to'. And I said, 'Yes, but it's just legitimating the whole thing of women being seen as objects'. And she got really on her high horse and said, 'Don't you come up here with all this clever talk' (Alexandra, a white working-class woman).

The women's changing language, their 'clever talk', was a problem mentioned by one black and three white working-class women. It could either lead to, or feed into, feelings that the women were distanced from their parental families by their education:

> My own family, my mother and my sisters and my brothers, there was a bit of conflict there . . . and I think one of the real issues was that my language changed, it developed. I was using different words, which became natural to use, and maybe sounded slightly pompous (Janice, a white working-class woman).

Their status as degree students could also distance the women from their brothers and sisters. Two black and five white working-class women felt that their siblings were ignoring what they were doing. In another five cases, where brothers or sisters had themselves studied for a degree there was felt to be a special affinity with them:

> It was lovely because for him [my brother] it does mean something, 'cos he understands. I mean he's got a degree himself. He understands the work and the achievement, you know (Angela, a white middle-class woman).

Because the women felt so different from 'normal' mothers who did not do degrees, and could also feel that unless somebody had studied for a degree themselves they could not understand what it was about, they felt especially close to members of their family who had a higher education. Their education could otherwise lead them to feel an 'alien' or an 'outcast' within their own and their partners' families. Five women spoke of themselves as distanced from their own family of origin in particular because of their studies.

Conclusion

The women's abilities to connect their educational lives within the home and within family relationships echo their abilities to connect their family lives into their academic experiences, as discussed in the previous chapter, and are linked to issues of power. In the family these issues were mostly centred around the power to define family life as a private sphere and to define women's responsibilities within it. Partners and parents were likely to believe that education should not enter the home and affect relationships within it, interfering with the women's domestic and emotional commitments, or lead the women to 'get above themselves'; or perhaps more accurately, to 'get above' partners and maybe also parents, by displaying their knowledge to them. Where the women's views on the way to have family and education coexisting in their lives concurred with these definitions then power battles, particularly with partners, were much less in evidence. These women felt that they were almost a different person at home with their partners, children and extended families:

> I have two separate lives as it were, which are very separate. I'm a student there, and that's that role I take on there. And then I come home and I very much fit into the role, you know. I'm a mother and a wife and what have you here. And even though I'm sort of disappearing upstairs to the study for hours on end, I'm not the student that I am at the poly (Judith, a white middle-class woman).

They could either be quite happy for this to be the case or to wish that what they saw as an imposed separation between their educational and family lives was not there. In these latter cases, as will be discussed further in the next chapter, the separation often occurred after an initial period of connection because of conflicts, actual or potential, between themselves and their partners. These women would have liked to have been like the women who did not 'put on different coats': 'I'm too old to change, you know, like kids do, you know. One personality at school and one at home' (Lynne, a white middle-class woman). The fact of women moving from initial connection to separation in order to avert conflict suggests, however, that women who pursued connection were likely to have partners who felt so threatened that their relationships came to an end. The power balances within their relationships had been disrupted to an extent that was unacceptable to their partners. These issues around the separation or connection of education with family life were not so relevant for the women's relationships with their children because they, as mothers, could hold the balance of power here and define the coexistence of family and education as they wished.

When considering the configurations of the women's personal relationships, however, the patterning of these relationships are not their own explanation. The structures and institutions in which this construction takes place must be addressed. Within this chapter there have also been some indications of race and class moulding some aspects of the women's experiences. The presence of these factors was not especially relevant in the women's relationships with their partners. Despite some analyses of the construction of masculinity that point to differences along the lines of race and class, these factors did not appear to have any great significance for the women's perceptions of the threats which their gaining an education posed to their partners. In the most private relationship within the private sphere, between a woman and a man, the effect of the women's having both family and education in their lives was less shaped by race and class and more by sex. However, class did operate to an extent within the women's relationships with parents, particularly in the case of white working-class women feeling that their education had distanced them from their families of origin and was censured by them. As will be seen in the next chapter, the women's perceptions of their places and identities within the worlds of education and 'the family' structured their separations and connections.

Notes

1 As was noted in Chapter 3, regarding the family as the woman's sphere and show-ing little interest or accommodation to it on the part of previous partners were reasons the women had given for the breakup of those relationships.
2 See Safilos-Rothschild (1976) on the link between power and the 'principle of least interest'. This postulates that the person with the most relational power is the one who is least involved in the relationship. However, although it might appear on the surface that disinterest on the part of men means they are less involved in relationships, in actuality they are much more dependent in terms of *receiving* interest.
3 Kathleen Rockhill (1987) has also referred to the way in which women gaining the 'symbolic power of education' (p. 164) is regarded as a threat by the men that they live with. She found these perceived threats could result in violence by the men towards the women, an effect also discussed later in this chapter.
4 See Marilyn Porter (1983) for similar findings about areas of expertise that are defined by men as male concerns.
5 This sexual threat is fear on the part of men that Rockhill (1987) has also noted when it comes to women gaining an education and which some of Annette Lawson's (1990) findings would appear to bear out.
6 What Bott regarded as sharing roles and obligations within the domestic sphere has been criticized by many feminists (for example, Stacey and Price, 1981) because she left the fundamentals of the overall sexual division of labour unques-tioned and taken-for-granted.

Chapter 7

Ways of Being

This chapter takes a closer look at certain themes that have been identified as running through the women's accounts. These themes are concerned with the separation or connection of their educational and family lives; the bases of educational and family ways of knowing and the authority or power they carry; and the theme of difference — differences between men and women, differences between women, and the difference (perhaps even deviancy) of being a mother and a student. It is concerned with the ways in which the women could 'be' in this situation — separating or connecting their educational and family lives in various ways. The practical and emotional ways in which the women either connected their family lives into academic learning and the education institution, or kept the two worlds separate, and the variety of ways in which they either integrated their educational knowledge and lives as students into their family lives or, again, kept them apart, have been set out and examined in the previous two chapters. Here, I pull together the various means of separation and connection, and construct an overall typology and continuum of the ways in which education and family can coexist in women's lives. I then draw out the links and inter-actions between the women's place in the typology and positioning on the con-tinuum, and their relationships with their partners.

The women's separations and connections also have implications for the way that women's lives are conceptualized and discussed. The values and priorities of the women concerned must be the base for understandings, and these may or may not be different from those of men. Differences between women are not so apparent when looking at their separations and connections in relation to their families. They are apparent, however, when looking at relationships outside of this, especially their friendships and their placing in the public world generally.

Education and Family in Women's Lives: A Typology

The idea of separations and connections of education and family in the women's lives was drawn from the apparent tensions between two ideological constructs outlined in Chapter 2: that of separated private and public worlds and a connecting feminine psyche. While ideological constructs such as these do not necessarily exist in reality, I have argued that they do help structure people's mature women students. In the women's accounts of the meanings of education and family for them, and their experiences of having the two in their lives, notions of both separations and connections have appeared in various forms. From these notions, three main ways in which the women had both education and family in their lives emerge. Some women wanted, and worked towards, connections and integrations between the two, some strived for a separation of the worlds. Others had a mix whereby they separated some aspects of education and family, but in other areas felt, and wanted, connections. The typology, on its own, appears essentially static. The different aspects of the women's separations or connections of their educational and family lives (in both directions) have also mainly been discussed as if they had a fixed quality to them, with women falling into one group or the other. Over time, however, women could move from one means of having family and education in their lives to another.

The connections and separations were frameworks for understanding that could evolve and change. For example, as was referred to in Chapter 5, one of the women, Michelle (white working-class), moved from wanting to feed her life experiences into her learning to regarding her experiences as irrelevant to academic learning. Nevertheless, she always spoke of discussing her studies with her husband. The reasons why Michelle and other women moved between separations and connections will be considered, as will other factors that affected whether the women wanted connections or separations in different circumstances, and the relevance of this for the effects of education upon their lives.

Connection of Education and Family

For the women who wanted connections, education was an indivisible part of all areas of their lives, as was their family. These women did not feel they wanted to, or could, divide themselves into being students and being mothers and partners. They talked of themselves as one person who did not act, feel or think differently in the education institution to the way they did at home, and vice versa.

These women wanted their children and partners to visit the university or polytechnic they attended, and the friends they made there to be part of their home lives. Their paid work and family experiences and knowledge were seen as feeding into their academic learning. They viewed education as a broad and personal process. They could express disappointment at the contractual nature of the relationship they had with their lecturers, expecting more personal relationships with people they regarded as their peers in many ways.

The knowledge that these women gained in higher education was fed back into their relationships with their partners and their children. They wanted their partner's support in domestic ways, but more importantly, they wanted their partners' interest, both in the domestic tasks undertaken and in their studies. Women who wanted connections wished to discuss what they learned with their partners and for their partners to be interested in this and in meeting their student friends. They also wanted to talk to their children and parents about what they were learning, and felt that their academic knowledge had affected the way they brought up their children.

Study truly spilled over into and affected all areas of their lives. These women regarded higher education as giving them confidence in their dealings with officials and professionals in public institutions, but they also felt that this confidence enabled them to be themselves more within the home in their personal relationships.

Separation of Education and Family

The women who wanted separations felt that their lives were divisible into parts. They switched from being a student to being a mother/partner and back again, usually on the bus or train journeys to and from their home and the education institution. They felt that their family life experiences were not relevant to their academic learning and/or that they were private matters. They spoke of feeling, acting, and thinking differently in the two separate worlds.

These women enjoyed 'cutting off' from their family selves and having a separate identity as a student. They preferred not to take partners or children to visit their place of study and, if they did so, felt uncomfortable at this meeting of the two worlds, or the two parts of themselves. They referred to higher education as not being part of 'real life', probably due to the feeling that they were escaping in some way when they went to the university or polytechnic. This feeling did not mean that they were dissatisfied with their home lives; they just valued each identity for its differences. Lecturers, too, were seen as having not experienced real life, were felt to be different people from the women, and thus a more intimate relationship with them was not looked for.

These women actively worked towards ensuring that being a degree student intruded upon their home lives as little as possible, and did not mix their student friendships with their home lives. While seeking some domestic support from partners they tried to ensure their own domestic input left partners and children unaffected by their other commitments. They did not expect, or want, their partners to show an interest in what they were learning or even in the more social aspects of being a student. They did not discuss what they were learning with their children and did not feel their academic knowledge had affected the way they brought up their children, other than perhaps acting as a role model. They were aware of making efforts not to show off their academic knowledge within the home and in personal relationships with partners or parents, but felt that education had given them a greater confidence when dealing with public officials or professionals.

Mixing Connections and Separations of Education and Family

These women fell between the connecting and separating approaches just outlined. For instance, they may have discussed what they were learning with their partners but not with their parents, and not have wanted to let home life experiences feed into their academic learning. They may have watched, and encouraged their children to watch, different types of television programmes but made efforts not to use academic language when talking. They may have wanted their student friends to visit their homes, but did not look for a less contract-based relationship with lecturers.

There were no particular patterns to these women's separations or connections except in one aspect. Crucially, the women who mixed connections and separations shared with those who separated education and family a sense of having two different parts to their lives. The separation was not so complete between the worlds because they did allow varying amounts of overspill. Importantly, they did not value having a separate identity in the same way as did the women who separated education and family. They sensed that they were 'switching hats' when they moved from the education institution to their family and back again, but this was because switching on and off felt like the only way of coping with the demands of the two areas.

Shifting Patterns on a continuum

There are difficulties in being precise about the number of mature women students who fit each of the above ideal types. There are several reasons for this. Few of the women's accounts accorded with all of the aspects of the patterns for the typology of connection and separation. Jennie (white working-class), for example, had all of the aspects of separation of education and family in her account of her experiences, bar some disappointment that she had not had more affective relationships with other students. A central feature of her account, however, was that she valued the other separations and enjoyed having an identity as a student that was distinct from that of her family identity as a mother and a wife. Lynne (white middle-class), on the other hand, had all the aspects of connections of education and family in her account except for a lack of desire for any more personally-based contact with lecturers.

It is probably more helpful to view the typology as a continuum made up of three linked strands, as shown in figure 7.1.

Figure 7.1: Education–family continuum

Connection of education and family	Connection with some aspects of separation	Mix of connections and separations of education and family	Separation with some aspects of connection	Separation of education and family

- -

valuing - - - - - - - - - - - - - - coping - - - - - - - - - - - - - - - valuing

- -

Integrated student and mother/partner identity	Distinct student and mother/partner identities

The top strand indicates the daily and actual aspects of connection and separation on both mental and physical levels, such as feeding the experiences in both worlds into each other. The bottom strand indicates identity within connection and separation, ranging from women viewing themselves as simultaneously both students and mother/partners to envisaging themselves almost as different people in different places. The middle strand represents the women's evaluations of this position; at either end placing a value on connection/integrated identity or on separation/distinct identities, but in the middle seeing a mixture of connections and separations with distinct identities as a way of coping rather than valuable.

Women could thus be located at various points along the overall continuum. At the time of their last interviews, sixteen women could be grouped towards the connecting end of the continuum, nine around the middle, and six towards the separating end of the continuum. If what the women actually did at this point in time alone is looked at, half the mature women students could be said to have education and family in their lives by connecting them, with the other half being proportionally more inclined towards some connections. Further complications are introduced, however, if what the women would have wanted is taken into account, as against their description of what actually occurred. Two factors in particular could affect this: geographical separation and, more importantly, their partners. Both produced a greater weighting towards the separating end of the continuum.

The geographical distance between the institutions the women attended and their homes operated not only in terms of physical miles; it also created some form of mental separation, even where this was not necessarily looked for. Geographical separation could therefore feed a separation of education and family life. Five women lived an hour or more's travelling time from their education institutions (although it was the nearest institution for all but one of them) and all commented to some extent on a separating effect. Wendy (white working-class), for example, travelled forty miles to and from the polytechnic. Although several of her student friends did occasionally make the journey to her home (thus becoming a small part of her home life) she felt that she would have become much more involved in her studies generally and socialized a lot more if it were not for the distance. Wendy felt that she was not a different person in the institution to the way she was at home. She did, however, feel that the geographical distance meant that there was some mental distance between the different parts of her life and she wished that this was not so:

> I suppose other people see it as two different lives, you know, sort of thing, but I don't. I thought, I sort of thought about it at first, you know. I thought, you know will I be a different person when I'm up there sort of thing? . . . It's just sort of two parts of my life really, you know. I think it's the distance more than anything, you know, it sort of being so far away.

Wendy also felt that if she had lived nearer to the institution and to other students her relationship with her husband would have become more strained. At the end of her first year her connective approach to the majority of the aspects of her education was revealing her husband's lack of interest in her studies.

This highlights another difference between what the women would ideally have liked and what they felt actually was the case — the role of their partners in their connections or separations. As already indicated, over time several of the women shifted to different points along the continuum. These shifts were either evident in their retrospective accounts (if final year or graduate students) or could be seen in the differences between their descriptions of their lives at the beginning and end of their first year of full-time higher education. Five women indicated that they had shifted (or in one case, intended to shift) along the continuum from connections towards a more separating approach to education and family over the period of their studies. Three women's accounts (all first year students) showed that they had moved towards a more connective approach over the year. All the women who made shifts spoke of serious problems in their relationships with their partners, and of their partners being threatened in the various ways outlined in the previous chapter. Those who moved towards connection spoke of conflicts with their partners that did not seem to have existed prior to their shift. Another nine women also talked of conflicts and threatened partners, and these women were part of the group towards the connecting and integrated identity end of the continuum. Connection of education and family was thus closely associated with conflict with partners. Only two women appeared to be able to connect up their educational and family lives continually with no repercussions for their relationships with their partners. Another was able to connect as much as she could (given the distance she lived from the institution) because her husband worked away from home during the week. As was mentioned in Chapter 6, no women appeared to make shifts towards separation of education and family because of their children's reactions to their studies. The role of the women's partners in creating a greater weighting towards the separation end of the continuum is thus a crucial one.

When such shifts are taken into account, just under two-thirds of the women (twenty) had, at least at some stage, taken a strongly connecting approach towards having education and family coexisting in their lives — or would have done so if they felt that they could. As will be discussed further below, if shifts towards connections or separations were to take place, these tended to occur around the end of the women's first year of study. This first year would seem, logically enough, to be a crucial period for setting the women's orientation. It was also an important time for any ramifications for their relationships with their partners.

Ending Relationships

The women who moved towards connecting education and family did so as part of wanting to be 'one person' — an issue that will be returned to later. Those women who moved towards connection, and those who continuously connected education and family, did not perceive separating the two worlds as an option, even if they acknowledged that their partners felt threatened. They just did not see how anyone could possibly have two separate identities. Instead, these women continued their attempts to draw their partners into a sharing of their education in ways that the majority of their partners did not appreciate. Apart from the two men who never appeared threatened, only two women's partners eventually responded positively to this continued connection:

I've seen him change in that three years while I was doing the degree . . . You know, I mean he really took it very personally in the end. And he was absolutely so sunk in this degree, you know, with me (Marcia, a 'mixed' race woman).

If attempts at sharing and connection did not work, one way out of the situation was for the women's relationships to come to an end. This happened to a quarter (eight) of the women. The final figure may, however, be higher. Those last interviewed at the end of their first year of study, who were undergoing problems, may have experienced their relationships with their partners ending later on. Wendy, for example, was unsure that her relationship with her husband would last in the long-term, and continued contact with one of the women means I am aware that her relationship broke up towards the end of her second year. Of those whose relationships had ended, most (six women) experienced the breakup sometime during their first year of study. One woman's relationship, however, finally finished towards the end of her second year. Another waited until she had graduated to end a relationship that she felt had been unsatisfactory, in terms of her partner's support and interest, for most of her time as a student. These women's partners had, as reported by the women, been obstructive to their integrating education into their family lives. Maureen (black working-class), for example, had felt herself to be a different and separate person at the polytechnic to the way she was at home:

Mixing with friends and family I'm more outgoing. I'm more sort of, you know, optimistic. A bit friendlier, you know. I think I'm a bit more serious at college because I want to get down to business.

She spoke, however, of her student self gradually coming home with her because 'switching on and off' did not seem right to her. Maureen did not directly link this to the ending of her relationship with her live-out boyfriend, but did feel that he was threatened by her becoming more knowledgeable about things.

The women thus saw no option but the end of their relationships with their partners, even though five of the relationships had been in existence for nine years or much longer. None said that they had originally sought a breakup when they entered full-time study, and only half of them felt that they had actively initiated the split when the conflict between themselves and their partners had become too great (the other half feeling that their partners had left them). As Stella (white, middle-class) remarked:

As it turned out it [doing the degree] was in competition with my relationship, but that isn't why I did it. I didn't do it because I had a bad relationship.

'Saving' Relationships

Those who moved from connection and integration towards separation and a feeling that they had two different identities, appeared to have done so in order to avoid or remedy problems in their relationships with their partners. As has been said, shifts from connections towards separations were never associated with the women having problems with their children alone. The sense of having two different lives was not one these women ideally wanted or that they valued. Although they were aware of making shifts in the ways they separated or connected their education and family lives, they often appeared not to link these shifts to saving their deteriorating relationships with their partners. Cathy (white middle-class), for instance, at the end of her first year, spoke of her boyfriend's lack of interest in her studies. At the beginning of the year she had felt him to be supportive, while not ecstatic, over her decision to become a full-time student. By the end, however, she felt that he was 'threatened' by her gaining an education, and said that their relationship was not as good as it had been when she started studying. She then, in another context, mentioned that she thought it would be better if she started separating off education:

> I think I'm going to have to be a lot firmer with myself. In fact I envisage spending a bit more time actually up at the poly and not coming home quite so quickly. Making use of the library facilities and things like that more, rather than feeling that I've got to sort of get a load of books and bring them all home.
>
> RE: Why do you think to do that?
>
> Because I think it would sort of make me do — be more likely to sort of get it out of the way and know that the time I've got left when I get home is free time.

Janice (white working-class) was unusual in being very clear about the link between the two — although she couched it in terms that referred to what was best for her rather than her husband. This may be because her account was a retrospective one, given after she had graduated:

> I made a conscious effort to keep the two lives totally separate. I no longer discussed what was going on, about what I was studying. It was more — anything that was discussed was about people that Cliff or the kids had met as well. But otherwise it was totally separate worlds.
>
> RE: Did you feel comfortable with that?
>
> No. No. I felt hurt that what I was interested in wasn't being supported. But at the time it seemed necessary to keep those two worlds separate because otherwise I think the conflict would have deepened . . . At the end why I separated it was because I felt I was, and still am, so determined, that I isolated it for my own protection to a certain extent because I didn't want the end and I knew he didn't want it either.

Janice felt that this shift in the way she had education and family coexisting in her life occurred towards the end of her first year of study. As already stated, for all the women for whom shifts in their patterns of connections and separations can be identified, this was around the time they took place. Again, most of those who had always kept their educational and family lives largely separate did not link their construction of distinct identities and worlds to a lack of conflict with their partners. Only two women who had continuously almost completely separated the two made such a link. Victoria (white middle-class), for example, at the end of her third year of study, was clear on this point, and intended to continue: 'I shall go on keeping, trying to keep, I don't know, a bit of distance between my home life my work and things'.

The women who separated their educational and family lives and selves seemed slightly more prone to be aware of what they were doing — almost as if it required conscious effort. Those women who moved towards connection, and those who continuously connected education and family, did not see how anyone could possibly have two separate identities. Women who connected their education and family — by far the majority initially — were therefore much more likely to just *be* a partner/mother/student without consciously splitting themselves between these two areas of their lines. This, taken in conjunction with discussions of time and of the divisions of labour within the private sphere in previous chapters, has ramifications for the ways we think about women's lives and women themselves.

'Strategy' and the 'Feminine Psyche'

Education and family required, and were perceived as requiring, very different things of the women. The ways of being a student in full-time higher education, and a female partner and mother, are socially constructed. These social constructions, as has been elucidated, are built around different value bases and assumptions that can be in conflict: the one objective, impersonal, unemotional and abstract, the other subjective, personal, emotional and anecdotal. The women regarded their part in family life and relationships as caring, represented by emotional, time and energy commitments. Their way of knowing things about their families was the result of the everyday process of caring about and for them. Higher education's knowledge was mainly about 'getting above' personal ways of knowing, and knowing within higher education was not necessarily linked to caring. Moreover, both education and family are greedy institutions which demand that women fulfill their different requirements to the full. The women wanted to, and attempted to, meet these requirements. The typology of separations and connections and the continuum of women's movements between them, set out above, could, therefore, be argued to be 'strategies' women may adopt in order to allow the two potentially conflicting and greedy institutions of higher education and family to coexist in their lives. Put starkly, women may either try to keep on top of the greediness of each and prevent clashes of values by separating them physically and mentally into different compartments; or they may attempt to amalgamate their greeds, so that feeding one is also feeding the other, and to meld their different value bases into one. There are, however, certain implications in using the word strategy to describe the women's experiences for a public and an academic audience — implications that echo aspects of the women's experiences within the public and academic world.

A Strategy or a Concern with Process?

The concept of strategy has been widely used as an explanatory device when looking at the ways in which women manage and work with particular situations. Julia Brannen and Peter Moss (1988) have described the com-partmentalizing attitudes towards home and employment on the part of new mothers returning to paid work as a 'strategy' adopted in order to manage the conflicting demands of being both mothers and full-time workers. Janet Finch (1983a) writes of wives utilizing 'coping strategies' for fitting their lives around the incorporating demands of their husbands' paid work, and Hilary Graham (1987) also designates the ways lone mothers use their greater powers of control (once without their male partners) over fewer material resources as 'coping strategies'. Laura Balbo (1987) argues women spend their lives continually putting together 'survival strategies' for themselves and their families. Many other examples of the use of the term strategy to explain aspects of women's lives could be cited (see Crow, 1989, for some of them).

The use of strategy as a means of analyzing social situations, however, carries all sorts of baggage and assumptions derived from its basis in masculinist activities and understandings. As such, the concept has the potential to undermine women's lives and understandings, and, for reasons discussed more fully else-where (Edwards and Ribbens, 1991), I do not use it to describe the typology and continuum of ways women may have both education and family coexisting in their lives. In using the term strategy as a description of the ways women deal with particular situations — including ways that, at first sight, may appear irrational and unacceptable — writers may be seeking to legitimate, and thus empower, women's actions and women themselves. They are, nevertheless, imposing a particular, and a particularly loaded, pattern of order upon women whose lives may well be founded upon a very different pattern.

This process, as will be discussed in relation to the mature women students, reflects the position of women with family responsibilities in the public world generally. Jane Ribbens and I have suggested that, because public world audiences are being addressed (particularly policy-makers) in the presentation of research findings, public world values and norms are invoked, using discourses that are derived from masculinist spheres of activity. In a similar vein, Dorothy Smith (1989) has written of the ways in which sociological discourse is often privileged above the actual discursive world in academic accounts of people's lives, in such a way that those whose lives are described fail to recognize them. In this sense, the ultimate effect of the use of the term strategy in relation to women's lives, particularly as it takes place in domestic settings, may be to distort, undermine and ultimately erode their own understandings and priorities. This has been shown to be the position of the mature women students within the education institutions. Their knowledge, gained within the private sphere, was often not acceptable as a legitimate way of knowing within academia (irrespective of whether or not they themselves wished to use local and particular knowledge in this way). Their position as working-class or black women, particularly, could be distorted or ignored. The point is one that has been made before by Margaret Stacey (1981) — that sociological language and concepts are rooted in public world understandings. Moreover, as was indicated in Chapter 5, the holders of knowledge generated in the private world have little status in the public world, unless they can also lay claim to a place of status in the public world (see also Edwards, 1993b). Admittedly, the term strategy would have allowed the attribution, to the women, of a sense of rational control over lives shaped by the often conflicting requirements of two very different institutions. There are, though, other problems, in addition to, and following on from, those outlined above.

The use of strategy to describe the ways that the mature women students had education and family coexisting in their lives places a focus upon the women themselves as successfully or unsuccessfully managing the two. Education institutions and the press have been interested in the research that forms the basis of this book. I have, for example, been asked whether or not marriage guidance facilities should be available within institutions and what advice I would give to mature women students. Indeed, several studies of mature students suggest that counselling facilities would help solve many of their problems (for example, see Osborn, Charnley and Withnall's, 1981, review). The questions, their answering, and the emphasis on counselling, imply that it is the women who must learn the appropriate strategy for managing education and family — albeit with professional help — drawing attention towards individuals rather than the institutions whose values and ethos are so contraposed. Moreover, my advice would have to assume that mature women students have certain ends in sight (other than gaining a degree), especially in relationships with their partners, which they then attempt to work towards. As has been said, this was rarely the case. The women were far more likely to orient themselves in particular socio-emotional ways rather than to pursue a goal.

The presence of clear and explicit large-scale goals contained within the concept of strategy implies that activities are directed towards goals. Activities are largely assumed to be means–ends motivated within rational frameworks. As Bernice Fisher and Joan Tronto argue, however, women's experience of caring within family life particularly, sits uneasily with motivations based on public realm rational, autonomous goal-direction: 'caring is about an orientation rather than a motivation' (Fisher and Tronto, 1990, p. 42). Only a minority of the mature women students (five) could be said to have recognized themselves as doing anything over and above just being mothers/partners and students, going about the everyday processes of their lives in the way they felt they should and to the best of their abilities. Even those few who were aware that they were being a certain way for a particular purpose or goal — that of keeping their relationships with their partners on an even keel — were still more concerned with the actual process. Jennie's (white working-class) explanation of how 'on the way home I sort of gradually switch from student-mode to mummy-mode' illustrates this point. She had initially not switched 'modes' because 'I was full of it [being a student], I thought it was great'. Her husband, however, she felt, had reacted to her enthusiasm by becoming depressed. Jennie had stopped being so 'full of it' at home, rarely discussing her studies with her husband. Having made this shift, her concern was the mode; the daily concerns and the process of being each.

Being a mother/partner and being a student may well be moulded by social expectations. Yet these social constructions of motherhood/partnership and studentship also contain the element of just being these things (even if they are, in the event, conflictual). The idea of adopting a strategy (other than attempting to be organized) was not something the majority of the women would even have recognized as appropriate in describing how they moved between family and education. Taking an overall, retrospective view, one might discern particular connecting or separating strategies and their outcomes in terms of the women's relationships with their partners. Yet for the women themselves the effects of the different ways they moved between education and family were, certainly initially for some and for the majority continued to be, unintended outcomes rather than goals they worked towards. Their only aim was to move between the two — a process rather than an end.

Process and Female Difference

The fact that the women themselves did not use, or would not necessarily recognize, the term 'strategy' as applicable is not a reason for abandoning it. The fact that the concept imputed a public world type of rationality with regard to outcomes, while the women's adoption of strategies could be said to bear only a limited relationship to any actual outcomes of their connections, separations and so on, is a valid reason. This is not to imply that the public world is rational and the domestic/women are irrational — just that domestic rationality has to be understood on its own terms, with goals that are linked to processes rather than means and ends:

> Men are socialised according to a means–ends rationality, where efficiency is the basic aim or value. By contrast, women are the typical bearers of rationality of care (care for and with human beings . . .). The concept of rationality takes on a different meaning when women's reality is considered (Lie, 1990, p. 110).

Others have also noted an orientation towards socio-emotional process on the part of mothers, even if just in passing. Berry Mayall (1990) stresses mothers' concern with 'now' and the give and take of daily living with their children, as against health visitors' emphasis on children's developmental stages. Brannen and Moss (1991) remark upon the concern of mothers in full-time paid work being rooted in the process of combining motherhood and full-time work, rather than with long-term career goals.[1] Arguments that women's rationality, as a concern with process for its own sake, is different from men's may also be supported by studies of helpseeking in marital disputes (Brannen and Collard, 1982; Hunt, 1985). These studies show that wives tend to hope for help which will be emotionally supportive (process), while husbands tend to look for advice and programmes of action (means–ends). The concern of the mature women students was, too, as has been said, to *be* a mother/partner and student in the ways they thought and felt fit to the best of their abilities. It was a concern with processes rather than goals; with activities and ways of being which are regarded as valuable in their own right, rather than as means to ends. This view largely held even when they switched their mode of being due to their partners' reactions to their studies (in terms of daily process, if not in terms of valuing). Moreover, most of the women had tried to connect up their educational and family lives and those who had desisted would have wanted, under ideal circumstances, to continue in this way. This would seem to come down, in the main, on the affiliative feminine psyche side of the ideological tension between connecting education and family, rather than on the side of separation of education and family in order to maintain a boundary between public and private spheres. Most of the women did not want to compartmentalize their lives in the way that men are commonly held to do.

It may well be, however, that even men and the public sphere are not totally means–ends motivated, and that they just present themselves in a way that conceals from view emotions and being. Feminist arguments that academic objectivity is merely a masculinist cover for subjectivity come to mind here. Furthermore, when it comes to women, a concern with process does not necessarily exclude compartmentalization as well. Attempts at a firm resolution of this question of women/process/connections as contraposed to men/means–ends/compartmentalization are beyond the scope of this book, particularly as it contains only women's accounts. Mature men students' ways of having education and family coexisting in their own lives cannot therefore be compared.

Differences and Being 'Different'

The issues of separation and connection were there for all of the women. No particular type of relationship seemed prone to ending as compared to another: three marriages came to an end (all first marriages), three cohabitations (all after a previous divorce), and two live-out relationships. No definite overall class and race patterns can be discerned either. When it came to the women feeling that their lives as students and as mothers/partners were divisible or indivisible, white and black women, and working-class and middle-class women, were just as likely to want connections and integrations, or just as less likely to want separations and distinctions. The sense of the privacy of what went on in the private sphere, in their relationships and in the home itself, varied among the women, as did their ideas on the extent to which educational and family knowledge fed into each other. These variations mainly were unrelated to the women's race and class, although the black women could be particularly conscious of the privacy of the details of their lives when asked to take part in interviews (Edwards, 1990b). The women's race and class also played a part in how they regarded themselves and their knowledge as placed within the public world of higher education particularly.

It would appear that more structural factors, such as race and class, asserted themselves in the women's relationships to public world knowledge, public world institutions and so on. They were, however, not so significant in their private world relationships, especially those with partners, and in their initial orientation to separation or connection. Regardless of race or class, the women could want, not want, or come to not look for, their partners' interest in what they were doing. Their partners seemed to be perceived as threatened, whatever their class or race, in much the same ways: by violations of the mental and physical privacy of the haven of the home, by a lack of attention from the women; and by the women's educational success. These threats appeared to be to their partners as *men*, which would imply that the factor of sex was of importance here, rather than race or class. In the private sphere and people's relationships within it, the more public world definitions of race and class are less significant. It is their gendered roles as partners and mothers that are relevant. Again, because no mature men students were included, it is not possible to be definite about this. Certainly men's family relationships can be disrupted and threatened if they become mature students (see Kirk, 1977). Whether or not the threats operate in the same way as for women is an open question. Would mature men students perceive their female partners as threatened by their success, for example? Would their female partners place such stress on the mental and physical privacy of the home as the male partners of the mature women students appeared to do, and would they resent the men's attention being directed elsewhere? Would some of their female partners resort to violence? And would race or class also play as little part in these threats and in these aspects of men's separations or connections as it has for the mature mother students?

Race did, however, appear to play an overt part for one of the black women in her relationship with her partner. Beverley had connected up her educational and family lives and had parted from her husband shortly after returning to full-time higher education. At the end of her first year, however, she indicated that she was moving towards a more separating approach to some aspects of education and family. For example, she was not so bent on integrating her lived experience with her academic learning, at least in the institutional sense. She started writing two essays for every one required to be handed in: '[One essay is] what you feel and what you know, and then write another one, you know, and give in the other one!' Moreover, her relationship with her estranged husband seemed to be moving towards a form of living-out. She also said that she had decided to stop the divorce proceedings she had instituted in case this was perceived as him no longer being 'good enough' for her, it seemed, as a black male:

> Because I'm interested in black issues, that again it — it's not coinciding with what I'm doing, you know. In your marital relationship, it's not ... There's a mixture of, a mixture of guilt, yeah, a mixture of identification ... [I stopped the divorce because] it's going against a whole lot of other things, you know. And at the moment you feel to finalize that would be like saying because I'm moving on in this, you know, this way you're not acceptable any more, and it's not that, you know.

Underlying Beverley's words seemed to be a sense of keeping solidarity with black people. Indeed, an area where race and class did play a part was in black and white working-class women's worries that education would somehow move them apart from their peers in an élitist way.

Friendships — Race and Class

Friendships between women, especially as mothers, are fully part of neither the private or public spheres. In some ways they could be said to mediate between them and, as an ambiguity, point up the difficulties of conceptualizing the two as dichotomies. There is now a growing literature on friendships, including studies concentrating on women's friendships. (For a review of many of them, see Allan, 1989, and Bell and Ribbens, 1993, forthcoming). A detailed examination of them is beyond the scope of this discussion. What is of importance here is the perceptions of the mature women students with regard to their relationships with friends, as affected by their education. These views point to particular differences between the women on the basis of race and class, and highlight their sense of being different generally (in the sense of deviancy) because they were students. Friendships, as Graham Allan (1989) argues, must be understood within their social context. They are influenced by social and material factors lying outside of the relationship itself.

While most (seven) of the white middle-class women had friends who had studied, often at degree level, the majority of the black and the white working-class women (five and nine, respectively) did not have many friends who had any experience of further or higher education. The women who had friends with degrees could usually share their experiences as a student with those friends. The women without such shared experiences often talked of not letting their friends become aware of their academic knowledge in case they were then regarded differently:

> I can relate to things more on the TV, you know, than like before when I was at home doing nothing. My friends think I've changed, you know . . . I find that I can't — if I start saying to them anything — we look at the telly and if something great's coming on like a documentary, I wouldn't say anything although I know something about it, you know. Maybe turn over, look at something else . . . I don't show them that I know much, you know, more than them or anything (Anna, a black woman).

Allan emphasizes the way in which notions of equality shape friendship relationships: 'Friendship is a bond in which issues of hierarchy and authority have no bearing' (1989, p. 20). Broad similarity of status, circumstances, background, orientation to life and so on, provide firm groundings for friendships. Any contradictions of such equalities through an altering of one person's status in relation to another, such as becoming far more educated, can mean that maintaining the friendship can become problematic. Indeed, several studies of women returning to full-time education show that they tend to lose contact with their previous friends (Levy, 1981; Suitor, 1987).

Being regarded as 'snobbish', 'stuck-up', or 'stand-offish', and being 'ostracized' because of their education, was a possibility mentioned by the majority of the black and the white working-class women, but only a third of the white middle-class women. As was noted in Chapter 5, the former were concerned to mention that gaining a higher education did not make them 'better' than people who did not have such an education. The women were quite happy to be told by other people that they were, and to think of themselves as, 'more confident', but they were unwilling to believe that they had changed in other ways. That is, while they valued and wanted the status that higher education gave them, they could find it difficult to deal with the ramifications of this:

> I mean I won't go round and say to someone, 'Oh, I'm doing a degree'. But, you know, if they do sort of realize I'm doing a degree they sort of think, you know, she's sort of either, not snobbish, but, you know, sort of up there and we're down there. Which isn't, you know, that's not me at all (Wendy, a white working-class woman).

This seems to mirror the position the women had previously seen themselves in with regard to public institutions and professionals. They had often regarded doctors, social workers, social security officials and so on, as 'up there', but felt that doing a social science degree had led them to understand the workings of 'the system'. They were able to question the place and expertise of the people operating 'the system'. The women no longer regarded themselves as 'down there'. This realization, however, left them in a different position from those who were still 'down there' — and those people were their former peers. Now it was the women themselves who might be regarded as 'up there' by their friends and acquaintances.

Education could thus threaten their friendships in the same way that it did their other intimate relationships, if they pursued any connections between education and friends:

> There have been people that I no longer see because we don't have anything in common any more. That sounds terribly snobbish and I don't mean it to. But like, for example, the girl next door . . . I mean she's very heavily involved in programmes like *The Bill* and *The Equaliser*, and all that kind of stuff. And I can't talk about — I don't watch them, I don't like them, and I think they present a false image anyway. And so I was saying, 'I don't really think that's a very fair example of how life is'. And I didn't see her again. She didn't ask me back and I didn't go back (Alexandra, a white working-class woman).

Similarly the women spoke of a lack of time in which to give friends the amount of attention they had done prior to their studies. Friendships could die off because of this, particularly if the women felt their education now meant they had little in common to talk about. While friends could prove supportive and interested in the women's studies regardless of their own educational level, separation, in the form of not discussing what they were doing and showing off their knowledge to friends, could be a way of allowing education and friendship to coexist. This was a course some women were more prepared to pursue with friends than they were with partners, even if ideally they would have liked to share their educational experiences. Helen (white working-class) had parted from her live-out boyfriend because she could not discuss what she was learning and her course generally with him, and yet with some of her friends she was prepared to avoid such topics for the sake of the friendship:

> Anything political, anything like that, I just don't talk about it. It's a no-go area . . . because of how they react and everything I'd just rather leave the subject alone.

The black and white working-class women often regarded themselves as now being able to talk and reason, as Sandra (black) put it, 'on a different level' — a level that was one many of their friends could not relate to. They could end up feeling themselves to be 'cut off' from the women they had previously regarded as the same as them:

> I mean especially when I went out during the summer holidays to work, I mean the people that I, you know, met like in the offices where I temped, it was just awful . . . It's really petty and I think god, I couldn't

stand this. You know, I just wouldn't fit. It's this feeling that you don't fit anymore . . . If I'd stayed like most women — I mean I don't feel I've got anything in common with some women of my age, or a certain group. There are a whole section of women that I meet that I feel I've got absolutely nothing in common with (Jenny, a white working-class woman).

This was particularly so for white working-class women. Although white middle-class women also thought of themselves as thinking about issues in a different way, they were now able to join their friends who had degrees: 'The fact that most of the people I knew were graduates and made assumptions that I was, and I felt I was lacking something' (Angela, a white middle-class woman). Friendships are important providers and maintainers of people's sense of social identity and belonging. The black women could still identify themselves as black, while the white working-class women especially could end up unsure of their class position and allegiances now they were educated.

As Geoff Payne and Pamela Abbott (1990) note, theorists concerned with class have paid little attention to the meanings of social mobility for people (as well as being gender-blind). Nicola Charles (1990), however, has explored some of these subjective, experiential aspects for women. She found that women's own background was of great importance to them, with inter-generational consistency giving them a clear sense of the class to which they belonged. If the women themselves broke this consistency, by being the first in a working-class family to go on to higher education for instance, they were left with a sense of belonging nowhere in class terms. Other studies (Heath and Britten, 1984; Abbott, 1987) have also indicated that level of education is important in relation to women's subjective class — the likelihood of a woman assigning herself to the middle-class increases with the level of education she attained.[2] The working-class mature women students could be said to be shifting at least their potential social class position, subjective and occupational, by gaining a degree level education; which was not always a comfortable process. Jenny, a white woman from a working-class background who had graduated, spoke about a particular instance that had brought it home to her:

When they come at the door and knock and interview, 'What does your husband do?' I said, 'I'm working-class, he's an electrician'. They look at me, you know. I said, 'Don't you want to know what I do?' Now why should it be his? Why should he classify what we are? I'm an academic, I have a degree, I'm a BSc.

The 'Pain of Being Different'

Whatever their friendship perceptions, all the women felt a sense of doing something unusual, perhaps even deviant. The women felt this within the higher education institution and they felt it outside of it; they were out on a limb on all sides. Within higher education they were not proper full-time students; students are not people with family responsibilities. Outside of the higher education institutions the women were different as well. Other mothers did not do the sort of thing they were doing.

Why were they students 'at your age, isn't it a bit late?' Why didn't they just get a job and earn some money instead of being so self-indulgent? These were comments the women often either reported that they had received from people, or that they themselves felt people were thinking even if they were not voicing them. Some of them had been told by friends, parents and so on, that they were 'mad', 'crazy', 'flipped my lid', for either giving up a paid job in order to be a student on a full-time degree course, or for not being satisfied with being a full-time mother and partner. Many, as we have seen, felt that nobody other than students in a similar position to themselves could possibly understand what they were doing and the pressures they were under. The women felt that they were forever having to justify what they were doing, both to others and to themselves. Some of the women (nine) also spoke of encouraging others to study (friends, partners, children, parents, women they spoke to in shops and so on) perhaps in an effort to make what they were doing less unusual, more within the sights of any woman-in-the-street: 'I always encourage women that I meet to — you know, often women say, "Oh, I'd love to do that". I say, "Well, go and do it"' (Jenny, a white working-class woman).

Enid Hutchinson and Edward Hutchinson (1986), in their study of women on Fresh Horizons courses, comment that those women who continued on to be full-time students in higher education set themselves apart from their contemporaries, and that relatives and friends often found these women's actions incomprehensible. In his preface to Earl Hopper and Marilyn Osborn's book on mature students, Ralf Dahrendorf writes of the 'people who have chosen an arduous way towards improving their life chances'; that 'in short, they are different, and being different hurts' (Hopper and Osborn, 1975, unpaginated). This is so for the women whose experiences have been explored in this book. They were different, and being different could be painful at times. Being different may, however, also have been something that the women recreated. In Chapter 3 it was noted that many of the women spoke of themselves as somehow set apart from their peers in their childhoods. There was something different about themselves and their families, most often spoken about in terms of their standing *vis-à-vis* the rest of their peer group and the community. Usually they were different because of their higher status in some ways — for instance, a car and telephone when not many others had them, the ability to read and write, a father in a white collar job and so on. And yet these things were not to be boasted about. Echoes of this situation occur in the women's accounts of not flaunting their new knowledge in front of friends. Perhaps the women were used to feeling different to others in some way from childhood, and this contributed towards propelling them into higher education later on in their lives; placing them once again in the position of difference and a different status. On the other hand, it may have been that, feeling themselves apart from their peers now, in their retrospective reconstructions of their childhood histories the women may have rewritten their positions so as to fit with their present perspectives.

This scenario, however, is not just about the women's psychological make-up; about their identities and consciousnesses only. Separations, connections and feelings of difference on the part of mature women students are not about personality types, but about a social system and social contexts that require certain behaviours and attitudes of women and which mean that women have particular personal and institutional experiences. The women's position within the higher education system and the individualizing hidden curriculum within higher education may well have contributed to this feeling of difference.

Notes

1 Brannen and Moss (1991) argue that on one level this attitude was because the women were highly oriented to the long-term planning of the lives of their children, but that on another level ideologies of marriage discouraged them from addressing long-term resource issues. Brannen and Moss, though, are themselves not addressing the issue of caring as a concern with process.
2 As most of the women in these studies seem to have had an unproblematic journey through the education system, this self-assignation, of course, also relates to the occupations they enter and maybe, therefore, to the men they meet and marry (Abbott and Sapsford, 1987).

Chapter 8

Equality in Different Worlds?

In the first chapter of this book a question was posed: does higher education have any effect upon women's placing in the public sphere, and upon their placing as partners and mothers within the private sphere? The women felt that they had gained confidence through being students in higher education. They regarded the status higher education gave them in their own and others' eyes as making a difference to the way they approached, and to the way they were treated by, public world officials. The power balance between themselves and those in authority was perceived as having shifted. Yet, within the higher education institutions themselves many of the women felt deviant, with some of their experiences devalued. Additionally, as will be seen, many of those who graduated found it difficult to find paid work they felt was commensurate with their graduate status. Their family responsibilities still constrained the type of employment they undertook. Indeed, little had changed with regard to the women's responsibilities within the private sphere as a result of their education. Their studies did, however, have some implications for the power balances between themselves and their male partners within their private worlds, although not in the ways that this is often conventionally measured.

This final chapter is concerned with questions of equality; in particular equality of experience within higher education and equality between men and women within 'the family'. The implications for teaching mature women students, and indeed all students, within higher education are examined. The women's separations and connections, their feelings of difference, and the problems that arise for them, can only be addressed if there is a flexible democratization of knowledge within higher educational institutions. The effects of the women gaining an education for themselves upon their position within their families, especially in relation to their partners, is then, finally, explored. Any effects must be viewed in the context of the women's active receipt of higher education, and within the context of the value bases of the social institutions that shape their lives.

Equality in the Public Sphere

Many of the women had mentioned factors surrounding their sex, race and class as responsible for low expectations of, and by them, educationally, during their period of initial schooling. Paralleling their experiences in higher education, the black women mainly perceived these low educational expectations in terms of race, while the white women felt these expectations operated in terms of their sex or, in the case of several of the white working-class women, sex combined with class. It would seem that once more in their lives the women's experiences made them feel they did not fit into the education system. Within higher education the women were not traditional students, coming straight to university or poly-technic from school after taking A-levels. Moreover, they had responsibilities other than studying, in the form of their families, which made demands upon their time, energy and attention. For those women who wanted to separate these family responsibilities and commitments, the higher education institutions reflected and reinforced this way of allowing education and family to coexist in their lives.

The women's private world knowledge was rarely valued nor, for the 'mixed' race, black and white working-class women, were their understandings often represented. In the previous chapter Michelle's (white working-class) shift with regard to connecting one of the aspects of education and family in her life was referred to. At the start of her first year of degree study she had talked about connecting up private and public knowledge. By the end, however, she regarded them as separate. This division could be linked to Michelle's worries that education might be potentially damaging to her relationship with her husband. She may have moved to a separation of the two in this area in order to protect it — although she did continue to discuss what she was learning with him. Another interpretation could be that, after a year of higher education, she was imbued with an ethos of public, academic knowledge as objective, impersonal and abstract. Links between relationships in the private sphere and higher education will be returned to again in the next section. On the other hand, the two-thirds of the women who, at least at some stage, desired connections between their education and family experiences found them difficult within the institution. This connection could even be just in the form of allowing their children to see where they studied. The lack of status accorded to their domestic roles within the institutions, as against public world roles such as paid or voluntary work, was again reflected and reinforced in the public world generally. The women felt that their status as students in higher education meant that public world professionals and others regarded them differently. They were listened to, and what they had to say accorded greater weight than it had been when they were just 'somebody's mum' or 'the woman behind the typewriter'. In the women's own eyes as well, higher education had status and gave them greater confidence when dealing with these public people. 'The system' had been demystified for them, and they could feel more confident even when simply taking faulty goods back to a shop.

Yet this can hardly be pointed to as equality within the public sphere. The women who had graduated sometimes found it difficult to gain employment. For example, three of the eight women who had already graduated when I first interviewed them had been looking for paid work unsuccessfully for over five months: 'Well, there's supposed to be a shortage of women, isn't there? They want the older woman back, but I can't see it happening. Not to me anyway' (June, a white working-class woman). Most ended up training for or taking traditional women's work in the caring professions. Of the fifteen graduate and third-year women (out of a total of twenty) who had obtained a place on a training course or paid work when I last interviewed them, two worked as playleaders, three were training for a job within primary or secondary education, three had gone into (untrained) social work, five had some form of clerical or administrative work, and two had found management posts within training agencies. Only six of these women had taken the type of paid work that they wanted to do, and that they regarded as a suitable reward for doing a degree. For the others, it was a question of who would have them and/or what fitted with their family responsibilities:

> I'm applying, for the moment, for local government, but I don't know. I'm applying for teaching as a sort of backstop . . . I mean you can always think of better things, but I mean, yeah, you are limited aren't you? I've got so many things against me (Jennie, a white working-class woman).

> I'm not sure that that's — teaching's what I want to do . . . I mean it's fairly good money for the — and convenient with the children for the holidays. I mean I hate to admit it but that is about the only reason I'm doing it (Victoria, a white middle-class woman).

These sorts of outcomes are consistent with other studies addressing mature students' job destinations (for example, Smithers and Griffin, 1986; Brennan and McGeevor, 1987).

That the women had not necessarily gained equality in the public world of paid work cannot be laid at the door of higher education alone. Indeed, as the women themselves acknowledged, the employment they took was not usually open to them before, and was often more interesting than the jobs they had done previously. Higher education does, however, bear some responsibility for the women's experiences as students.

Equality of Experience within Higher Education

Within the first chapter it was argued that higher education institutions were generally more concerned with increasing student numbers than with what students experienced once they were within the institutions. Higher education, as we have seen, could shut out the family side of the women's lives. It made similar greedy demands of the women as were made of students without their family responsibilities. The image most of the women held of being a student was that of the bachelor boy whose only other call upon his time apart from study is his leisure. The bachelor boy, however, should he wish to, can respond to the greedy demands of degree study at any time, and it was this image of being a student that the women strove to meet. They could end up blaming themselves for their inability to be organized enough to meet the standards set by this image. The women could also be disappointed in their expectations of higher education and of lecturers. The contractual nature of their relationships with lecturers, in particular, was a surprise to most of them, and yet this appears to be the direction in which higher education is moving.

There have been changes in how education institutions operate, from primary through to higher education:

> In a slow but clear fashion, the education institutions have taken on the characteristics of business rather than professional organizations for the pursuit of teaching and learning (David, 1989, p. 157).

Miriam David argues that along with the shift towards business characteristics within education has gone a concomitant shift towards, in the case of higher education, students making individual choices as consumers, and away from any form of equality of opportunity for unrepresented groups: 'Individualism and competitiveness as root values replace notions of academic community and scholarship' (David, 1989, p. 174). Despite moving with these shifts, higher education has done little to change the image held by the women of what being a student was about, either in its publicity or in its practice. At a time when institutions are concerned with their corporate image and with selling this image to business, industry and so on, it would seem that higher education generally could do with an effective public relations exercise concerning what a student within a business organization can expect.

There may, however, be other areas in which higher education — or at least social sciences within it — could change in order to promote some equality of opportunity. This change has often been argued for in the form of equality of opportunity for access to higher education (for example, the provision of crèche facilities). But the issue has also been addressed in the form of equality of opportunity of experience within higher education. Despite, or more likely because of, the image of a student that the women measured themselves against, the majority of them recognized that they were not equal to the traditional 18-year-old students once within higher education — either those that they studied alongside or their friends or partners who had been students at the 'proper' time.

There have been calls by some feminists and others for curriculum changes in order to deal with issues of equality of experience for women in education. Mary Belenky and colleagues (1986) argue that, for women's learning to be such that it empowers them, lecturers should take as their starting point not the discipline-based knowledge, but the student's knowledge. Students' work should not be evaluated against that of other students and the 'blind objectivity' of the discipline, but against the student's own past work. Forms of teaching presentation that hide from view the 'process of gestation' and present only a polished final product should be jettisoned. Belenky and colleagues, along with others such as Nell Noddings (1984) and Shulamit Reinharz (1984), have argued for an approach that treats the student as an independent subject, rather than as an object. Such an approach is said not to be opposed to objectivity, so long as this is not defined as self-extrication, but attempts to meld it with subjectivity. Belenky and colleagues:

> ... emphasize connection over separation, understanding and acceptance over assessment, and collaboration over debate ... accord respect to and allow time for the knowledge that emanates from firsthand experience ... instead of imposing [lecturers'] own expectations and arbitrary requirements ... encourage students to evolve their own patterns of work based on the problems they are pursuing (p. 229).

They add, 'These are the lessons we have learned in listening to women's voices' (p. 229).

Yet, if all the voices of the mature women students whose experiences are presented here are listened to, it must be recognized that a third of them were not keen to integrate at least their private family experiences with their studies (or vice versa), either in the learning that Belenky and colleagues are referring to, or in other ways. Additionally, more of the women eventually felt unable to connect their family and educational lives. Arguably this situation may to an extent have been the result of becoming socialized to higher educational values. In the main the women had entered higher education wanting something more than just an educational qualification for use in the market place. Admittedly, future employment opportunity was an important factor for the women. Many of them did, however, wish to be able to draw upon, and place in context, certain aspects of their own life experiences as part of the learning process within higher education. Nevertheless, some flexibility with regard to the extent of the connectedness of the personal with the academic should be allowed for.

Jenny Shaw, in her reconsideration of the development of the social sciences as led by the structure of the discipline (the 'ideas approach'), rather than by the 'structure' of those studying them, has urged a changed relationship between teaching and research. Shaw, too, argues for a 'democratization of knowledge' — this time as aided by placing research skills, utilized in the investigation of contemporary issues, at the core of the undergraduate curriculum. This is as against the traditional tendency to keep substantive topics and research methods separate (Gubbay, 1991). Shaw's argument is:

> . . . based on the recognition that in a comprehensive university there will be many older students who are ready to embark on research projects, and indeed do their degrees by dissertation much sooner than most 18-year-olds. A more investigative approach to social science would be more in tune with the needs and experiences of older students (1986, p. 217).

Additionally, Jane Ribbens (1991) argues that autobiographical work can be 'very effectively' used within academic courses to consider the meanings surrounding privately-based experiences, to examine existing publicly-based academic forms of knowledge and understandings, and to explore the relationship between individual experience and wider social patterns. She illustrates the practical way a course can be structured so as to allow personal experiences to be integrated into academic learning if the student so wishes.

Shaw's and Ribbens' proposals are both more concrete and allow for flexibility, as compared to many other advocates of curriculum change. Providing opportunities for all students to go deeply into areas that are of importance to them, providing them with the techniques to do so, and valuing these areas in the concrete way of assessment, would allow women who wished to do so to render visible their domestic and other experiences. It would also allow the pursuit of issues of sex, race and class, where women saw these factors as important, while not penalizing those who, for whatever reason, do not wish to make their private lives public. It is not only mature women and other students who may benefit from such curricular and epistemological changes; it has been argued they would enhance lecturers' intellectual development as well (Sperling, 1991).

Building degree level study around the requirements and needs of non-traditional, rather than around traditional, students may go part of the way towards enabling mature women students to experience equality of learning experience within higher education. It does, however, challenge some of the fundamental bases of higher education's structure in terms of epistemology and pedagogy. Moreover, whether or not such changes are achievable — whether equality of access and the mandates of business organizations such as higher education are compatible with equality of experience within the higher education system — is debatable. Nevertheless, while being a student within higher education remains constructed around bachelor boys, mature women students will always feel themselves to be deviants who fail to meet the greediness of the institution, and can never be proper students. This conclusion, of course, still leaves their deviancy from proper motherhood and inequalities within the private sphere unaddressed.

Equality in the Private Sphere: The Role of Higher Education

The language of equality, of sharing, tended to cover over inequalities within the women's relationships with their partners in the private sphere of their homes. It was only when the women's partners refused to share the women's education with them — to connect into it themselves — that inequalities in their relationships became clear to the women, and even then this process did not operate for all of them. Some women moved towards an approach to education and family in their lives which, because they no longer sought connections, no longer required their partners to respond to their studies. Some women never looked for their partners to share their education in the first place. While separations and connections could operate in the women's relationships with others, such as their children, within the private sphere, only their partners' reactions to their studies could cause them to shift their ways of having the two in their lives. If they did not shift, it was only their relationships with their partners, not with their children, that came to an end.

The ending of a long-term relationship between a man and a woman, especially where there are children present, is often viewed as something to be avoided. Particular interest groups have defined the significance of problems in these relationships in particular ways. Rendered as classifiable, reducible and, thereby, treatable, the problems are 'medicalized' (Morgan, 1985). The desire to define the nature of the problems, and thus prevent them, is a fairly recent phenomenon historically. Marriage in particular, and 'the family' generally, have latterly carried a heavy 'public script' (Clark and Haldane, 1990). They are invested with natural and traditional values, and with significance for the state of the nation overall:

> The family [has been elevated] to a high position of responsibility for the welfare of its members, for exercizing freedom of choice in the selection of private and/or state welfare provision — schools, health care, housing and so on — and for responsibility for morality, discipline and the transmission of British cultural values (Williams, 1989, p. 176).

Problems such as high divorce rates and lone parenthood thus become legitimate material for public debate and for social action because of their supposed threat to cherished values. For eight mature women students, however, the end of their relationships with their partners was not purely a problem, but was to a large extent a solution to a problem (whether they took this course themselves or their partners took it for them). For several other women it was either a potential solution that they had rejected, or was still an option for the future.

Ending relationships with partners was a solution to inequalities that could no longer be obscured in those relationships, and within which moves towards equality proved impossible. Michael Hardey (1990) states that the lone mothers whom he interviewed felt that any future partnership with a suitable man inevitably necessitated returning to conventional sex-based divisions of responsibility. He states that the women were keen to retain the control they had over their own family and home. In this case, both those women who had ended their relationships with their partners and those whose partners had left them also felt that they had regained control of their lives. Nevertheless, they all spoke of having a future relationship with another partner — this time, though, a relationship in which there was to be equality between them and the men: 'I certainly would go for different things. It would be on a much more level, equal footing' (Lynne, a white middle-class woman); 'I like men in my life. I don't want to cut myself off from men. But the new man, the man that sees women as an equal, not as somebody to be patronized' (Alexander, a white working-class woman). Unlike the lone mothers Hardey interviewed, these women could envisage relationships that did not mean a return to previous divisions of responsibility. Higher education had probably played some part in this.

All but one of the women spoke of higher education as giving them confidence. While for some this feeling could be termed a public confidence that operated in their dealings in the public world, for others it was a more private confidence that operated within their more personal relationships. Gaining a higher education for themselves had given these latter women the confidence to both demand equality of a relationship or to leave it, as well as the financial potential to back this up:

> I think it [the degree] makes you reassess things. I don't think it's inevitable, but I think lots of men can't cope with the situation, and lots of women do look at things in a new light. You know, I realized that he [my ex-boyfriend] was undermining my confidence terribly, and in fact I, you know, I can do things by myself. I don't need him, you know. I don't think I'm bitter. If I had a good relationship I'd probably live with someone again. I don't know. I know I don't have to. That's what it is, I don't have to (Stella, a white middle-class woman).

> [If] you had the education that I've just experienced and then you'd got the job that I've just experienced, you wouldn't go into a power relationship within the home that exists, would you? You couldn't accept it surely? But even if you did accept it as soon as it went bad you would have access to a job to get out of it . . . Well, that's my education. It's taken me a long time to get to that point (Gillian, a white working-class woman).

Higher education gave some of the women the confidence to demand equality within their present relationships — with the accompanying conflict with their partners. Gayle (white working-class), who had experienced problems with her partner over 'making space' for her studies at home, said:

> I'm much more confident about things I feel about things. Much more ready to express them ... I think I've actually been more forthright about the way I feel about things in general and in particular with our relationship. I think I've probably been less prepared to, to give ground than I would've done in, you know, the past maybe.

When I asked Beverley (black), who had withdrawn from divorcing her husband, if she thought they would eventually resume their relationship fully, her reply was in terms of any potential for equality within the relationship:

> I don't know, I can't say. I can't say at the moment. It's really — because the relationship wouldn't be a balanced one, right. And I don't know if that's possible yet ... He's supportive, but I think it's a selfish supportiveness, you know. It's a supportiveness where if you support me maybe at the end of the day there's some — you know!

If, however, there was no response from their partners to the women's desire for equality, women who continued to connect up their lives, while they could not envisage separate identities, could envisage independence and personal autonomy for themselves in a way they had not been able to previously. As Annette Lawson (1990) puts it, they could speak of 'I' rather than 'we'. Wendy (white working-class), who was referred to in the previous chapter as not being sure that her relationship with her husband would continue in the long term, said:

> Education has affected me tremendously. I mean over the last two or three years I think I've completely changed. I think I'm a completely different person. I'm more confident now, you know ... Because I think now that if I had to live my life on my own I could do it, whereas before I don't think I — you know, I would have been sort of terrified.

The women who moved towards separation because of conflicts with partners could envisage separations between education and family. On the other hand, they could not envisage independence; they could not visualize an 'I' rather than a 'we':

> I can't really want to go [leave the marriage]. It's a sort of battle with yourself really, isn't it, rather than with the other person? ... I mean it's got — I suppose it's a fear of being lonely. You know, because okay you've got friends, but friends are not there all the time (Jenny, a white working-class woman).

It would be unwise, however, to point to higher education as a deterministic change agent that leads those mature women students who gain access to it to reconsider their relationships with men within their private spheres and to want equality. Independence as a lone female parent could still be seen as inequality, in that along with independent control goes all the responsibility, unshared. More importantly, postulations such as this one tend to regard higher education as transmitted to passive recipients. Women's receipt of higher education, and higher education itself, is more complex. There needs to be an understanding of the process as one in which there is active participation on the part of women, albeit within a context of option-limiting social structural constraints. The perceptions and circumstances of women on the receiving end of higher education must be taken into account. Those circumstances include her partner and the contradictory ethos of family and of higher education itself. Within them the women actively created varying ways of having education and family coexisting in their lives, and could value them. Some of the women were active in ensuring that higher education affected their private lives and relationships as little as possible; others were active in working towards integrations of the two so that each affected the other (successfully or otherwise). Some of the women's partners actively worked towards resisting any connections with education within the relationship (again, successfully or otherwise), a few others accommodated them, and some did not have to face the situation at all. Some women shifted their pattern of having education and family in their lives when faced with conflict with their partners, others did not. Nevertheless, it is interesting to consider briefly the particular effect of a social science education within the various configurations.

A Social Science Education

Kim Thomas's (1990) study of both ends of the science–humanities subject divide (i.e. physics/physical science and English/communication courses) shows that across the disciplines, higher education's values and beliefs covertly marginalize women. It may be, however, that different disciplines do play a role in women's separations or connections. For example, physical science subjects may even more firmly encourage a separation between women's educational and family lives. While social science does not often turn the spotlight on itself and on higher education's hidden curriculum, it does examine other areas of social life. It may be that the social sciences are more likely than other disciplines to make students connect with and reflect upon their own social situations, and that this would especially be the case where feminist perspectives and teaching methods were part of courses. Social science, and feminist social science in particular, provides a critical vocabulary with which to look at social institutions such as 'the family'.

There certainly are indications that the social science courses the women studied played an important role. The women reported their partners as, in part, threatened by their education because it might somehow give them a greater insight into the men's motivations, and was shown to have affected their knowledge about their children's schooling. With regard to the former particularly, this form of threat would be less likely if the women were studying the physical sciences. On the other hand, this may have encroached even further on the men's supposed area of competence, and thus enhanced another form of threat.

Whether or not studying the social sciences especially encouraged a desire for connections, rather than separations, of family and education is another matter. It must still be borne in mind that it was the women themselves who chose to study social sciences, and that they overwhelmingly attributed this to aspects of their life experiences making them interested in the subjects that are social sciences' concern. It may be that more personally-based factors had a role to play in their orientations towards separations or connections. Helen Weinreich-Haste's study of undergraduates across a range of disciplines found that the discipline they were studying linked to aspects of their identity and values more strongly than did sex. As she notes:

> It is an interesting question as to why this relationship [between discipline and values] should be. Does it precede the experience of university, in some way determining choice? Or is it a consequence of socialization within university — in which case is it the result of membership of social groups, the anticipation of professional roles, or the outcome of learning to think about social issues in ways particularly associated with the context of different disciplines? ... Other data [suggests] there is already ... a clear pattern of general intellectual orientation to science, arts, technology, or social sciences which does relate to politics and to social and personal values (Weinreich-Haste, 1984, p. 130).

In other words, preceding experience plays an important part in students' choice of which discipline they study and the values and orientations they hold.

A Particular Psyche?

While shifts in the way the women had education and family coexisting in their lives can be linked to their relationships with their partners, what originally made them receive and perceive education as an integral or a separate part of their lives is another question. If connection is part of the feminine psyche, why did a third of the women not attempt many, if any, connections in the first place? Was their feminine psyche less developed in some way? Belenky and colleagues (1986), in their examination of women's separating or connecting epistemological positions, suggest that the social forces operating on women's formative childhood years continue to shape their experience; separating or connecting family backgrounds producing separating or connecting women. For these women though, no differences stand out in their backgrounds as pointing to their future separations or connections. However, Helen's (white working-class) account of her childhood contained many images and anecdotes that appeared to stress both her parents' separating approach to life. Yet, she herself took a connecting approach to education and family in adulthood. There are also the questions of why some women can envisage a move towards separation when conflict with their partners ensues because they have made connections, and why others cannot envisage separation but can envisage independence? For those interested in what motivates individual women to attempt to have both education and family in their lives in certain ways further exploration is obviously needed. Here, however, my intention has been to show that these ways exist in the first place.

Conclusion

My main concern has been to offer an explanation of and for women who are in a particular position. I have examined the social context under which education and family coexist in women's lives — that is, that both are greedy but have distinct, antipathetic, value bases that are weighted differently in particular contexts. The ramifications of this for the women themselves have been explored. It would, however, be interesting to hold men up to a model constructed around women's experiences rather than having to hold women up to models constructed upon male experience (see Gilligan, 1982; Belenky *et al.*, 1986). Lawson (1990) suggests that, generally speaking, women are more affected by a return to education than are men. It may be that a similar analysis to the one employed here, applied to mature partner/father/students, might find that men were also strung out along the three-stranded continuum posited in the previous chapter (p. 131), but with an opposite weighting towards the separation end. Indeed, perhaps the whole male-female psyche/difference theory would be better conceptualized as a continuum. Account could then be taken of those who, particularly with regard to any race or class aspects, did not fit into such dichotomized categories, and a more comprehensive explanation offered of their lives.

The unique intrapersonal and private partnership between a man and a woman, and the network of kinship relationships surrounding it, are not individually drawn scenarios. They have, particularly in the form of marriage, complex structural and institutional dimensions. The politics of male-female relationships are echoed throughout society. Higher education has a structural and institutional dimension that reflects this politics. Both 'the family' and higher education can be said to act in concert in particular ways for women; as social institutions they, in fact, favour a separating approach to education and family in women's lives. Family, as a bounded private sphere calls for separation so that outside concerns do not intrude upon the minutiae of its everyday life and relationships, while higher education invites a separative approach so as to ensure objectivity and attention to abstract concepts. Nevertheless, there is also ambiguity. Women's caring within 'the family' can lead them to seek affiliations across the public/private divide. While higher education requires the separation of family life on the part of the women, it can also give them the confidence to want connections, and to want to be a connecting whole person. The latter issue can be illustrated by two similar sorts of accounts from women who had both attended the same course at the same university. For Gayle (white working-class) the confidence gained from being in higher education had helped to give her an integrated identity, and allowed her to make connections between education and family despite conflict with her husband: 'I suppose doing this course has actually made me much more of *a* person than a lot of different people. It's kind of brought me together much more'. Gillian (white working-class), however, while she had wanted education and family to coexist in her life in connective ways, had felt that neither allowed this. It was only after she graduated and went on a training course that encouraged connections of her experiences with her learning, and after she and her boyfriend had ended their relationship, that she felt that this had happened:

> All my experiences seemed to come together. I wasn't somebody who
> was a voluntary worker, I wasn't just somebody who had got a degree, I
> was actually a whole person. Sort of elements all sort of drawn together.

The women who felt that higher education had made them one person valued this
connected, integrated identity just as much as the women who appreciated the
separate identity it gave them.

The role of higher education within the family-education couple, and as a
resource or identity that women can use to gain equality within their private
worlds and relationships, is double-edged. Which side predominates depends
upon the woman, her preferred way of allowing education and family to coexist
in her life and, importantly, the circumstances under which she attempts their
coexistence. Those circumstances are often dictated by the expectations, values
and requirements of both the masculinist institution of higher education and the
individual men with whom women have relationships. While higher education
policies and institutions concern themselves with inputs and outputs and privilege
disciplines over students, and while the balance of male identity depends on
a masculine/feminine demarcation that associates loss of power with loss of masculinity, combining education with family life (and relationships with men
especially) will never be easy for women. The issues would appear to centre
around not women's education but *men's education*.

Appendix: The Women Interviewed

Women Interviewed at Beginning and End of Their First Year of Study

Anna: age 25; black.
Two children aged 3 and 5.
Seven-year relationship with her boyfriend, an engineer, who was not a member of her household.

Anne: age 39; white working-class.
Four children aged 5, 9, 13 and 16.
Married for seven years to an unemployed factory worker.

Beverley: age 35; black.
Four children aged 10, 13, 16 and 17.
Married for seventeen years to a restaurant owner. Relationship ended.

Cathy: age 45; white middle-class.
Two children aged 17 and 19.
Three-year relationship with her live-in boyfriend, a graphic designer.

Jackie: age 43; white working-class.
Two children aged 18 and 22.
Four-year relationship with her boyfriend, a self-employed builder, who was not a member of her household.

Lynne: age 35; white middle-class.
Two children aged 13 and 17.
Nine-year relationship with her live-in boyfriend, a self-employed builder. Relationship ended.

Maureen: age 36; black working-class.
One child aged 6.
Four-year relationship with her boyfriend, a teacher, who was not a member of her household. Relationship ended.

Michelle: age 26; white working-class.
Two children aged 2 and 6, plus pregnancy halfway through her first year.
Married for two years to an unemployed plumber.

Sandra: age 35; black.
Six children aged between 3 to 15, plus pregnancy halfway through her first year.
Married for seventeen years to a computer operator.

Val: age 37; black.
Three children aged 9, 16 and 19.
Ten-year relationship with her boyfriend, an engineer, who was not a member of her household.

Wendy: age 23; white working-class.
One child aged 7.
Married for seven years to an area manager.

Women Interviewed at the Beginning and End of Their Third Year of Study

Alexandra: age 42; white working-class.
Two children aged 16 and 18.
Married for twenty years to a self-employed decorator.
Relationship ended.

Angela: age 38; white middle-class.
One child aged 10.
Eight-year relationship with her boyfriend, a teacher, who was not a member of her household.

Carol: age 31; white middle-class.
One child aged 1 — pregnancy during the second year of her degree.
Married for two years to an executive manager.

Gayle: age 29; white working-class.
Two children aged 2 and 8 — pregnancy during the first year of her degree.
Married for three years to a social worker.

Helen: age 34; white working-class.
One child aged 15.
Three-year relationship with her boyfriend, a coach driver, who was not a member of her household. Relationship ended.

Jane: age 25, white middle-class.
One child aged 4.
Married for two years to a tree surgeon. Relationship ended.

Jennie: age 34; white working-class.
Three children aged 8, 11 and 12.
Married for fifteen years to a laboratory technician.

Judith: age 40; white middle-class.
Two children aged 8 and 11.
Married for nineteen years to a teacher.

Lorraine: age 31; white middle-class.
One child aged 8.
Six-year relationship with her live-in boyfriend, a social worker.

Madeline: age 27; white middle-class.
One child aged 1 — pregnancy during the second year of her degree.
Married for two years to a solicitor.

Paula: age 26; black.
Two children aged 1 and 6 — pregnancy during the second year of her degree.
Seven-year relationship with her live-in boyfriend, a used car dealer.

Victoria: age 34; white middle-class.
Two children aged 7 and 9.
Married for eleven years to an area manager.

Women Interviewed After They Had Graduated

Gillian: age 40; white working-class.
Three children aged 15, 17 and 20.
Four-year relationship with her live-in boyfriend, an accountant. Relationship ended.

Irene: age 34; black.
Four children aged 6, 13, 15 and 16.
Eleven-year relationship with her boyfriend, a mechanic, who was not a member of her household.

Janice: age 37; white working-class.
Five children aged between 8 and 18.
Married for twenty years to a self-employed builder.

Jenny: age 46; white working-class.
One child aged 14.
Married for seventeen years to an electrician.

June: age 46; white working-class.
Four children aged 18, 21, 23 and 25.
Married for twenty-seven years to a manager.

Kim: age 25; 'mixed' race.
One child aged 2 — pregnancy during the first year of her degree.
Two-year relationship with her live-in boyfriend, a local government officer.

Marcia: age 36; 'mixed' race.
Two children aged 12 and 14.
Three-year relationship with her boyfriend, a carpenter, who was not a member of her household.

Stella: age 38; white middle-class.
Three children aged 5, 17 and 19.
Fifteen-year relationship with her live-in boyfriend, a lecturer. Relationship ended.

References

ABBOTT, P. (1987) 'Women's social class identification: Does husband's occupation make a difference?', *Sociology*, **21**, 1, pp. 91–103.

ABBOTT, P. and SAPSFORD, R. (1987) *Women and Social Class*, London, Tavistock.

ABEL, E.K. and NELSON, M.K. (1990) 'Circles of care: introductory essay', in ABEL, E.K. and NELSON, M.K. (Eds) *Circles of Care: Work and Identity in Women's Lives*, Albany, State University of New York Press.

ACKER, S. (1980) 'Women, the other academics', in EQUAL OPPORTUNITIES COMMISSION, *Equal Opportunities in Higher Education*, Report of an EOC/SRHE conference at Manchester Polytechnic, Manchester, EOC.

ACKER, S. (1981) 'No woman's-land: British sociology of education 1960–1979', *Sociological Review*, **29**, 1, pp. 77–104.

ACKER, S. (1984) 'Women in higher education: What is the problem?', in ACKER, S. and WARREN PIPER, D. (Eds) *Is Higher Education Fair to Women?* London, SRHE/NFER-Nelson.

ALIBHAL, Y. (1989), 'Burning in the cold' in GIEVE, K. (Ed.) *Balancing Acts: On Being a Mother*, London, Virago.

ALLAN, G. (1989) *Friendship: Developing a Sociological Perspective*, Brighton, Harvester/Wheatsheaf.

ALLAN, G. (1990) 'Insiders and outsiders: Boundaries around the home', in ALLAN, G. and CROW, G. (Eds) *Home and Family: Creating the Domestic Sphere*, Basingstoke, Macmillan.

ALLAN, G. and CROW, G. (1990) 'Introduction', in ALLAN, G. and CROW, G. (Eds) *Home and Family: Creating the Domestic Sphere*, Basingstoke, Macmillan.

AMOS, V. and PARMAR, P. (1981) 'Resistance and response: The experiences of black girls in Britain', in McROBBIE, A. and McCABE, T. (Eds) *Feminism for Girls: An Adventure Story*, London, Routledge and Kegan Paul.

ANDERSON, D. and DAWSON, G. (Eds) (1986) *Family Portraits*, London, Social Affairs Unit.

ANYON, J. (1983) 'Intersections of gender and class: Accommodation and resistance by working-class and affluent females to contradictory sex-role ideologies', in WALKER, S. and BARTON, L. (Eds) *Gender, Class and Education*, London, Falmer Press.

ARNOT, M. (1983) 'A cloud over co-education: An analysis of the forms of transmission of class and gender relations', in WALKER, S. and BARTON, L. (Eds) *Gender, Class and Education*, London, Falmer Press.

ARNOT, S. (1985) 'Current developments in the sociology of women's education', *British Journal of Sociology of Education*, **6**, 1, pp. 124–30.

ATTWOOD, M. and HATTON, F. (1983) ' "Getting on". Gender differences in career development: A case study in the hairdressing industry', in GAMARNIKOW, E., MORGAN, D., PURVIS, J. and TAYLORSON, D. (Eds) *Gender, Class and Work*, London, Heinemann.

BACKETT, K. (1982) *Mothers and Fathers*, Basingstoke, Macmillan.

BALBO, L. (1987) 'Crazy quilts: The welfare state debate from a woman's point of view', in SASSOON, A.S. (Ed.) *Women and the State: The Shifting Boundaries of Public and Private*, London, Hutchinson.

BANKS, O. (1981) *Faces of Feminism*, Oxford, Martin Robertson.

BARRETT, M. and McINTOSH, M. (1982) *The Anti-Social Family*, London, Verso.

BELENKY, M.F., CLINCHY, B.M., GOLDBERGER, N.R. and TARULE, J.M. (1986) *Women's Ways of Knowing: The Development of Self, Voice, and Mind*, New York, Basic Books.

BELL, L. and RIBBENS, J. (1993, forthcoming) 'Isolated housewives or complex maternal worlds? The significance of social contacts between women with young children in industrial societies', *Sociological Review*.

BLACKIE, S. and CLARK, D. (1987) 'Men in marriage counselling', in LEWIS, C. and O'BRIEN, M. (Eds) *Reassessing Fatherhood*, London, Sage.

BLACKSTONE, T. (1976) 'The education of girls today', in MITCHELL, J. and OAKLEY, A. (Eds) *The Rights and Wrongs of Women*, Harmondsworth, Penguin Books.

BOOTH, A., JOHNSON, D.R., WHITE, L. and EDWARDS, J.N. (1984) 'Women's outside employment and marital stability', *American Journal of Sociology*, **90**, pp. 567–85.

BOSE, C.E. (1987) 'Dual spheres', in HESS, B.B. and FERREE, M.M. (Eds) *Analyzing Gender: A Handbook of Social Science Research*, London, Sage.

BOTT, E. (1957) *Family and Social Networks*, London, Tavistock.

BOULTON, M.G. (1983) *On Being a Mother: A Study of Women and Pre-School Children*, London, Tavistock.

BOWLES, G. (1983) 'Is Women's Studies an academic discipline?', in BOWLES, G. and DUELLI KLEIN, R. (Eds) *Theories of Women's Studies*, London, Routledge and Kegan Paul.

BRANNEN, J. (1988) 'The study of sensitive subjects', *Sociological Review*, **36**, 3, pp. 552–63.

BRANNEN, J. (1990) 'Dual earner households in early parenthood: Some methodological considerations in the interpretation of data', paper presented at the British Sociological Association Annual Conference, Surrey University.

BRANNEN, J. and COLLARD, J. (1982) *Marriages in Trouble: The Process of Seeking Help*, London, Tavistock.

BRANNEN, J. and MOSS, P. (1987) 'Dual earner households — Women's financial contribution after the birth of the first child', in BRANNEN, J. and WILSON, G. (Eds) *Give and Take in Families: Studies in Resource Distribution*, London, Allen and Unwin.

BRANNEN, J. and MOSS, P. (1988) *New Mothers at Work: Employment and Childcare*, London, Unwin Hyman.

BRANNEN, J. and MOSS, P. (1991) *Managing Mothers: Dual Earner Households After Maternity Leave*, London, Unwin Hyman.

BRENNAN, J.L. and MCGEEVOR, P.A. (1987) *The Employment of Graduates From Ethnic Minorities*, London, Commission for Racial Equality.

BROWN, C. (1984) *Black and White Britain: The Third PSI Survey*, London, Policy Studies Institute.

BRYAN, B., DADZIE, S. and SCAFE, S. (1985) *The Heart of the Race*, London, Virago.

BYRNE, E. (1978) *Women and Education*, London, Tavistock.

CHAFETZ, J.S. (1989) 'Gender equality: Towards a theory of change', in WALLACE, R.A. (Ed.) *Feminism and Sociological Theory*, London, Sage.

CHARLES, N. (1990) 'Women and class — A problematic relationship?', *Sociological Review*, **1**, pp. 43–89.

CHEAL, D. (1991) *Family and the State of Theory*, London, Harvester/Wheatsheaf.

CHODOROW, N.J. (1978) *The Reproduction of Mothering*, Berkeley, University of California Press.

CHODOROW, N.J. (1989) *Feminism and Psychoanalytic Theory*, Cambridge, Polity Press.

CLARK, D. and HALDANE, D. (1990) *Wedlocked?*, Cambridge, Polity Press.

CLARK, D. and SAMPHIER, M. (1983) 'Public attitudes to marital problems', *Marriage Guidance*, Autumn, pp. 2–8.

COLLINS, P.H. (1990) *Black Feminist Thought: Knowledge, Consciousness and the Politics of Empowerment*, London, Harper Collins.

COMER, L. (1982) 'Monogamy, marriage and economic independence', in WHITE-LEGG, E., ARNOT, M., BARTELS, E., BEECHEY, V., BIRKE, L., HIMMELWEIT, S., LEONARD, D., RUEHL, S. and SPEAKMAN, M.A. (Eds) *The Changing Experience of Women*, Oxford, Martin Robertson/Open University.

COMMISSION OF THE EUROPEAN COMMUNITIES (1991) *A Guide to Higher Education Systems and Qualifications in the European Community*, London, Kogan Page.

COONTZ, S. (1988) *The Social Origins of Private Life: A History of American Families 1600–1900*, London, Verso.

COSER, L. (1974) *Greedy Institutions: Patterns of Undivided Commitment*, New York, Free Press.

COSER, R.L. (with L. COSER) (1974) 'The housewife and her greedy family', in COSER, L. *Greedy Institutions: Patterns of Undivided Commitment*, New York, Free Press.

COULTAS, V. (1989) 'Black girls and self-esteem', *Gender and Education*, **1**, 3, pp. 283–94.

CREHAN, K. (1986) 'Women, work and the balancing act', in EPSTEIN, T.S., CREHAN, K., GERZER, A. and SASS, J. (Eds) *Women, Work and the Family in Britain and Germany*, London, Croom Helm.

CROW, G. (1989) 'The use of the concept of "strategy" in recent sociological literature', *Sociology*, **23**, 1, pp. 1–24.

DALE, J. and FOSTER, P. (1986) *Feminists and State Welfare*, London, Routledge and Kegan Paul.

DAVID, M. (1980) *The State, the Family and Education*, London, Routledge and Kegan Paul.

DAVID, M. (1983) 'Sex education and social policy: A new moral economy', in WALKER, S. and BARTON, L. (Eds) *Gender, Class and Education*, London, Falmer Press.

DAVID, M. (1984) 'Women, family and education', in ACKER, S., MEGARRY, J. NISBET J. and HOYLE, E. (Eds) *Women and Education*, London, Kogan Page.

DAVID, M. (1985) 'Motherhood and social policy — A matter of education?', *Critical Social Policy*, **12**, pp. 28–43.

DAVID, M. (1986) 'Teaching family matters', *British Journal of Sociology of Education*, **7**, 1, pp. 35–57.

DAVID, M. (1989) 'Education', in MCCARTHY, M. (Ed.) *The New Politics of Welfare: An Agenda for the 1990s?*, London, Macmillan.

DAVIDOFF, L. (1979) 'The separation of home and work? Landladies and lodgers in nineteenth and twentieth century England', in BURMAN, S. (Ed.) *Fit Work For Women*, London, Croom Helm.

DAVIDOFF, L. and HALL, C. (1987) *Family Fortunes: Men and Women of the English Middle Class 1780–1850*, London, Hutchinson.

DAVIES, K. (1990) *Women, Time and the Weaving of the Strands of Everyday Life*, Aldershot, Gower.

DEEM, R. (1978) *Women and Schooling*, London, Routledge and Kegan Paul.

DEEM, R. (Ed.) (1980) *Schooling for Women's Work*, London, Routledge and Kegan Paul.

DEEM, R. (1981) 'State policy and ideology in the education of women 1944–1980', *British Journal of Sociology of Education*, **2**, 2, pp. 131–43.

DEEM, R. (1983) 'Gender, patriarchy and class in the popular education of women', in WALKER, S. and BARTON, L. (Eds) *Gender, Class and Education*, London, Falmer Press.

DEEM, R. (1986) *All Work and No Play: The Sociology of Women and Leisure*, Milton Keynes, Open University.

DEEM, R. (1988) 'Feminism and leisure studies: Opening up new directions', in WIMBUSH, E. and TALBOT, M. (Eds) *Relative Freedoms: Women and Leisure*, Milton Keynes, Open University Press.

DEPARTMENT OF EDUCATION AND SCIENCE (DES) (1987) *Higher Education: Meeting the Challenge*, London, HMSO.

DEPARTMEN OF EDUCATION AND SCIENCE (DES) (1991) *Mature Students in Higher Education 1975–1988*, London, HMSO.

DOMINELLI, L. (1988) *Anti-Racist Social Work*, Basingstoke, Macmillan.

DOYAL, L. (1990) 'Hazards of hearth and home', *Women's Studies International Forum*, **13**, 5, pp. 501–17.

DYHOUSE, S. (1989) *Feminism and the Family in England 1880–1939*, Oxford, Basil Blackwell.

EDWARDS, R. (1990a) 'Access and assets: The experiences of mature mother-students in higher education', *Journal of Access Studies*, **5**, 2, pp. 188–202.

EDWARDS, R. (1990b) 'Connecting method and epistemology: A white woman interviewing Black women', *Women's Studies International Forum* **13**, 5, pp. 447–90.

EDWARDS, R. (1993a) 'An education in interviewing; Placing the researcher and the research', in RENZETTI, C.M. and LEE, R.M. (Eds) *Researching Sensitive Topics*, Newbury Park, Sage.

EDWARDS, R. (1993b) 'Shifting status: Mothers' higher education and their children's schooling', in DAVID, M., EDWARDS, R., HUGHES, M. and RIBBENS, J. *Mothers and Education: Inside Out? Exploring Family-Education Policy and Experience*, Basingstoke, Macmillan.

EDWARDS, R. and RIBBENS, J. (1991) 'Meanderings around "strategy": A research note on strategic discourse in the lives of women', *Sociology*, **25**, 3, pp. 477–89.

EHRENSAFT, D. (1981) 'When women and men mother', *Power And Politics No. 3: Sexual Politics, Feminism and Socialism*, London, Routledge and Kegan Paul.

EICHENBAUM, L. and ORBACH, S. (1984) *What Do Women Want?*, London, Fontana.

EICHLER, M. (1980) *The Double Standard: A Feminist Critique of Feminist Social Science*, London, Croom Helm.

EICHLER, M. (1981) 'Power, dependency, love and the sexual division of labour', *Women's Studies International Quarterly*, **4**, 2, pp. 201–19.

EISENSTEIN, H. (1984) *Contemporary Feminist Thought*, London, Unwin.

ELSHTAIN, J.B. (1981) *Public Man, Private Woman*, Princeton, Princeton University Press.

EVANS, M. (1983) 'In praise of theory: the case for Women's Studies', in BOWLES, G. and DUELLI KLEIN, R. (Eds) *Theories of Women's Studies*, London, Routledge and Kegan Paul.

FAMILY POLICY STUDIES CENTRE (1988) *Family Policy Bulletin 5*, London, FPSC.

FARKAS, G. (1976) 'Education, wage rates, and the division of labour between husbands and wives', *Journal of Marriage and the Family*, **38**, pp. 473–83.

FINCH, J. (1983a) *Married to the Job: Wives' Incorporation in Men's Work*, London, George Allen and Unwin.

FINCH, J. (1983b) 'Dividing the rough and the respectable: Working-class women and pre-school playgroups', in GAMARNIKOW, E., MORGAN, D., PURVIS, J. and TAYLORSON, D. (Eds) *The Public and the Private*, London, Heinemann.

FINCH, J. (1984) *Education as Social Policy*, Harlow, Longmans.

FISHER, B. and TRONTO, J. (1990) 'Towards a feminist theory of caring', in ABEL, E.K. and NELSON, M.K. (Eds) *Circles of Care: Work and Identity in Women's Lives*, Albany, State University of New York Press.

FONER, N. (1979) *Jamaica Farewell: Jamaican Migrants in London*, London, Routledge and Kegan Paul.

FORSTER, P. and SUTTON, I. (Eds) (1989) *Daughters of DeBeauvoir*, London, The Women's Press.

FRIEDAN, B. (1965) *The Feminine Mystique*, London, Victor Gollancz.

GAILEY, C.W. (1987) 'Evolutionary perspectives on gender hierarchy', in HESS, B.B. and FERREE, M.M. (Eds) *Analyzing Gender: A Handbook of Social Science Research*, London, Sage.

GERSON, K. (1985) *Hard Choices: How Women Decide About Work, Career and Motherhood*, Berkeley, University of California Press.

GIEVE, K. (1989) 'Introduction', in GIEVE, K. (Ed.) *Balancing Acts: On Being a Mother*, London, Virago.

GILBERT, L.A. and HOLAHAN, C.K. (1982) 'Conflicts between student/professional, parental and self-development roles: A comparison of high and low effective copers', *Human Relations*, **35**, 82, pp. 635–48.

GILLIGAN, C. (1982) *In a Different Voice: Psychological Theory and Women's Development*, London, Harvard University Press.

GILLIGAN, C. (1986) 'Viewpoint: Reply by Carol Gilligan', *Signs: Journal of Women in Culture and Society*, **11**, 2, pp. 324–33.

GITTINS, D. (1985) *The Family in Question: Changing Households and Familiar Ideologies*. Basingstoke, Macmillan.

GLENN, E.N. (1987) 'Gender and the family', in HESS, B.B. and FERREE, M.M. (Eds) *Analyzing Gender: A Handbook of Social Science Research*, London, Sage.

GOLDTHORPE, J.H., LOCKWOOD, D., BECHOFER, E. and PLATT, J. (1969) *The Affluent Worker in the Class Structure*, Cambridge, Cambridge University Press.

GONIN, C. (1984) 'Work and marriage', *Marriage Guidance*, Spring, pp. 2–10.

GORDON, T. (1989) 'Feminist mothers: Reflections on tensions in research in action', paper presented at the British Sociological Association Annual Conference, Plymouth Polytechnic.

GOULD, K. (1988) 'Old wine in new bottles: A feminist perspective on Gilligan's theory', *Social Work*, **33**, 5, pp. 411–5.

GRAHAM, H. (1982) 'Coping, or how mothers are seen and not heard', in FRIEDMAN, S. and SARAH, E. (Eds) *On the Problem of Men*, London, Women's Press.

GRAHAM, H. (1983) 'Caring: A labour of love', in FINCH, J. and GROVES, D. (Eds) *A Labour of Love: Women, Work and Caring*, London, Routledge and Kegan Paul.

GRAHAM, H. (1984) *Women, Health and the Family*, Brighton, Harvester.

GRAHAM, H. (1987) 'Being poor: Perceptions and coping strategies of lone mothers', in BRANNEN, J. and WILSON, G. (Eds) *Give and Take in Families: Studies in Resource Distribution*, London, Allen and Unwin.

GREENO, C.G. and MACCOBY, E.E. (1986) 'Viewpoint: How different is the different voice?', *Signs: Journal of Women in Culture and Society*, **11**, 2, pp. 310–6.

GROVE, V. (1987) *The Compleat Woman. Marriage, Motherhood, Career: Can She Have It All?*, London, Chatto and Windus.

GUBBAY, J. (1991) *Teaching Methods of Social Research*, Norwich, University of East Anglia.

HAMNER, J. and SAUNDERS, S. (1983) 'Blowing the cover of the protective male: A community study of violence to women', in GAMARNIKOW, E., MORGAN, D., PURVIS, J. and TAYLORSON, D. (Eds) *The Public and the Private*, London, Heinemann.

HAMNER, J. and SAUNDERS, S. (1984) *Well Founded Fear: A Community Study of Violence to Women*, London, Hutchinson.

HARDEY, M. (1990) 'Lone parents and the home', in ALLAN, G. and CROW, G. (Eds) *Home and Family: Creating the Domestic Sphere*, Basingstoke, Macmillan.

HARDING, S. (1986) 'The instability of the analytical categories of feminist theory', *Signs: Journal of Women in Culture and Society*, **11**, 4, pp. 645–65.

HAREVEN, T. (1982) *Family Time and Industrial Time: The Relationship Between the Family and Work in a New England Industrial Community*, New York, Cambridge University Press.

HARTMANN, H. (1981) 'The family as the focus of gender, class and political struggle: The example of housework', *Signs: The Journal of Women in Culture and Society*, **6**, 3, pp. 366–94.

HEATH, A. and BRITTEN, N. (1984) 'Women's jobs do make a difference', *Sociology*, **18**, pp. 475–90.

HEWLETT, S.A. (1988) *A Lesser Life: The Myth of Women's Liberation*, London, Sphere Books.

HM INSPECTORATE (1991) *Aspects of Education in the USA: Quality and its Assurance in Higher Education*. London, HMSO.

HOCHSCHILD, A. (1975) 'The sociology of feeling and emotion: Selected possibilities', in MILLMAN, M. and KANTER, R.M. (Eds) *Another Voice: Feminist Perspectives on Social Life and Social Science*, New York, Anchor Books.

HOCHSCHILD, A. (1990) *The Second Shift: Working Parents and the Revolution at Home*, London, Piatkus.

HOMER, M., LEONARD, A. and TAYLOR, P. (1985) 'Personal relationships: Help and hindrance', in JOHNSTON, N. (Ed.) *Marital Violence*, London, Routledge and Kegan Paul.

HOOKS, B. (1982) *Ain't I a Women? Black Women and Feminism*, London, Pluto Press.

HOPPER, E. and OSBORN, M. (1975) *Adult Students: Education, Selection and Social Control*, London, Francis Pinter.

HUMM, M. (1987) 'Autobiography and "bell-pins"', in GRIFFITHS, V., HUMM, M., O'ROURKE, R., BATSLEER, J., POLAND, F. and WISE, S. (Eds) *Writing Feminist Biography 2: Using Life Histories*, Studies in Sexual Politics 19, Manchester, University of Manchester.

HUNT, P. (1985) 'Clients' responses to marriage counselling', *Research Report 3*, Rugby, National Marriage Guidance Council.

HUTCHINSON, E. and HUTCHINSON, E. (1986) *Women Returning to Learning*, Cambridge, National Extension College Publications.

JACKSON, D. (1990) *Unmasking Masculinity: A Critical Autobiography*, London, Unwin Hyman.

JAGGAR, A.M. (1983) *Feminist Politics and Human Nature*, Totowa, Rowman and Allanfield.

JOHNSTON, R. and BAILEY, R. (1984) *Mature Students: Perceptions and Experiences of Full-time and Part-time Higher Education*, Sheffield, PAVIC, Sheffield City Polytechnic.

KANTER, R.M. (1977) *Men and Women of the Corporation*, New York, Basic Books.

KERBER, L.K. (1986) 'Viewpoint: Some cautionary words for historians', *Signs: Journal of Women in Culture and Society*, **11**, 2, pp. 304–10.

KIRK, P. (1977) 'The tip of the iceberg: Some effects of OU study on married students', *Teaching At a Distance*, **10**, pp. 19–27.

LAND, H. (1989) 'Girls can't be professors, Mummy', in GIEVE, K. (Ed.) *Balancing Acts: On Being a Mother*, London, Virago.

LAWSON, A. (1990) *Adultery: An Analysis of Love and Betrayal*, Oxford, Oxford University Press.

LEVY, J.A. (1981) 'Friendship dilemmas and the inter-section of social worlds', in LOPATA, H.Z. and MAINES, D. (Eds) *Research and the Interweave of Social Roles: Friendship*, Greenwich, JAI Press.

LEWIS, C. and O'BRIEN, M. (1987) 'Constraints on fathers: Research, theory and clinical practice', in LEWIS, C. and O'BRIEN, M. (Eds) *Reassessing Fatherhood*, London, Sage.

LEWIS, D.K. (1983) 'A response to inequality: Black women, racism and sexism', in ABEL, E. and ABEL, E.K. (Eds) *The Signs Reader: Women, Gender and Scholarship*, London, University of Chicago Press.

LEWIS, J. (undated) 'Public/private and explaining the position of women', unpublished paper, London School of Economics.

LEWIS, J. (1984) *Women in England 1870–1950: Sexual Divisions and Social Change*, Brighton, Wheatsheaf.

LEWIS, J. (1986) 'Anxieties about the family, and the relationship between parents, children and the state in twentieth-century England', in RICHARDS, M. and LIGHT, P. (Eds) *Children of Social Worlds: Development in a Social Context*, Cambridge, Polity Press.

LEWIS, J. and MEREDITH, B. (1988) *Daughters Who Care: Daughters Caring for Mothers at Home*, London, Routledge and Kegan Paul.

LIE, S.S. (1990) 'The juggling act: Work and family in Norway', in LIE, S.S. and O'LEARY, V.E. (Eds) *Storming the Tower: Women in the Academic World*, London, Kogan Page.

LOVELL, A. (1980) 'Fresh Horizons: The aspirations and problems of intending mature students', *Feminist Review*, **6**, pp. 93–104.

LURIA, Z. (1986) 'Viewpoint: A methodological critique', *Signs: Journal of Women in Culture and Society*, **11**, 2, pp. 316–21.

McDONALD, G.W. (1980) 'Family power: The assessment of a decade of theory and research 1970–1979', *Journal of Marriage and the Family*, November, pp. 841–54.

McILROY, J. (1989) 'The great reform of the universities', in BRENTON, M. and UNGERSON, C. (Eds) *Social Policy Review 1988–9*, Harrow, Longmans.

McINTOSH, N. (1981) 'Adult learners and their needs', in ASHTON, S. and PEDDER, S. (Eds) *Adult Learners in Higher Education*, papers presented at a conference held at the Polytechnic of North London.

McLAREN, A. (1985) *Ambitions and Realisations: Women in Adult Education*, London, Peter Owen.

MARTIN, J., POWELL, J.P. and WIENEKE, C. (1981) 'The experiences of a group of older unqualified women at university', *Women's Studies International Quarterly*, **4**, 2, pp. 117–31.

MASON, J. (1990) 'Reconstructing the public and the private: The home and marriage in later life', in ALLAN, G. and CROW, G. (Eds) *Home and Family: Creating the Domestic Sphere*, Basingstoke, Macmillan.

MAYALL, B. (1990) 'A joy or a hassle: Child healthcare in a multi-ethnic society', *Children and Society*, **4**, 2, pp. 197–224.

MAYNARD, M. (1990) 'The reshaping of sociology? Trends in the study of gender', *Sociology*, **24**, 2, pp. 269–90.

MERCER, K. and JULIEN, I. (1988) 'Race, sexual politics and black masculinity: A dossier', in CHAPMAN, R. and RUTHERFORD, J. (Eds) *Male Order — Unwrapping Masculinity*, London, Lawrence and Wishart.

MILLAR, J. and GLENDINNING, C. (1989) 'Gender and poverty', *Journal of Social Policy*, **8**, 3, pp. 363–82.

MITCHELL, J. (1971) *Woman's Estate*, Harmondsworth, Penguin Books.

MORGAN, D.H.J. (1985) *The Family, Politics and Social Theory*, London, Routledge and Kegan Paul.

MORGAN, D.H.J. (1986) 'Gender', in BURGESS, R.G. (Ed.) *Key Variables in Social Investigation*, London, Routledge and Kegan Paul.

MORRIS, L. (1990) *The Workings of the Household: A US-UK Comparison*, Cambridge, Polity Press.

MOUNT, F. (1982) *The Subversive Family*, London, Jonathan Cape.

MURPHY, M.J. (1985) 'Marital breakdown and socioeconomic status: A reappraisal of the evidence from recent British sources', *The British Journal of Sociology*, **36**, 1, pp. 81–93.

NEW, C. and DAVID, M. (1985) *For the Children's Sake: Making Childcare More Than Women's Business*, Harmondsworth, Penguin.

NODDINGS, N. (1984) *Caring*, Berkeley, University of California Press.

OAKLEY, A. (1974) *The Sociology of Housework*, Oxford, Martin Robertson.

OFFICE OF POPULATION, CENSUSES AND SURVEYS (OPCS) (1989a) *Mature Students: Incomings and Outgoings*, London, HMSO.

OFFICE OF POPULATION, CENSUSES AND SURVEYS (OPCS) (1989b) *General Household Survey: Preliminary Results for 1988*, OPCS Monitor, London, HMSO.

OFFICE OF POPULATION, CENSUSES AND SURVEYS (OPCS) (1991a) *General Household Survey: Preliminary Results for 1990*, OPCS Monitor, London, HMSO.

OFFICE of POPULATION, CENSUSES and SURVEYS (OPCS) (1991b) *Population Trends 65*, London, HMSO.

ORTNER, S. (1974) 'Is female to male as nature is to culture?', in ROSALDO, M.Z. and LAMPHERE, L. (Eds) *Women, Culture and Society*, Stanford, University of Stanford Press.

OSBORN, M., CHARNLEY, A. and WITHNALL, A. (1981) *Review of Existing Research in Adult and Continuing Education: Educational Information, Advice, Guidance and Counselling for Adults*, VI, Leicester, National Institute of Adult and Continuing Education (England and Wales).

OSBORN, M., CHARNLEY, A. and WITHNALL, A. (1984) *Mature Students. Review of Existing Research in Adult and Continuing Education*, 1 (rev), Leicester, National Institute of Adult and Continuing Education (England and Wales).

PAHL, J. (1985) *Private Violence and Public Policy*, London, Routledge and Kegan Paul.

PASCALL, G. (1986) *Social Policy: A Feminist Analysis*, London, Tavistock.

PATEMAN, C. (1983) 'Feminist critiques of the public/private dichotomy', in BENN, S.L. and GAUS, J.F. (Eds) *Public and Private in Social Life*, London, Croom Helm.

PAYNE, G. and ABBOTT, P. (1990) 'Beyond male mobility models', in PAYNE, G. and ABBOTT, P. (Eds) *The Social Mobility of Women: Beyond Male Mobility Models*, London, Falmer Press.

PHILLIPS, A. (1987) *Divided Loyalties: Dilemmas of Sex and Class*, London, Virago.

PHOENIX, A. (1987) 'Theories of gender and black families', in WEINER, G. and ARNOT, M. (Eds) *Gender Under Scrutiny: New Inquiries in Education*, London, Hutchinson.

PLECK, J.H. (1985) *Working Wives, Working Husbands*, Beverley Hills, Sage.

POLLERT, A. (1981) *Girls, Wives, Factory Lives*, London, Macmillan.

PORTER, M. (1983) *Home, Work and Class Consciousness*, Manchester, Manchester University Press.

PURVIS, J. (1991) *The History of Women's Education in England*, Milton Keynes, Open University Press.

RAPOPORT, R. and RAPOPORT, R. (1971) *Dual Career Families*, Harmondsworth, Penguin.

RAPOPORT, R. and RAPOPORT, R. (1976) *Dual Career Families Re-examined*, Oxford, Martin Robertson.

RAPP, R., ROSS, E. and BRIDENTHAL, R. (1979) 'Examining family history', *Feminist Studies*, **5**, pp. 174–95.

REID, P.T. (1990) 'African-American women in academia: Paradoxes and barriers', in LIE, S.S. and O'LEARY, V.E. (Eds) *Storming the Tower: Women in the Academic World*, London, Kogan Page.

REINHARZ, S. (1984) *On Becoming a Social Scientist*, New Brunswick, Transaction.

RIBBENS, J. (1991) *The Personal and the Sociological: The Use of Student Autobiography in Teaching Undergraduate Sociology*, Oxford, Oxford Polytechnic.

RIBBENS, J. (1993) 'Having a word with the teacher: On-going negotiations across home-school boundaries', in DAVID, M., EDWARDS, R., HUGHES, M. and RIBBENS, J. *Mothers and Education: Inside Out? Exploring Family-Education Policy and Experience*, Basingstoke, Macmillan.

RIBBENS, J. (1993, forthcoming), *Mothers and Their Children: Towards a Feminist Perspective on Childrearing*, London, Sage.

RILEY, D. (1983) 'The serious burdens of love? Some questions on childcare, feminism and socialism', in SEGAL, L. (Ed.) *What Is to Be Done About the Family?*, Harmondsworth, Penguin.

ROBINSON, E. (1980) 'Course design and structure', in EQUAL OPPORTUNITIES COMMISSION, *Equal Opportunities in Higher Education*, Report of an EOC/SRHE conference at Manchester Polytechnic, Manchester, EOC.

ROCKHILL, K. (1987) 'Gender, language and the politics of literacy', *British Journal of Sociology of Education*, **8**, 2, pp. 153–67.

ROSALDO, M.Z. (1974) 'Women, culture and society: A theoretical overview', in ROSALDO, M.Z. and LAMPHERE, L. (Eds) *Women, Culture and Society*, Stanford, University of Stanford Press.

ROSALDO, M.Z. (1980) 'The use and abuse of anthropology: Reflections of feminism and cross-cultural understanding', *Signs: Journal of Women in Culture and Society*, **5**, 3, pp. 389–417.

RUDDICK, S. (1989) *Maternal Thinking: Towards a Politics of Peace*, London, The Women's Press.

SAFILOS-ROTHSCHILD, C. (1976) 'A macro- and micro-examination of family power and love: An exchange model', *Journal of Marriage and the Family*, May, pp. 335–62.

SASSOON, A.S. (1987) 'Women's new social role: Contradictions of the welfare state', in SASSOON, A.S. (Ed.) *Women and the State: The Shifting Boundaries of Public and Private*, London, Hutchinson.

SCOTT, S. (1985) 'Feminist research and qualitative methodology: A discussion of some of the issues', in BURGESS, R.G. (Ed.) *Issues in Educational Research: Qualitative Methods*, London, Falmer Press.

SEIDLER, V. (1989) *Rediscovering Masculinity: Reason, Language and Sexuality*, London, Routledge.

SHARISTANIAN, J. (1987a) 'Introduction: Women's lives in the public and domestic spheres', in SHARISTANIAN, J. (Ed.) *Beyond the Public/Domestic Dichotomy: Contemporary Perspectives on Women's Public Lives*, Westport, Greenwood Press.

SHARISTANIAN, J. (1987b) 'Conclusion: The public/domestic model and the study of contemporary women's lives', in SHARISTANIAN, J. (Ed.) *Beyond the Public/Domestic Dichotomy: Contemporary Perspectives on Women's Public Lives*, Westport, Greenwood Press.

SHARPE, S. (1984) *Double Identity: The Lives of Working Mothers*, Harmondsworth, Penguin.

SHAW, J. (1986) 'What should be done about social science in higher education?', in FINCH, J. and RUSTIN, M. (Eds) *A Degree of Choice? Higher Education and the Right to Learn*, Harmondsworth, Penguin.

SMITH, D.E. (1987) *The Everyday World as Problematic: A Feminist Sociology*, Boston, Northeastern University.

SMITH, D.E. (1989) 'Sociological theory: Methods of writing patriarchy', in WALLACE, R.A. (Ed.) *Feminism and Sociological Theory*, London, Sage.

SMITHERS, A. and GRIFFIN, A. (1986) 'Mature students at university: Entry, experience and outcome', *Studies in Higher Education*, **11**, 3, pp. 257–68.

SOKOLOFF, N.J. (1980) *Between Money and Love: The Dialectics of Women's Home and Market Work*, New York, Praegar.

SPENDER, D. (1981) 'Education: The patriarchal paradigm and the response to feminism', in SPENDER, D. (Ed.) *Men's Studies Modified: The Impact of Feminism on the Academic Disciplines*, Oxford, Pergamon Press.

SPENDER, D. (1982) *Invisible Women: The Schooling Scandal*, London, Writers & Readers.

SPENDER, D. (1983) 'Theorising about theorising', in BOWLES, G. and DUELLI KLEIN, R. (Eds) *Theories of Women's Studies*, London, Routledge and Kegan Paul.

SPENDER, D. (1985) *For the Record: The Making and Meaning of Feminist Knowledge*, London, The Women's Press.

SPERLING, L. (1991) 'Can the barriers be breached? Mature women's access to higher education', *Gender and Education*, **3**, 2, pp. 199–213.

STACEY, M. (1981) 'The division of labour revisited or overcoming the two Adams', in ABRAMS, P., DEEM, R., FINCH, J. and ROCK, P. (Eds) *Practice and Progress: British Sociology 1950–1980*, London, George Allen and Unwin.

STACEY, M. and PRICE, M. (1981) *Women, Power and Politics*, London, Tavistock.

STACK, C.B. (1986) 'Viewpoint: The culture of gender: Women and men of colour', *Signs: Journal of Women in Culture and Society*, **11**, 2, pp. 321–4.

STANLEY, L. and WISE, S. (1983) *Breaking Out: Feminist Consciousness and Feminist Research*, London, Routledge and Kegan Paul.

STONE, K. (1983) 'Motherhood and waged work: West Indian, Asian and white mothers compared', in PHIZACKLEA, A. (Ed.) *One Way Ticket*, London, Routledge and Kegan Paul.

SUITOR, J.J. (1987) 'Friendship networks in transition; Married mothers return to school'. *Journal of Social and Personal Relationships*, **4**, 4, pp. 445–61.

THOMAS, K. (1990) *Gender and Subject in Higher Education*, Buckingham, SRHE/Open University Press.

THOMPSON, J. (1983) *Learning Liberation: Women's Response to Men's Education*, London, Croom Helm.

THOROGOOD, N. (1987) 'Race, class and gender: The politics of housework', in BRANNEN, J. and WILSON, G. (Eds) *Give and Take in Families: Studies in Resource Distribution*, London, Allen and Unwin.

Tolson, A. (1987) *The Limits of Masculinity*, London, Routledge.

Ungerson, C. (1983) 'Women and caring: Skills, tasks and taboos', in Gamarnikow, E., Morgan, D., Purvis, J. and Taylorson, D. (Eds) *The Public and the Private*, London, Heinemann.

Ungerson, C. (1986) 'Introduction: Women and education policy', in Ungerson, C. (Ed.) *Women and Social Policy: A Reader*, London, Macmillan.

US Department of Education (1988) *Digest of Education Statistics 1988*, Washington, National Centre for Education Statistics.

Walby, S. (1990) *Theorising Patriarchy*, Cambridge, Basil Blackwell.

Walkerdine, V. and Lucey, H. (1989) *Democracy in the Kitchen: Regulating Mothers and Socialising Daughters*, London, Virago.

Weil, S. (1986) 'Non-traditional learners within traditional higher education: Discovery and disappointment', *Studies in Higher Education*, **11**, 3, pp. 219–35.

Weinreich-Haste, H. (1984) 'The values and aspirations of English women undergraduates', in Acker, S. and Warren Piper, D. (Eds) *Is Higher Education Fair to Women?* London, SRHE/NFER-Nelson.

Westwood, S. (1984) *All Day, Every Day: Factory and Family in the Making of Women's Lives*, London, Pluto Press.

Williams, F. (1989) *Social Policy: A Critical Introduction. Issues of Race, Gender and Class*, Cambridge, Polity Press.

Williams, J., Cocking, J. and Davies, L. (1989) *Words or Deeds*, An occasional paper, London, Commission for Racial Equality.

Willie, C.V. and Greenblatt, S. (1978) 'Four "classic" studies of power relationships in black families: A review and look to the future', *Journal of Marriage and the Family*, November, pp. 691–4.

Wolpe, A.M. (1976) 'The official ideology of education for girls', in Flude, M. and Ahier, J. (Eds) *Educability, Schools and Ideology*, London, Croom Helm.

Wolpe, A.M. (1978) 'Education and the sexual division of labour', in Kuhn, A. and Wolpe, A.M. (Eds) *Feminism and Materialism*, London, Routledge and Kegan Paul.

Woodley, A., Wagner, L., Slowey, M., Hamilton, M. and Fulton, O. (1987) *Choosing to Learn: Adults in Education*, Milton Keynes, SRHE/Open University.

Yeatman, A. (1987) 'A feminist theory of social differentation', paper presented to the American Sociological Association Annual Meeting, Chicago, Illinois.

Young, M. and Wilmott, P. (1975) *The Symmetrical Family*, Harmondsworth, Penguin.

Index

Council on Education's Office of
    Minorities in Education 6
Crehan, Kate 32, 33
culture 22, 26
curriculum 6–7, 82, 150–2

Dahrendorf, Ralf 145
David, Miriam 4, 6, 25, 150
Davidoff, Leonore 22
Davies, Karen, 64
Deem, Rosemary 3, 5, 64, 70
de Beauvoir, Simone 31
Department of Education 4, 5, 6
difference
    feelings of 43, 59, 86–88, 93, 126,
        140–46
    from lecturers 94
    from other students 96–9
    theory 20–34, 139–40, 157
dissertations 99
division of labour 105–10, 119
    children's involvement 119
    extended family influence 123
    male involvement 67, 74, 104,
        106–7
    see also domestic; emotion
domestic
    sphere see private sphere/world
    standards 77–9
    violence 117–8, 127n
Dyhouse, Carol 3

education
    and family continuum 131–3
    and family typology 128–131
    as resource 2, 105
    equality 1–5, 147–58
    meaning in adulthood 50–60, 129
    meaning in childhood 45–7
    policies and family life ideologies
        39–43
    power 1, 3, 4, 105, 117–9
    race 9
    remedial 42
    return to 54–6, 80
    status 12
    subordination 1–5
    see also higher education
Eichler, Margrit 107
Eisenstein, Hester 23–4, 25
Elshtain, Jean 11–2
emotions 14, 70–3, 112, 140
    anger 71
    division of labour 75, 107–10

guilt 70, 72, 73, 80, 121
    power 69, 71–2
equality
    friendship 142
    in private sphere 152–5
    in public sphere 147–9
    sex 106, 153–4
    through education 1–5
    within higher education 149–52

family
    and education continuum 131–3
    and education typology 128–131
    as invisible in higher education 84–6
    complementary roles 39, 40, 42
    dominant matriarchs 42
    effect of higher education on 104–126
    extended 51, 52, 75, 122–3
    extended in childhood 39, 40, 42
    greedy institution 62–3
    ideologies 32
    ideologies and education policy 39–43
    knowledge 51, 112, 136, 137, 148
    meaning in adulthood 49–53
    meaning in childhood 43–5, 145, 156
    mental presence in higher education
        89–90
    nation 152
    physical presence in higher education
        90–3
    shared parenting 20, 34–5n
    structures 48–9, 130n
    symmetrical roles 33, 40, 42
    see also paid work
feminine mystique 2
feminine psyche 20–34, 52, 128, 139,
    156, 157
feminists 21, 23, 25, 52, 150
    and education 2–5, 82
    and family 104
    black 1, 2, 22–3
    white 1
Finch, Janet, 4, 27, 67, 109, 137
Fisher, Bernice 63, 138
Foner, Nancy 8
Friedan, Betty 2, 3
friendships 76, 141–4
    class and race 141–4
    educational level 142, 143
    in childhood 45
    threatened 143
    time 143
    with other students 96–9, 114, 129,
        130, 132

176

Oakley, Ann 40
organisation 11, 15, 63, 73–7, 80, 81n
Ortner, Sherry 20, 22
Osborn, Marilyn 145

paid work 2–4, 13, 18, 27, 29, 31–3, 39,
   41, 42, 56, 59, 64, 70, 73, 84, 105,
   116, 139, 148–9
   and family 31–3, 35n, 67, 75, 81n, 137,
   139, 149
   power 105–6, 116
parents
   disapproval 124
   distanced from 125, 126
   sharing education 125
   support 124
partners 8, 9, 16n, 91, 92, 105–7, 129,
   130, 133, 138, 154
   as threatened 13, 110–9, 127n, 133–5,
   140, 155
   ending relationships 10, 133–4, 140,
   152–4
   family structure 48–9
   level of education 118
   role in separation or connection
   132–3
   saving relationships 134–6
   sharing education 108, 110, 119, 133,
   134
   support and dis/interest 107–10, 134
   see also division of labour
Pateman, Carole 26
Pascall, Gillian 4–5
Payne, Geoff 144
Pegg, Angie 31
Phillips, Anne 9, 23, 35n
Phoenix, Anne 27
Piercy, Marge 14
Pollert, Anna 31
Porter, Marilyn 32, 127n
power 2, 6, 8, 9, 11, 23, 24, 64, 104–7,
   115, 119, 122, 123, 127n
   black women 23
   children 119, 122
   division of domestic labour 69, 74
   education 1, 3, 4, 98, 112, 117–9
   emotional 69, 71–2, 107
   extended family 122–3
   masculinity 117–9
   principle of least interest 127n
   public/private worlds 18, 20
   resource theory 105
pregnancy 38, 42, 44, 45, 93, 103n
Price, Marion 2, 3

privacy 19, 25, 28, 44, 49–51, 60n, 88–9,
   123, 140, 141
   class and race 28, 140
   of family life 28, 44, 51, 88–9, 112
   of home 28, 111–2
   sexual relationships 88–9, 114
private sphere/world 14–5, 17–34, 43,
   45, 84, 104, 105, 119, 122, 123, 127,
   128, 137–8, 140, 148, 157
   education 2–3
   equality 152–5
   subordination 18
process 138–140, 146n
public/private 34n
   as ideology 27, 128
   boundaries 17, 18, 22, 25, 27, 29–31,
   32, 44–5, 47, 50, 51, 139, 157
   confusing usages 18
   criticisms of 21–6
   culture 20, 93
   dichotomies 26–7
   theory 19–20
public sphere/world 14–5, 17–34, 45,
   50, 56, 72, 84, 93, 105, 107, 128,
   137–40, 148
   confidence in 100–2
   education 2
   equality 148–9
   subordination 18

race
   and class 8
   confidence 100
   education 42, 99
   friendship 141–4
   higher education 6, 99
   ideological forces 27
   in childhood 38
   masculinity 118
   partner relationships 48, 140–1
   perceptions of 9
   privacy 28, 140
   public/private theory 22–3
   women 22–3, 33
Rapp, Rayna 25
rationality 137, 139
Reinharz, Shulamit 150
Ribbens, Jane 52, 137, 151
Rich, Adrienne 4
Rockhill, Kathleen 127n
role conflict/theory 10–3, 23, 33
Rosaldo, Michelle 19–20, 22–4
Ross, Ellen 12
Ruddick, Sarah 51